P9-DXF-724

CALGARY PUBLIC LIBRARY

MAR   2017

Praise for

THE
MINDBODY
SELF

"The MindBody Self is an absolute masterwork, combining science, anthropology, and the wisdom of the heart—all easily accessible and beautifully written and explained. Mario's use of language goes right into my bone marrow. Just reading the difference between a ritual and routine is life changing, not to mention the thousands of other gems of meaning and understanding strewn throughout this book. It should be required reading for everyone on the planet who wants to live their very best and most fulfilling life."

— Christiane Northrup, M.D., *New York Times* best-selling author of *Goddesses Never Age* and *Making Life Easy*

"This is the new medicine of the 21st century! Dr. Mario Martinez's The MindBody Self is a wellspring of state-of-the-art discoveries, rock-solid science, and practical wisdom that gives us the formula for a long and vibrant life. In a conversational style that's easy to read, yet packed with timeless wisdom, Martinez leads us on an 11-chapter journey of self-discovery that reveals the hidden links between our family, our culture, and our life's potential. I especially appreciate the 'debriefing' section at the end of each chapter that gives us the opportunity to apply what we've just read immediately in our lives. If you're ready to move beyond the conventional theories of aging and discover your personal code of extraordinary potential, The MindBody Self is your personal prescription for success. I love this book!"

— Gregg Braden, *New York Times* best-selling author of *The Divine Matrix, The God Code,* and *Resilience from the Heart*

"Mind-blowing, heart-opening, and life-changing! Dr. Martinez combines the latest scientific research with ancient spiritual principles to reacquaint us with our Unconditioned Self, which is creative, abundant, and powerful beyond measure."

— Robert Holden, Ph.D., author of *Shift Happens!* and *Authentic Success*

"One does not have to agree with every assertion in this book to recognize that in The MindBody Self *Dr. Martinez combines informed cultural analysis, original thinking, and refreshing insights to create a helpful new theory of wellness. Best of all, he offers a well-wrought methodology that will enable people to shed their culturally derived limited selves and become the agents, the fully empowered co-creators of their health."

— Gabor Maté, M.D., author of *When the Body Says No: Exploring the Stress-Disease Connection*

"There is genius at work in these pages. Dr. Martinez presents ideas and techniques that are so startlingly original and innovative that they actually expand the reader's capacity for astonishment. The MindBody Self *is a must-read book for therapists, physicians, and transformational change agents of every kind."

— Gay Hendricks, Ph.D., author of *The Big Leap* and coauthor of *Conscious Loving Ever After*

THE
MINDBODY
SELF

ALSO BY DR. MARIO MARTINEZ

The MindBody Code

The Man from Autumn

THE
MINDBODY
SELF

HOW LONGEVITY
IS CULTURALLY LEARNED
and the
CAUSES OF HEALTH
ARE INHERITED

DR. MARIO MARTINEZ

HAY HOUSE, INC.
Carlsbad, California • New York City
London • Sydney • Johannesburg
Vancouver • New Delhi

Copyright © 2017 by Mario Martinez

Published and distributed in the United States by: Hay House, Inc.: www.hay house.com® • *Published and distributed in Australia by:* Hay House Australia Pty. Ltd.: www.hayhouse.com.au • *Published and distributed in the United Kingdom by:* Hay House UK, Ltd.: www.hayhouse.co.uk • *Published and distributed in the Republic of South Africa by:* Hay House SA (Pty), Ltd.: www.hayhouse.co.za • *Distributed in Canada by:* Raincoast Books: www.raincoast.com • *Published in India by:* Hay House Publishers India: www.hayhouse.co.in

Indexer: Jay Kreider
Cover design: Tricia Breidenthal
Interior design: Pamela Homan

All rights reserved. No part of this book may be reproduced by any mechanical, photographic, or electronic process, or in the form of a phonographic recording; nor may it be stored in a retrieval system, transmitted, or otherwise be copied for public or private use—other than for "fair use" as brief quotations embodied in articles and reviews—without prior written permission of the publisher.

The author of this book does not dispense medical advice or prescribe the use of any technique as a form of treatment for physical, emotional, or medical problems without the advice of a physician, either directly or indirectly. The intent of the author is only to offer information of a general nature to help you in your quest for emotional, physical, and spiritual well-being. In the event you use any of the information in this book for yourself, the author and the publisher assume no responsibility for your actions.

Cataloging-in-Publication Data is on file at the Library of Congress

Hardcover ISBN: 978-1-4019-5128-3

10   9   8   7   6   5   4   3   2   1
1st edition, March 2017

Printed in the United States of America

SUSTAINABLE FORESTRY INITIATIVE

Certified Sourcing
www.sfiprogram.org
SFI-01268

SFI label applies to text stock only

To my son, Patrick, and to my daughter, Lauren,
who are my heroes and my inspiration.

Contents

Introduction

These are turbulent times we live in. And there is no shortage of solutions on offer to smooth the way. Virtually any approach you can think of to solve problems in your inner or outer world—your relationships, your purpose, your physical health, your sense of self, your place in the world—has been laid out somewhere by someone as a path to a better life. I said any approach you can think of—but the fact is you cannot *think* your way to a better life. Change is not something your mind can accomplish alone. It's not something your body can do all by itself, either. You need them both together.

It's likely you already have an intuitive understanding—perhaps a sophisticated and finely honed understanding—of the way the mind and the body dialogue with each other. The science of *biocognition* that I have been developing and teaching over the past two decades takes this understanding to a new level: My concept of the *mindbody* describes not two separate entities having mutual impacts on each other, but an essential, indivisible oneness. The concept of the *mindbody code*, which I unpacked in my first book, explains the "coauthoring" of mind and body, cognition and biology, within a cultural context. It gives a name to the language you learn from your culture that allows you to interpret your world.

In the book you're holding now, I will delve more deeply into the cultural conditions that shape our lives, our health, our very selves. You'll discover a *mindbody cultural science* that illuminates how you coauthor your reality in collaboration with everything around you, and biocognitive tools you can use to change outworn patterns and create a healthier, happier, fuller life.

A New Language of the Self

The mindbody cultural language you will learn in this book has the flexibility needed to engage the turbulent challenges in your life with new and effective strategies that provide experiential solutions rather than intellectual explanations. We'll replace rigid boundaries of learned helplessness with permeable horizons of potential empowerment, genetic sentencing of disease with propensities influenced by cultural beliefs, and aging as inevitable deterioration with learning healthy longevity at any age. Based on revolutionary mindbody science research, we'll debunk reductionist myths that view human biology as mechanistic processes void of cultural influence in the causes of health and longevity. You will learn why and how what you perceive is a culturally woven world, rather than a perception void of cultural contexts. But more important, you will learn that you can reweave your cultural fabric to release what no longer serves you and reclaim the personal excellence you were taught to ignore.

We're self-organizing and self-regulating mindbody fields of living information coauthoring our world in cultural contexts, using an inseparable collaboration of mind *and* body to find meaning in what our cultures teach us to believe. Consequently, our biology confirms what we believe, and unfolds based on what we plan to become. But I do caution that all these fine goals of expanding our human potential cannot be reached with mere wishful thinking and quick-fix formulas. We learn what does not serve us well with coauthors that intentionally or unwittingly impose their cultural beliefs on us. If personal change were a matter of reasoning, we could simply end our woes by recognizing the harm they are causing us. But we know how perplexed we feel when we fail to change what we wish to disengage. The concepts I introduce offer a cultural vision to understand, embody, and change what up to now did not appear possible. To understand with our mind what goes on with our body is necessary but not sufficient to achieve lasting change. The reason is that learning is a mindbody experience—we can't change what we learn by only engaging what the mind experiences. In other words, rather than mind over matter, mind and matter are coauthors in cultural contexts.

I will explain technical terminology without "dumbing down" the information I want you to assimilate. I strongly believe paradigm shifts require new language that provides novel ways to approach old problems and new turbulence. Rather than making unrealistic promises that sound more like clever marketing schemes than good science, I will show you methods that I developed and refined during more than 25 years of clinical neuropsychology practice. This does not imply, however, that everything will work for all. But the reason I believe it will work for most is that you will learn how your culture weaves the fabric of your selfhood, how you participate in the process, and most important, how you can change what appears immutable. Two of the main reasons why these methods work are the ways they incorporate what life sciences have so arrogantly ignored: 1. Cultural beliefs coauthor our biology. 2. Meaning, rather than survival of the fittest, is the driving force of our humanity.

My interest in providing effective ways to make lasting mind-body changes comes from the shortcomings I see in some of the alternatives offered by the health-care professions. Although we should not discard the impressive advances in medical diagnostics and treatment, it does not follow that we should buy the notion that aggressive intervention is the best way to confront all of our ailments. Our body is much more than organs interacting as parts of a mechanical system. One of the problems with understanding the difference between mechanical versus organic models is that our mindbody has characteristics of both. There's no denial that the heart pumps blood and that blood pressure is the force of the pumping. When the pumping process fails to work, there's no better *acute* remedy than biochemical or mechanical intervention. But the major mistake that reductionist medicine makes is to assume that because mechanistic intervention works, our biology is mechanical. The mechanical intervention works only when there's a mindbody breakdown that eventually reaches a critical physical dysfunction. But before this happens, in addition to pumping blood, the heart makes its own regulating hormones that can be affected by shame causing inflammation, and love regulating the rhythm of the pumping. These statements are not New Age poetics. Instead, they are based on scientific research from the interdisciplines of psychocardiology, neuroanthropology, cultural neuroscience, and psychoneuroimmunology (PNI). I refer to "interdisciplines" because, quite simply, the Renaissance concept of one discipline explaining everything is no longer tenable: We need to take a broader and more fully integrated view. My training in clinical neuropsychology taught me to understand the limitations of the sick brain, leaving me clueless about the potential power of the healthy brain. I learned strategies to diagnose and rehabilitate pathological damage, but next to nothing about the causes of health. I am grateful for my lessons on brain pathology, and also excited to show you how I integrate the discoveries of different disciplines to develop tools that can change your life.

But this book is about much more than arguing for an integration of the best of medicine with mindbody science. I share results of my investigations of healthy centenarians (100 years or older) worldwide as well as other extensive research to argue that healthy longevity is learned rather than inherited, and that the causes of health are inherited rather than learned. This does not mean, however, that you should sit passively and wait for your health to unfold. What I will show you is that cultures weave the reality we perceive and strongly determine how our biology should respond.

I bring together interdisciplines that are not communicating their discoveries with each other, and I'll explain the practical aspects of results that remain buried in highly technical journals. But more important than giving you a rundown of research data, I'll show you ways to apply their results to deal with issues of health, longevity, relationships, and self-esteem. You will find that the brain is cultural, our social systems are still tribal, and Western and Eastern cultures differ in how their biology responds to stress, illness, and other life challenges. We cannot change our DNA, but we can certainly culturally influence how our genes express disease and the causes of our health.

The MindBody Self offers a new vision that challenges the technology of doom with scientific evidence for hope. The shift I propose goes from mind and body communication to *mindbody* communication in cultural contexts. In this paradigm, mind influences the body based on how culture influences the mind. The paradigm-shifting language I use opens pathways that are not available in conventional methods aimed at changing unwanted behavior. For example, my term *coauthorship* forges awareness that our actions are mutually sculpted with others rather than unilaterally created. In the back of the book you'll find a glossary with definitions of the new terms I introduce. If you imagine language as instructions for interpreting your world, then when the existing evidence can no longer explain what you see, you need different interpretations (language) to incorporate your new worldview. For example, *cultural portal* is one of the terms I introduce to argue that growing older is the passing of time, whereas *aging* is what you do with time based on your cultural beliefs. Middle age is one of the cultural portals. When it begins, your culture will tell you how to behave and dress and what to expect—all without any biological evidence to support that stage of your life. But if you're not aware that you're in a *cultural fishbowl*, you will age according to what your culture tells you rather than your biology. Fortunately, there are ways to come out of the portals, as healthy centenarians and other cultural rebels (outliers) are able to do.

HOW TO NAVIGATE THE BOOK

The book is divided into 11 chapters, with one recurring theme and many pathways to change what no longer serves you well. My main objective is to show you how to change the cultural consciousness that maintains a cluster of unwanted behaviors, rather than simply modifying a behavior. For example, it may be difficult to break a self-sabotaging habit, but when you experientially change a consciousness of unworthiness, the cluster of behaviors that support self-sabotaging is no longer sustainable.

The chapters are written in a sequence designed to let you assimilate the information in stages. But if you prefer, you can read the topics that most interest you initially, and then return to the sequence at any time. The content is designed as a resource that goes beyond reading the book through once. You can return to review the concepts and their applications anytime you face overwhelming challenges.

At the end of each chapter, you'll find exercises to help you assimilate and apply the concepts you learn. The tools consist of contemplative methods, embodied imagery, and incidental learning; I developed them in my clinical neuropsychology practice and have taught them to my patients and in hundreds of my workshops worldwide. Feedback from people who have used the tools has helped me improve their effectiveness and simplify their applications. When you try the exercises, take advantage of the Glossary to clarify any of the new concepts and terms you encounter. You'll also find an extensive bibliography to support the new concepts I introduce, and to use as a resource if you are interested in the academic and research foundation of mindbody science.

Chapter 1 introduces how selfhood is sculpted by culturally defined principles, and how we gradually develop a self-image that may not reflect what we really are or want to be. Cultures establish portals to define how we should experience the passing of time. At the end of the chapter I provide techniques to break away from the cultural lessons that go against your best interest and suggest ways to deal with the coauthors (the people and events collaborating with you to shape your consciousness and your experience) that want to keep you tied to your past.

Chapter 2 takes you *beyond the pale* (tribal boundaries) and shows you how cultures set consequences, "for your own good," to keep you from leaving the mindbody confinements of the tribe. I'll show you ways to increase your independence without dishonoring your cultural heritage, with the understanding that there's a difference between dishonoring and disagreeing with the cultural lessons you were dealt.

Chapter 3 shows how perception is culturally learned, and how symbols taught by *cultural editors* (people given contextual power: parents at home, doctors in hospitals, teachers in classrooms) affect your biology. You'll learn how symbols become *biosymbols* when your biology assimilates their meaning, and how to recontextualize (change the mindbody meaning of) symbols that affect you in negative and restrictive ways.

Chapter 4 provides a thorough understanding of why control, permanence, and other existential concepts are illusions that can deeply disappoint you when you fail to conquer them. When you understand how to focus on what you can change rather than what's beyond your control, dread of the unknown is downgraded to fear of the known, allowing you to resolve what appeared unworkable. This chapter's tools are designed to resolve major fears found in all cultures, and to free you from self-entrapment.

Chapter 5 explores why self-esteem is culturally constructed and how you can change what you were taught to believe about your cultural self that diminishes your worthiness. You'll be able to see why our mindbody responds more to the belief that we are loved than to the love we are given. You'll understand why public figures who are idolized by their fans struggle with accepting massive love, and how this process applies to your own life in how you give and receive love. Tools include ways to move from giving and taking with expectations, to offering and receiving for the intrinsic value of the process.

Chapter 6 offers evidence to debunk the notion that family illnesses are a genetic life sentence. The latest research shows that the way genes express disease or health has more to do with cultural beliefs than genetics. Tools are provided to enhance the causes of health and diminish the expression of disease. The causes of health are discussed, as well as how to access them within your culture.

Chapter 7 shows you how the digital culture of laptops, video games, and cell phones is interfering with family rituals that enhance immunological function. But rather than giving up technology, you'll learn ways to benefit from the advantages of digital communication, without replacing the social bonding that's essential for your health and longevity. I also explain how we become emotionally attached to digital companions (cell phones, Internet, media) at the expense of family time, and how to balance your attention between people and technology. You'll also learn why many stress-related illnesses like gastrointestinal disorders, high blood pressure, and reflux can be related to excessive use of computers and cell phones, especially during meals.

Chapter 8 provides most of the scientific evidence for the power that culture has over our health, relationships, and longevity. You'll experience how our brain perceives the world weaved with cultural interpretations, why Eastern and Western cultures interpret their world differently, and why gene expression differs based on cultural interpretations of the world. I provide methods that integrate the best of Eastern and Western cultures to enhance your health and quality of life.

Chapter 9 refutes, based on good science, the theories of aging that assume we lose cognitive and physical capacities with the passing of time. I share the results of my extensive fieldwork with healthy centenarians that show genetics only accounts for 25 percent of their longevity. You'll learn why healthy longevity can be learned at any age, and how to incorporate *centenarian consciousness* into your life.

Chapter 10 covers the psychology of adversity and how to use principles of uncertainty to successfully navigate abrupt changes in your life. Most important, you'll learn why people who intuitively know how to apply these principles of uncertainty are not affected negatively by major stresses in their lives. Tools are provided to confront adversity without letting it make you sick.

Chapter 11 is a compilation of concepts and lessons that I've been refining for more than 25 years. The chapter consolidates lessons from the previous chapters to give you a compass, rather than a map, that you can use to identify challenges and approach them with proven tools. The concept of cultural portals is expanded to show you the unique mindbody consequences of being in each portal (childhood, adolescence, young adulthood, middle age, and old age). Additionally, you'll see how, by understanding the restrictions and obstructions of each portal, you can choose to step out and not be affected by their limitations.

The Mindbody Self takes you on a new journey that shows you how the science of hope is overwhelming the myths of doom. How you have inherited the resilience to handle adversity in ways that may appear magical, although they are based on credible scientific evidence. But like any new journey, this one requires courage to challenge old ways of doing things, and patience to let your cultural brain assimilate the new ways. Courage because known misery causes less anxiety than unknown joy, and patience because dysfunctional ways are long-term unwanted companions that require time to vacate your consciousness. The good news is that we are designed to choose meaning over survival of the fittest, and love over fear. But it takes entering worthy paths to embrace the personal excellence that has always been within you. Enjoy your paradigm shift.

chapter 1

Coauthoring the MindBody Self

N othing happens in a vacuum. From the moment of conception we are coauthors with our cultural contexts. I use the word *coauthors* because we are not passive recipients in a world that happens *to* us. Instead, the world—or, more precisely, *our cultural world*—happens *with* us. We engage our world in contexts that are culturally constructed to make sense based on the collective reality we share with our tribes. For the purpose of the journey we'll undertake in this book, I define *culture* as the agreements a group shares about aesthetics, ethics, health, transcendental beliefs, power, rituals, and other beliefs that determine their collective identity. The agreements are communicated with a common language shared within the group. The language can be as broad as to include nations (English, Japanese, Italian, German), subgroups within nations (gangs, teams, fraternities, professions), as well as across nations (global organizations, religions).

Whereas the culture is the set of agreements that identify a group, the tribe is the group that assimilates and lives by the agreements.

I am purposely giving working definitions of *culture* and *tribe* because as you delve into my theory and practice of mindbody cultural science, you will realize how human complexity can't be contained within fixed labels and boundaries. In fact, human civilization did not advance much until the more daring members of the tribe broke from their physical enclosures (the pale), and their limiting concepts of the world (belief horizons), to face the "ice monsters" that turned out to be mere ice caps.

In this chapter I illustrate how you become your mindbody self. *Within the pale,* consciousness is not recognized until you venture *beyond the pale.* The rules change, and many of the characteristics that you learned to function in the tribe will lose their effectiveness when you move on to explore on your own. Why? Because rather than personal flaws, when you move beyond collectivist thinking, you lack the tools to succeed in a place that requires dropping known scripts and engaging novelty. For example, when you're living at home, the rules are set by your parents; moving out requires discovering your own rules. Tribal living revolves around cooperation and compliance, but when you venture out on your own, you realize that you can set limits with others that you were not able to do in the tribe. This interplay of complying with tribal rules and questioning their function is necessary for the healthy development of your cultural self.

THE CULTURAL RULES WITHIN THE PALE

If you take a moment to ask yourself who and what you are, you will find a cluster of categories that relate to your gender, body, job, family—unending labels that you might take for granted. If you continue to explore, you'll find that these identity tabs can only make sense when you relate them to each of their opposites and their contexts. Let me explain what appears obvious but has profound implications for how your brain learns. You know you're woman because there are men, you can be brother because there are sisters, and so on. Additionally, depending on the conditions (contexts), you can be a "good" woman, or a "bad" brother, because you are a coauthor with your context. One cultural self does not fit all contexts, and one culture does not represent all cultures. In the "Cultural Brain" chapter, I'll explain how our brains assimilate and interpret information based on our cultural premises, but now what I want you to consider is that we construct our identity from *relational opposites* (man–woman, young–old, tall–short, heavy–thin), and bring meaning to our actions based on *contextual demands* (appropriate here–inappropriate there, trusting here–suspicious there). I argue that the relational and contextual components of our constructed reality are heavily influenced by our cultures. Examples: Men's potbellies are a symbol of affluence in India, and a sign of being out shape in the U.S.; belching after a meal is a sign of approval in China, and lack of good manners in Britain; eye contact indicates forthrightness in most Western cultures, and disrespect in some Eastern cultures; the adage "the squeaky wheel gets the grease" is taught in the U.S., and "the nail that stands out gets pounded down" is a standard in Japan. American children's stories end with "and they lived happily ever after," and in France they end with "and they had many children."

Additional cultural variability exists in the relational opposites and the contextual demands influencing the development of cultural selfhood: In Pakistan the generic "uncle," "aunt," and "grandparent" family labels are not used because they are determined by the patriarchal or matriarchal lineage. Thus, "paternal uncle," "maternal aunt," and "paternal grandfather" replace the generic labels accepted as sufficient familial identity in other cultures. In the 1990s Korean Airlines had a significant number of plane crashes due to the reluctance of first officers to question their captains' judgment. The Korean culture has a strict deferential language to address superiors, and does not encourage questioning authorities.

You can see how the conditions that influence your sense of self vary widely depending on your culture. But the objective of creating tribal identity within their respective pales remains the same across cultures. It does not mean, however, that tribal members are clones functioning identically within the pale. Instead, imagine the mindbody self as having identity horizons rather than rigid boundaries. These horizons are required for the flexibility needed to navigate relational and contextual conditions without losing cultural selfhood. You can very quickly experience the challenge to your cultural self when you travel to countries with customs very different from yours. Imagine if you travel from a culture where belching in public is rude, and you are compelled to produce a loud burp to show your host approval for the meal. Actually, it could be fun if you can step out of your cultural self for the evening.

The Disguised Cultural Lessons

Most of the cultural lessons we learn at home and in school during the development of our cultural self are straightforward: be fair, be honest, love your parents, get along with others. There are other cultural lessons, however, that are just as profound in creating tribal consciousness, but their influence is not as easily recognized. These lessons are disguised in children's lullabies, fables, epic stories, allegories, heroics, and other culture-specific narratives. They implicitly teach what we should fear, admire, and idealize, as well as the aspirations, ethical conduct, and judgment expected for the mindbody self to be accepted by the tribe. I'll elaborate on my example about the different endings of children's stories in France and the U.S.: The French stories associate happy endings with having more children, while American stories focus on living happily ever after. In her book *Medicine and Culture,* Lynn Payer suggests that the French cultural value placed on having children, as reflected in their fables, may help explain why young French women have fewer hysterectomies than their American counterparts. I propose that these imbedded cultural lessons influence how the medical, religious, and social practices are formulated in a tribe.

In the "Cultural Brain" chapter, I'll explain in greater detail how cultural beliefs affect medical diagnosis, prognosis, and treatment of disease, as well as how aging and longevity are perceived.

The Digital Culture

The considerable influence of the Internet, new media, and digital technologies on the development of the mindbody self and the roles they play in contemporary society, culture, business, politics, the arts, and everyday life is undeniable. In the past 60 years most modern societies have transitioned from the extended family (parents, children, and grandparents) to the nuclear family (parents and children). But in my view, what is most concerning is how the digital culture replaces cultural rituals that have powerful bonding and communication value for the family. In the 1960s children's television programs began to successfully compete with and gradually replace the storyteller role of grandparents. What was gained in the general developmental learning aids provided by the children's programs came at a price of losing the individual family histories passed on with narratives from grandparents. There's no question these children's programs provide valuable early childhood psychosocial development, particularly for children growing up with single parents and absent grandparents. But the loss of the grandparent's valuable role as mediator between parents and their children is undeniable as well.

Next, the cell phone and video games arrived to compete with the communication of parents and their children during meals. Not only has the television become a popular dinner guest, now when families go out to dinner, the new guests are cell phones and video games. We have all seen families eating out, with all engaged in their intimate digital world void of dinner conversation. Adding to the impersonal dimension of the digital culture is the text messaging replacing eye-to-eye communication and ear-to-ear phone conversations. What I find most amusing is that while the telephone replaced the telegraph, text messaging is replacing the telephone: the digital telegraph wins.

We could certainly write off these innovations as the price we pay for progress. I am certainly not complaining about the digital inventions. In fact, I am writing this book on my MacBook Air, and I do not romanticize the days when Hemingway wrote his manuscripts on his Corona typewriter. What I am addressing here is the loss of powerful cultural rituals established through trial and error since the beginning of our *Homo sapiens* presence on this exciting planet of ours. Instead, I am proposing a practical middle way that can allow us to incorporate the benefits of the digital culture with the wisdom of our tribal rituals. In other words, if the proverbial devil's advocate asks, "Should I cut off your right or left hand?" the answer should be, "Neither, because I'm learning how to use both hands in more creative ways." In the applications section at the end of the chapter, I'll show you some methods to manage and learn from the challenges created by the digital culture.

THE POWER OF RITUALS

We're gradually building a language and discovering pathways to understand how our cultural self develops and gains complexity. Rituals have a prominent place in the coauthoring of collective and individual cultural identities. But before venturing on, I'll define *ritual* and differentiate it from *routine*. Although these terms are commonly used interchangeably, they are culturally different. In my theory of biocognitive science, ritual *is a behavior or event that gives inclusive meaning to the individual, family, or culture*. A ritual identifies what we are about and our belongingness in a culture: breaking bread with family, celebrating special occasions, marriage, rites of passage. Routine *is a behavior or event that one must do with regularity*. A routine is what we do to maintain status quo: taking a shower, grocery shopping, work schedules. In some instances the difference can be fuzzy, but let me offer ways to help you differentiate. If you take a shower to be clean, it's a routine, but if your showering has ceremonial meaning, then it's a ritual. If you go for a walk to stay in shape, it's a routine, but if the purpose of your walk is to commune with nature, you are performing a ritual. The ultimate purpose differentiates routine from ritual. The former has functional value; the latter has symbolic meaning.

If my definitions remain fuzzy, explore the difference in the *felt meaning* (how you experience interpretations) of your mindbody patterns and cultural scripts. If you experience ceremony, communion, decorum, elegance, you've discovered your rituals. If they lack these exalted felt meanings, you have identified your routines. There are several reasons why most definitions lack the complexity to convey deep cultural meaning:

One definition does not fit all possible contexts.

As the variability of cultural contexts increases, the meaning and function of a definition decreases. For example, the definition of kindness works in most contexts where its cultural meaning is shared. The function and definition of kindness shift, however, when you eat meat with vegetarians who believe killing animals for consumption is barbaric.

One definition does not fit all cultural portals.

As you transition *cultural portals* (culturally defined life stages), the meaning and function change according to the collective agreements that define each portal. The portal of "middle age" in one culture may start at age 45 and end at age 60, while in another culture middle age goes from age 30 to age 50.

Which cultural self would you like to be? In the "Life beyond the Pale" chapter, I'll explain in greater detail how cultural portals are determined and how they influence the development of cultural selfhood. Then, in the "Entering a Biosymbolic World" chapter, we'll look into how cultural beliefs (assigned meaning) influence our health and longevity.

The Value of Cultural Narrative

Noting the limitations of definitions, we can begin to appreciate why narratives are so prevalent in all cultures. If an image is worth a thousand words, a story is worth a thousand images. Because narrative precedes the invention of written language, it has to evoke compelling images that can be remembered and applied in different contexts. Storytelling had a survival value that gradually became the developing agent for the mindbody self: After you learn to survive you can discover who you are. And although written language is the most phenomenal human invention, it is limited to what the brain can transfer from spoken language to written symbol.

As a writer I am keenly aware of how difficult it is to convey what I am thinking using a written language that limits what I could express in oral narrative. Additionally, storytelling allows questions to enrich cultural meaning and expand contexts. For example:

A few monks were traveling through a rain forest and had to stop when they reached a river too deep to cross. One monk suggested they build a raft. They cut some trees, built the raft, and crossed the river. Before resuming their path, one monk proposed they take the raft with them. Another monk asked, why would they want to carry a heavy raft? The first monk responded, "In case we encounter another river." And the inquisitive monk replied, "If there is another river there will be other trees."

This simple story conveys allegories of practicality, risk taking, faith, and many other cultural lessons. And although it's an improvement over stating a message in specifically defined terms, it is still limited by written language. The storyteller can give immediacy and force to the cultural lessons by mimicking facial expressions, tone of voice, movements, and many more experiences that could take a book to approximate the richness of one oral narrative. Oral narrative can come closer to conveying the subtle richness of imagination than the diminished presence of written words. In addition to receiving the content, in oral communications we experience the human voice, whereas with written words we experience the paper.

Just as I suggest finding a middle way with the digital culture, we should also look for creative methods to incorporate the richness of storytelling with the technology of our modern life. For instance, a new approach to diagnostics called *narrative medicine* is a prime example of balancing information gained from highly technical medical equipment with the patients' own stories of how they view their illness, their recovery, and their contributions to their healing. This apparently "unscientific" method of gathering data is one of the most valuable tools anthropologists use to study cultures based on the unadulterated narratives gathered from tribal members. The *Evidence-Based Medicine* (EBM) manual sets the standards for excellence in medical practice. It defines EBM as "the integration of best research evidence with clinical expertise and patient values." Although the scientific approach in EBM is essential, in practice, patient values are given the least weight, and patient culture is seldom considered. Thus most of the "evidence" continues to be defined by research results (some with rats), instrument measurements, and clinical observations, without much contribution from the patients' felt meaning of their maladies. In the "Biocognitive Tools for Life" chapter, I'll have more to say about the shortcomings of EBM and how it can be enhanced with mindbody cultural science methods.

I hope I am illustrating how my approach to the life sciences intends to integrate, refine, and balance the best that technology has to offer with the infinite wisdom of cultures. Although modern medicine has been studying the immune system since Élie Metchnikoff discovered, more than 100 years ago, that phagocytes (immune cells that literally eat foreign bodies) destroy pathogens rather than spread disease (as it was believed at the time), in fact the immune system has been refining how to express the causes of health for more than 2 million years!

ETHNOGRAPHY OF THE MINDBODY SELF

Ethnography is the branch of anthropology that systematically studies people and cultures. Ethnographers observe the culture from the point of view of members in the tribe and painstakingly avoid biasing their findings with their own personal or academic views. Listening to the stories people tell us allows us to learn how they view themselves in different contexts, their aspirations, beliefs, and worldviews. If we listen to narratives from a few people belonging to a group, we begin to see patterns of thought that reflect essential components of their tribe. But just as important is how the individuation of the mindbody self varies within groups: from criminal gangs to New England fishermen, we find how personal affectations and tribal idiosyncrasies coauthor cultural selfhood.

Recall stories you were told about your family—its routines, rituals, hierarchical structure, how you were characterized—and you will discover some of the coauthoring influences that shaped your cultural self. Who were the heroes, the black sheep, the comedians, the successes, and the ne'er-do-wells? You may discover you're a bit of some and more of others. The good news is that you can *become* what you want to be when you learn how you *became* who you are. But this does not happen at the drop of a hat, because your established cultural self does not readily yield to your best intentions. By the way, the idiom about the hat (which indicates something happening very quickly) came from Ireland and was later used in the 'American Old West. Originally, before a bell took its place, the signal to start a boxing match in Irish pubs and cowboy saloons was to drop a hat and wait until it hit the floor. But to someone not familiar with the culture, the drop of the hat would make no sense.

A family ethnography can identify the stories that are coauthored and how the *characteristics* assigned to each member gradually mold the *character* of its cultural self. Imagine you're designated the "intelligent" characteristic in your family. They come to you for advice and you feel respected and admired. That sounds good so far, but what happens when you move on to another subculture where your designation is ignored or no longer recognized? You enter the turbulence of self-doubt and begin to compensate by becoming a dysfunctional version of your bestowed character: the know-it-all. You've seen these types: they struggle to let you know how smart they are, and when they fail to convince you, their anger surfaces to mask their perceived failure.

But this loss of function can also go from negative to positive. In this scenario you're the chosen "black sheep" of the family. You're used as examples of what not to be, family members avoid or pity you, and your selfhood begins to live out your assigned script. You leave your tribe and find new coauthors to confirm your "badness." And believe me, there are plenty of anchors out there very willing to dance misery with you. (You'll read more about anchors of misery in the next chapter.) Fortunately, a few begin to see your goodness and challenge your negative image by treating you with kindness. This triggers a principle that you will thoroughly learn in this book: *Given that love-based emotions are more evolved than fear-based condemnations, our human tendency is designed to overwhelmingly gravitate toward our benign essence.* Then the black sheep among us can entertain the possibility that family labels are pronouncements rather than sentences, and that hope is a powerful agent of change on the journey of self-hood. But . . . all is not well. The recontextualizing processes I am describing seldom work for sociopaths, who see love as weakness and kindness as an opportunity to manipulate. It's highly unlikely that sociopaths would be interested in this book. If any sneak in, however, I invite them to consider that their selfhood has salvageable attributes they could learn to nourish with the lessons I'll share with all.

So as not to miss an opportunity to illustrate cultural symbolism, let's look at why "black sheep" got such a raw deal. Traditionally, English shepherds disliked black sheep because their fleece was not suitable for dyeing and consequently was worth less than that of white sheep. Although the color black has been used derogatorily to describe Africans or African descendants, its original negative connotation is unrelated to race. As far back as 2nd-century Rome, the black color was associated with death. In ancient times, it was thought the body had four fluids called humors that determined one's physical and mental health; black bile was one of the four humors, and it was an indicator of sadness, melancholy, depression, and possible impending death. The use of the word *black* to identify a race started in the 14th century, 1,200 years after its association with death. On the other end of the spectrum, some Asian countries associate death with the color white.

In social psychology, the *black sheep effect* refers to an interesting group identification phenomenon—again, unrelated to race or ethnicity. It refers to the tendency for group members to evaluate more harshly an in-group member who expresses offensive behavior than an out-group member guilty of the same offense.

Making group identification processes more complex is the *in-group overexclusion effect*: When presented with vague information to determine if someone belongs to a group, the tendency to exclude increases. By now you're probably thinking, *Why is this guy trying to confuse me with all this psychobabble?* I suggest that if you're patient with me, the social psychology maze we're exploring will reveal intriguing secrets about your cultural selfhood. Let's review the terms and expand their implications.

The black sheep effect: If you're strongly identified with a group and someone in your group screws up, you will judge your own group member more severely than a person from another group who has committed the same indiscretion. Why would you not try to protect your own group members? Here's the answer: You are protecting your group's integrity by strongly disapproving of its "bad" members, not really caring as much if other groups have screwups.

The in-group overexclusion effect: When you're trying to determine if someone belongs to your group and the information available is ambiguous, you will tend to find more reasons to exclude than to include the individual. In other words, you will be more selective with your rules of inclusion if the characteristics you're observing are not clear. Here, the group's integrity is protected in a different way: When in doubt, don't let them in.

The need to protect the integrity and safety of the tribe and its subgroups is primal. You can see now why exclusion or expulsion from tribes is so threatening to the safety and belongingness of cultural selfhood.

Universal Propensities

Although tribes vary in their inclusion/exclusion rules, common language, and mores, there are universal human propensities that transcend cultural differences. We can view cultures as variations of the same fabric. And the foundation of this human fabric is built on our proclivity *to belong*, *to be understood*, and *to be valued*. I strongly contend that, independent of where you look worldwide, you will find as many cultural variations of the same three primal propensities as there are tribes. But why are they so vital to our existence? They are the pathways to finding meaning and love: *Who am I? What am I doing here? Who cares?* In the chapter "The Causes of Health" I'll show you what can happen with our health and longevity when one or more of these pathways is neglected or blocked.

Selfhood is coauthored in a cultural complexity that can be accessed, understood, and recontextualized to be the best you want to become. This is not empty poetics; it is a paradigm shift that offers cogent answers to the life sciences that focus more on managing pathology than discovering the causes of health.

Tools to Explore Your Cultural Self

In this section you'll learn how to progress from theory to practice. We'll transition the concepts you learned with your mind to a mindbody language that translates your intentions to sustainable actions. Rather than replace one behavior with another, you'll learn a mindbody language that recontextualizes the felt meaning of the *operative consciousness* (mind-set) where the behavior resides. For example, quitting smoking (target behavior) and merely replacing it with jogging (alternative behavior) does not access the operative consciousness of self-devaluation that maintains *all* dysfunctional distractions. We assimilate and archive in memory the wholeness (bioinformational field) of mindbody communication with its coauthored meaning in cultural contexts: *mindbodycultural oneness*. For example, learning to enjoy tobacco involves forcing the lungs to tolerate hot, toxic smoke until the nicotine receptors can trigger pleasure in a context where smoking has social value. But the smoking can expand to contexts where the function changes from pleasure to anxiety distractor. As the contextual functions diversify, the simple act of smoking progresses from pleasure to lifestyle, and from addiction to curse.

Then you try "logical" strategies to quit smoking: nicotine patches, smoking-cessation clinics, brute-force abstinence, increasing fear of lung cancer, and other interminable ways to give up what you "reasoned" is no longer in your best interest. If you succeed with "reasonable" *mind* interventions, you're most likely replacing a mindbody-driven action with a thought-driven alternative action. But since thoughts are in the domain of mind, and the target behavior gained mindbody contextual complexity that defies reason, you may succeed with substituting smoking with jogging, while simultaneously replacing smoking with eating. I call this process *succeeding with the effect and failing with the cause.*

So, rather than blaming yourself for failing to change unwanted behavior, I invite you to learn the proper tools that will show you how the problem lies in underestimating the complexity of your cultural self, rather than in lacking will or conviction to honor your promises.

Instead of using the analogy of a sanitized laboratory with mechanical instruments to change behavior (rat psychology), we're going to contextualize a theatrical stage on which you are the coauthor of your play (narrative mindbody science). As you discover the *characteristics* you coauthored to mold the *character* of your cultural self, you gain expertise to become the director of your play. And when you do, you empower your mindbody language to transcend reasoning so you can experientially change your dysfunctional scripts: *recontextualizing the cause to change the effect.*

Setting the Stage

Since the mindbody language I'll teach you is experiential, it must be communicated void of the usual thought chatter that distracts your intentions and derails your actions. The stage we're constructing is a field of quietude reached through a contemplative mode, which is not the same as relaxation. I'll explain the difference: Relaxation is a reduction of muscle tension to reach serenity. Contemplation *is* serenity. Rather than the overused term *mindfulness*, contemplation is a mindbody experience that allows internal-external observation *and* reflection void of the habitual distractions played out by the mind to avoid knowing the body. In other words, first you learn to reduce distractions, then you bring in the cultural scripts that you want to change. Think of first quieting the audience before it can concentrate on the play.

The Contemplative Path

We'll use the contemplative method as the experiential stage to assimilate what you will learn in each chapter. The contemplative stage allows the players to experience their dysfunctional scripts to identify how they were contextualized and the coauthors that helped incorporate them and support them. I suggest that before applying the contemplative method, you practice it until the distractions become passing observations without much derailment. The contemplative experience is the internal stage during which you bring your cultural self to change the operative consciousness that feeds its dysfunctional scripts. The objective is to free yourself of mental noise: moving from judging content to observing without judgment. Let me give you narrative examples of the progressive stream of awareness you may experience during your practice.

The Distractions Stage

I am sitting quietly with my eyes closed. I notice tension in my shoulders and I try to relax them. I remember I am not supposed to relax them. I notice I just got distracted with the thought of what I am not supposed to do. I try to concentrate, and recognize I am not supposed to try to concentrate. I begin to feel frustrated, and the thought surfaces of opening my eyes and quitting. I tell myself I can do it. I realize I am not supposed to give myself encouragement . . .

See why the Buddhists call these distractions "monkey mind"? Our minds jump from one thought to another like monkeys jumping from one tree to another.

First Glimpses of the Contemplative Stage

I continue to sit quietly with my eyes closed. I observe blankness. I observe the thought of no thoughts. I observe my smile. I sense peace for a few seconds without interpretation. I smile and observe the muscles that moved to create the smile. I get excited about what I am accomplishing, and allow the excitement and accomplishment to pass with less derailment. I am experiencing observing the observer . . .

In this initial contemplative state, you begin to experience short periods of thought-free awareness. At first, the excitement of reaching these *serenity glimpses* ejects you from the serenity you just entered. Gradually the excitement is experienced without derailing you from the state of serenity. Why? Because joy and serenity are one, but the surprise of experiencing joy when expecting stillness is what causes the derailing excitement. When you learn to experience joy and serenity as one, the jolt of excitement transitions to *elated quietude*. These terms may seem paradoxical because our minds try to impose cause and effect on inseparable wholeness. And if these explanations appear more esoteric than scientific, I urge you to suspend judgment until you read the "Permanence, Control, and Other Illusions" chapter. You'll learn what cultural neuroscience has discovered about what the brain does during contemplation.

The Contemplative Stage

I observe the sensations of where my body touches the chair, my feet meet the ground, and my eyelids cover my eyes. I observe a stream of blankness void of thoughts. I observe hearing sounds outside and the pulsations of my heart inside. I flow without experiencing guidance and ownership. I observe my fear of losing selfhood as it enters and departs my field of thought-free awareness. I observe sensations of elated quietude. I observe the thought of not wanting to come out of my serenity. I observe the thought of trusting my mindbody to determine when to end my contemplative experience . . .

In this deeper level of awareness, you have longer periods of contemplation: observations void of interference and interpretations. Distractions lose their derailing effect, and you begin to experience content without assigned meaning: neutral percepts. Fragmented sensations transition to holistic experiences. Boundaries become horizons, and horizons lose their delineations: consciousness without contexts.

Once you can remain in the contemplative stage, you can incorporate the players and scripts that you want to change. This will be the *reflection* part of the contemplative method you will learn. But please note that you don't have to be in constant contemplative awareness before starting the exercise. This only happens after much practice. Fortunately, all you need for now is to reduce some of the distractions and interpretations. But if you have not been able to achieve the level you want, don't worry. You will improve as you practice the mindbody process I am going to show you next:

- Choose a comfortable time and place at home without obligations to others. Recognize this is your time because you're worth it.

- Sit quietly and *observe* what your mindbody is doing. You can do this with your eyes open or closed. What are the sensations, emotions, and thoughts that occupy your awareness? Observe them dispassionately, like clouds entering and exiting your field of awareness. If you give in to your mind chatter, you will engage endless reruns.

- You're in a contemplative state when you can observe your field of awareness without judging content, and acknowledging without attachment.

- If you encounter internal or external distractions, observe them without interpretation or attachments and let them return to where they came from. They're not yours, but they can become obstructions if you let them seduce you.

- By not attempting to relax, you release your tension. By not attempting to interpret your experience, you become your experience. Most important, by not intending to create a stage of serenity, you become serenity.

- The stage is now set to recall dysfunctional scripts from your past and to change the felt meanings that support them. You learned to quiet the audience. Now you bring the players and their scripts to the stage: from contemplative observation to contemplative reflection.

Let's start with the challenges of the digital culture. If the topic does not apply to you, replace it with one you want to explore. The technique can be applied to anything you want to change. Remember, start all exercises in the contemplative stage to reduce mind-chatter distractions.

Balancing Digital Culture and Cultural Rituals

- Choose one digital cultural condition that interferes with family coherence. For example, texting during dinner interfering with family conversations.

- Recall the scripts that play out the condition you want to change. For example, your children bring their cell phones or video games to the dinner table, and you try to compete for their attention.

- Feel the sensations and emotions you experience when you play out the frustrating reruns.

- Choose the most frustrating script. For example, when you tell your daughter to turn off her cell phone and she keeps texting or hides her phone under the table.

- Identify the salient emotion: anger, frustration, helplessness, sadness, or any other emotion.

- Notice where and how the emotion manifests in your body: stomach tension, tight jaw, rigidly held shoulders.

- Now observe these sensations and feelings as they ebb and flow in your field of awareness.

- Return to the contemplative stage for the next act by focusing on observing the sensations/ emotions, and defocusing from how they feel. For example, "I am observing (awareness) increased heartbeat, heat around my chest, and so on," rather than "I am angry with my daughter because she disobeys me." Although subtle, this shift from *mind* interpretation to *mindbody* witnessing has profound recontextualizing value that I will discuss at the end of this exercise.

- Explore your creativity by looking for options that fuse the function of the digital culture with the meaning of the cultural ritual. For example, imagine meeting with all the players (family members) and proposing a new script (family experience) to address the dinner disruptions. After suggestions from each member, the kids decide on a new ritual: Pre-dinner texting for 30 minutes replaces the texting during dinner. Although they most likely already text before dinner, *ritualizing* the behavior lends it identity and importance. At the end of the exercise, I'll expand on the power of rituals.

- As you're imagining (in the contemplative stage) the new ritual for your kids, identify the sensations/emotions that surface: resolution, bonding, doubt.

- Notice where and how the emotions manifest in your body: pleasant warmth around your stomach, proud expanding shoulders, sensed anticipation around your legs.

- Observe how these sensations and feelings ebb and flow in your field of awareness.

- Return to the contemplative stage to end the play by focusing on observing the sensations/emotions and defocusing from how they feel. For example, "warm stomach, expanded chest," rather than "I am happy and proud about my creativity." Remember, the shift from mind interpretation to mindbody witnessing has profound recontextualizing value.

- Commit to discussing your new ideas with your family and to incorporating whatever fusing ritual the group decides to adopt.

- End the exercise by observing your surroundings to discover something new: the subtle colors of your curtains, a spot on the wall, how the light from the window hits your chair, and so on. In the Debriefing section I will explain why novelty seeking is a good way to end the contemplative experience.

Debriefing

As I noted in the Introduction, I introduce experiential exercises at the end of each chapter and explain the mindbody processes involved. The themes of the chapter lay out its conceptual framework, and the exercises provide practical applications leading to sustainable change. As you progress through the book, you'll learn more advanced applications of the contemplative method to change difficult scripts that challenge your life. Each chapter varies in the method of winding down your mind. This allows you to discover which procedure works best for you.

Since this is the first chapter of the book, I've included a debriefing to thoroughly explain the process of the contemplative method. Also, I chose a fairly benign example from the digital culture (texting) that you can use as a starting point before moving on to tackle more complex disruptive behavior. In the chapters ahead, I'll include debriefings for certain aspects of the exercises that call for further explanation.

Value of the Contemplative Method

Why not use relaxation or mindfulness instead of contemplation? Because they only cover the first component of the contemplative process: Relaxation reduces muscle tension and mindfulness clears the mind by focusing attention on your immediate present. One relaxes the body and the other quiets the mind. As you know by now, quietude is necessary for sustained awareness but not sufficient to achieve experiential change. The contemplative method you're learning includes the main components of progressive relaxation and mindfulness, but it also converges the objectives of one-pointed (Samatha) and analytic (Vipassana) Tibetan Buddhist meditation. In the "Permanence, Control, and Other Illusions" chapter, I'll have more to say about differences in these methods.

You're welcome to use your own quietude techniques, but note that the contemplative method provides the quietude phase to end mind chatter *and* the discursive reflection phase to experientially "dress rehearse" the desired scripts.

The Quietude Stage and the Discursive Contemplation Phase

To change a culturally contextualized mindbody script, you need to minimize distractions. Once you reach the quietude stage, you can move to the discursive contemplation (experiential dialogue) during which the unwanted scripts can be challenged by more desirable options. Returning to the theater metaphor: Imagine reading a new script for a play while surrounded by noisy people. Also imagine learning a script without rehearsing it onstage. In the rehearsal you experience how *all* of you learns the new material. If you attempt this process in your *disembodied mind* (head trip), you'll get answers that are limited by what your intellect can extract from the total mindbody experience.

Introducing New Rituals

Cultures are confronted with paradigm shifts that challenge established social norms. The introduction of the automobile transitioned the horse-driven carriage to the horseless carriage mind view. But it was more than replacing the horse with the engine: The coachmen became cabdrivers, hay gave way to gasoline, and pollution went from horse manure to carbon monoxide. Although less dramatic, the digital culture exploded access to information and depersonalized communication. Although the shifts could be good or bad for cultural coherence, they are inevitable.

I propose throughout this book that if we learn to ritualize the best of the new and allow it to coexist with the wisdom of the old, we will be nourished by the progress.

Now you can see why I suggested in the experiential exercise to ritualize text messaging without disrupting the wisdom of breaking bread with family. For the digital generation, texting is a habit that could be elevated to ritual. When we ritualize a set of behaviors, we validate them and give them cultural status.

Novelty for Experiential Closure

As you gain proficiency in the mindbody language, you will appreciate the value of *novelty* in health and longevity. For now I'll explain its function in ending the contemplative exercises. When you diminish internal chatter and delve into a contemplative state, there's a disconnection with your external world. This causes your brain to shift from intellectually engaging *alterity* (otherness) to experientially dialoguing with your internal cultural self. Let me bring these heady concepts down to earth. But rather than dumbing down the language, I invite you to engage your intellect and hopefully fall in love with how mindbody science explores the complexity of what you may take for granted.

Alterity is a concept mostly studied in anthropology and grossly ignored in psychology and medicine. But things are changing: The field of cultural neuroscience discovered that the brain processes concepts of selfness and otherness differently based on cultural beliefs. One brain does not fit all.

However, to avoid digressing too much, I'll explain why novelty is one of the best ways to end a contemplative exercise. In fact, novelty is an excellent choice to end any meditation. Finding novelty is the fastest path to reconnecting with your external world after exploring your internal experiences. Why? Because the moment you engage novelty you enter mindfulness—maximum here-and-now awareness. You don't have to meditate for years in a cave to learn mindfulness. Novelty *is* mindfulness because the moment of discovery is the most immediate experience of here and now.

Next we progress from your cultural self within the pale to what happens when you go beyond the pale. Let's move on to the next chapter when you're ready.

chapter 2

Life beyond the Pale

In addition to pursuing the objectives you want, it's also necessary to create the context that supports your results. There's a subtle but essential biocognitive difference between working toward a defined goal and creating the conditions that allow the goal to thrive. If, for example, you want to improve your health, you might decide to eat well, exercise, and meditate. These may be necessary actions that lead to health, but they are not sufficient to create the context where health thrives. Achieving health requires a *mindbody* state coherent with the cultural beliefs that support more than the absence of illness. The pursuit of health within a culture that believes family illnesses are genetic sentences that cannot be changed imposes a major conflict between the goal and the conditions that support the goal.

Cultural beliefs are learned from individuals who are given the authority to determine a collective reality. These *cultural editors* do more than establish what should take place *within the pale*; they also set the admonitions to limit beliefs considered *beyond the pale*. And although their power may appear insurmountable, the moment you recognize that their cultural shackling requires your inadvertent permission, you gain access to a path of liberation that can only be stopped by your fear of displeasing your captors.

I argue that cultural beliefs are embodied in our biology, and they determine how we attribute mindbody cause to our actions based on the cultural portals we embrace. For instance, if you inhabit the cultural portal of "middle age," what happens within that construct will be perceived with middle-age consciousness. You begin to act, feel, dress, and look middle-aged, and if you happen to challenge the imposed reality, the admonitions can go something like this: "What do you mean you want to change professions? You should be planning for your retirement." "Why are you dressing like that? Do you want to look like a teenager?" These constraining statements, supposedly offered "for your own good," keep you within the designated portal, and your mindbody gradually acquiesces to a cultural collusion that will compel you to remain within the pale. *Cultures are powerful contributing architects to your reality, but you are the coauthor of their influence.*

THE STRUCTURE OF CHANGE

Many of the biocognitive principles I teach are counterintuitive. Why? I'll first answer this question with another question. Why do you think change can be so difficult when you want to move beyond your pain? It should be intuitively obvious and simple to choose joy over misery. Yet when you try to move away from the unwanted, the solutions are far from obvious and simple. And the reason is that we learn the patterns and behaviors that do not serve us well either with *paradoxical intentions* or during *initially functional conditions*.

Paradoxical intentions: taking up dangerous drugs to feel accepted; knowingly entering a toxic relationship to relieve your loneliness; choosing to engage in dangerous behavior to test your courage; avoiding people who can contribute to your personal growth so you can feel self-sufficient; doing what you hate about your parents to prove a point.

Initially functional conditions: suppressing anger when dealing with abusive parents; delaying personal needs to care for siblings in neglectful families; using illness to avoid attending school when you're being bullied.

But since the negative factors in paradoxical intentions eventually take their toll, and the initially functional conditions gradually lose their value, you're perplexed when you attempt to reverse what was once simple and functional. The simple becomes complex and the functional turns dysfunctional: The *butterfly effect* sneaks up to welcome chaos. Suddenly, the logical tools that served you well when life was simpler are no longer viable remedies.

I am borrowing the chaos-theory term *butterfly effect* to help illustrate the complexity of cultural change. Chaotic pathways are known to be highly sensitive to initial conditions. Metaphorically, the flapping of butterfly wings in the Amazonian forest shakes pollen off a flower that can make an oxen sneeze, increasing the force of the wind until two weeks later it progresses into a sandstorm in the Sahara Desert: thus, the butterfly effect.

Although mindbody processes are not chaotic in the technical sense, an initially simple behavior can gain cultural complexity as it is repeated in different contexts. Taking the example of the child who was not permitted to express anger in abusive conditions, what was once a straightforward emotional suppression gains complexity when the anger is withheld during any other condition. Anger becomes a prohibited emotion inaccessible to reasonable change.

Knowing how an undesired behavior gains cultural complexity across time can help us decipher the conditions for achieving desired change. Let's explore how complexity can be navigated.

The cultural language we learn to gain acceptance or to protect us from dangerous situations becomes a valuable tool not easily replaced with untested alternatives. The power of this initially desirable language lies in that it satisfies two essential sociocultural needs: *acceptance* and *safety*. And since the intended effects work well in these two specific contexts, there's an implicit reluctance to speculate with new strategies that may bring back painful memories. In the example of using dangerous drugs to gain peer acceptance, what may be mostly remembered when there's a need for change is the isolation felt before complying with the requirements to belong to the group. Of course, these processes are not consciously connected to the faulty logic that maintains behavior that no longer serves us well. As social beings we're willing to pay dearly for belongingness and security.

The cultural editors that coauthor our culturally constructed reality can be additional blocking agents when we attempt to change what no longer serves us. Just because we recognize that our present strategies are no longer useful, it does not follow that cultural editors are willing to change a language that they coauthored with you. Why not? Several reasons: Change may require giving up their authority over you; it may mean that you'll no longer need them on your journey; and most important, it means having to change their own strategies for acceptance and security. An expired ecosystem is not relinquished without a struggle.

The coauthors of change are individuals who are willing to explore worthy options and who support your invitation for acceptance and safety under benign conditions. They are the people who replace the misery in your life with opportunities to coauthor the level of joy that you believe is too good to be true. But you will find that instead of actively seeking these coauthors of change, you should create the conditions that will flawlessly entice them to share your new path.

Filling the vacuum created when you give up the strategies that no longer serve you is imperative to achieve sustainable change. If not diligently filled with worthy alternatives, a vacuum tends to attract known misery more readily than unknown joy. Why? Because, since an unknown future can cause more turbulence than a known present, there's reluctance to rock the boat even when it makes you seasick.

Anchors of Misery

We encounter some people who are committed to misery as a way of life, who seem to thrive in their woes. Some we choose as friends and others choose us as families. While some of these anchors of misery need to be released altogether, with others you may choose to limit their toxicity around you. But I strongly recommend that guilt should never be your reason for keeping toxic people in your life. There are healthy ways to deal with those you choose to endure. The key is to find a worthy reason that lifts your humanity when you choose to be around them. Worthiness takes care of the ethical component of your decision, but the duration and frequency of your contacts determines your protection against coauthoring their toxicity.

I believe there are evil people who choose to live in their darkness, and who enjoy instilling pain on the innocent. Fortunately, the infamous sociopaths I encountered when working as a correctional psychologist in a maximum-security prison are less common than Hollywood would have you believe. After observing the palpable evil in these criminals, I can still report that most people are toxic because of their fear of love rather than because they are evil. For these anchors of misery, love becomes toxic when it exceeds their capacity to experience joy.

At the end of this chapter I'll teach you experiential methods to set healthy emotional limits, but now I'll share some insights that may help you decide who stays and who must be excluded from your wellness journey. The first question to ask is how your life will change if you drop this person or if you reduce your involvement. Sometimes we maintain relationships with anchors of misery because we happen to share a history with them. Something like: "I've known this person since elementary school," or "She knew my grandmother when we were children." These types of reasons touch on two important cultural components: 1. Shared time as bonding agent; 2. Shared history that includes having known some of your favorite family members or valued friends. The first connects them with your personal history, and the second associates them with someone you love. These are powerful bonding factors, independent of the coauthored toxicity.

By considering what would happen if you dropped these people from your life, you can determine what you need to fill the vacuum they will create. In the two bonding examples above, it will require creating new history with worthy coauthors and disconnecting the emotional associations you made with the toxic person and your loved ones. As you know, this is easier said than done. But you'll be pleased to learn that the difficulty stems from trying to use intellectual reasoning to solve unreasonable emotional processes. This imposition of mind over matter can explain why change requires more than motivation and logic. Academic logic is not the same as *cultural logistics*. The former follows sequential reasoning; the latter seeks tribal meaning. This distinction does not mean that one strategy is better than the other. Instead, while logic is a human invention, it was created by cultural minds in a collective consciousness that is more expansive than the invention. The philosopher Michael Polanyi, in his book *The Tacit Dimension,* alludes to what he calls "tacit knowledge" when he suggests that "we can know more than we can tell." I am inviting you to explore how to experience more than you think you can tell.

Cultural Logistics versus Academic Logic

We are taught very early in school how to think logically and how to detect flaws in our reasoning. Logic is a necessary tool to help us choose our best options and maintain consistency in our lives. But parallel to our logical world we have an underlying force I call *cultural logistics*. This cultural dimension predates logic and serves a different purpose. It can be consistent with logical thinking in some contexts, and it can also suddenly switch to tacit codes with cultural parameters that defy conventional reasoning. I'll be more specific to avoid esoteric explanations that get fuzzy and lack substance.

Members of the Ndani tribe in West Papua, New Guinea, cut off a finger as a way of showing their grief at funeral ceremonies. To further express their love, they bury their amputated finger with the deceased. The logic of condolence without amputation is trumped by the tribal meaning of grief. If this seems like a ritual limited to "primitive" cultures, I'll remind you of a similar phenomenon—although less dramatic—in which some highly paid athletes with college degrees will not shave as long as they are winning games, or will not wash their socks for fear of losing games. More specifically, Michael Jordan reportedly never played a professional game without wearing a pair of gym shorts from his alma mater, the University of North Carolina, under his Chicago Bulls uniform. Get the picture? We're cultural beings who live out our rituals and occasionally engage logic in our daily existence. I am obviously pushing the envelope to prove my point, but take time to discover how many of your own rituals defy logic.

THE PRICE OF LIFE BEYOND THE PALE

I hope that as I continue to introduce you to the realm of mindbody anthropology, you will begin to engage your world with a cultural mindfulness that can help you realize that you're much more than your genetic endowment. In fact, I propose that your genes are mostly expressed based on the cultural perception you learned to help you find purpose and meaning in your life. In the chapter "The Cultural Brain," I'll go into more details about gene expression. For now, let's look at the practical implications of how cultural beliefs affect you when you venture beyond the pale. Anytime you try to change behavior, good or bad, always look at the function it is serving. You may be amazed to find how clever your mindbody can be in order to comply with your intentions. Nothing happens without a function; some continue to serve you well, while others turn rogue when they lose their initial purpose. Some initial functions are developmental: an infant crying when hungry, pointing to objects before learning language, and so on. These processes are so essential to our survival that we continue to use them in disguised ways throughout our lives. Most strategies work well, but the difficulty occurs when we fail to recognize their initial function as well as when they are no longer viable.

The strategies we learn to function within the pale are designed to serve the collective needs of the tribe. Your primal needs for acceptance and safety are met because there's an investment in your future contributions to the tribe. Rather than for Machiavellian reasons, most tribes work for the collective good. So when does the problem begin? As you increase your self-reliance, you decrease your dependence on the tribe, and although acceptance and safety continue to be basic needs, you're willing to risk them in search of your own identity.

You can begin to appreciate how the transition from dependence to independence is a subtle and profound process. The need for acceptance and safety changes, but what may not be so obvious is that the strategies that work well within the pale become counterproductive when applied beyond the pale. Adding to the complexity is the resistance you encounter from the cultural editors who are invested in keeping you from stepping out of the collective mind-set. At that time, the proverbial "for your own good" becomes the rationalization for admonishing your digressions.

Life beyond the pale can be the most exhilarating time of your life, but it requires a different compass to navigate uncharted paths. Whereas before you relied on tribal wisdom to confront turbulence, now you have to explore the dynamics of self-reliance.

Navigating Uncharted Pathways

Tribal wisdom is contextual: You learn to use a hammer to drive nails, but when confronted with a screw, all the acquired hammering skills must be replaced with learning how to use a screwdriver. Although this is an obviously transparent example, it's not intended to insult your intelligence or to bore you. In my biocognitive theory, lessons are grounded on the most basic scenarios to illustrate how sensitivity to initial conditions can progress from the mundane to a highly complex *field of bioinformation*: a dance where mind influences the body and culture influences the mind.

I'll define "simple" as a condition where cause and effect are easily determined, and it turns to "complicated" when determining cause and effect becomes more difficult. But *complicated* and *complex* are not the same. Situations progress from simple to complicated differently than from complicated to complex. By definition, complexity is a highly variable state where cause and effect are not determinable. The best we can do is to find correlations that show the highest probability of having causal value. Without jumping into technical complexity theory, let me land this concept with plain language.

We can track weather patterns and make predictions until they lose their linearity: prediction from point A to point B breaks down. When patterns lose their linearity, they go from point A to unknown multiple points. And you may rightfully ask, "What the hell does all this have to do with a book that's supposed to help me learn longevity and the causes of health?" Well, following the style of your question, here's my answer: It has a hell of a lot to do with how our brains function to make sense of simple, complicated, and complex situations. And if we don't understand the difference, we will continue to be perplexed when we fail to change what no longer serves us, when we try to learn longevity, and when we try to access the causes of our health. So what do you think now? If you stick with me, you will engage your brilliance and your patience in a way that will increase mastery of your destiny.

THE COMPLEXITY COMPASS

Now that you know how rules change drastically when you enter complexity, I'll introduce you to a tool that can guide you in times of complex turbulence. Simple and complicated turbulence require drawing from strategies that worked during prior similar conditions. Past knowledge becomes your functional tool. But whereas in simple and complicated conditions you can go from the hammer to the screwdriver, complexity requires dropping the hammer and navigating the turbulence in a way that will help you discover new strategies. If you skip this phase, however, you will enter perplexity rather than complexity. The former causes anxiety and the latter offers an opportunity for discovery—fear versus a date with novelty.

A linear compass always points to true north, but the complexity compass I propose points to the novelty in turbulence. So rather than looking for familiar patterns, you should detect what is the most unique component of the turbulence. Sometimes the uniqueness could be the most out-of-order or intriguing aspects of the turbulence. Once you detect the novelty, then you begin to look for correlations without concern for logical reasons: *what appears to go together without apparent reasons.*

Let's clarify using a common example: You're used to relying on others to give you driving directions because you were taught by your cultural editors that you're not good at finding your way around. Then you move to a new city and get lost in the middle of heavy traffic. You panic because, in addition to feeling lost, you *believe* you're not good with directions. At the end of the chapter I'll show you how to deal with the turbulence, but for now let's explore the complexity compass. Finding novelty: Go to the traffic lane that is moving fastest; look for the most relaxed driver in cars around you; look for the most inviting place to stop and recalculate your route; take the opportunity of feeling lost to challenge the label of being "bad with directions."

You may have noticed that none of my suggestions offer a solution to get you from point A to point B. Instead, they guide you to discover novelty rather than engage helplessness. Why? Because to resolve simple and complicated turbulence requires finding cause, but complexity requires finding novel correlations that gradually lead you to exit the turbulence. If this section seems confusing, it should. The reason is that you're entering a new paradigm that will help you understand why complex change is so difficult to implement. It's important to recognize, however, that the difficulty stems from using the wrong compass.

Let's look at the wisdom of finding novelty in the traffic example above.

1. Turbulence causes anxiety because it reduces your sense of control. You feel helpless in the middle of heavy traffic because you don't know how to proceed.

2. Discovering novelty increases control. You go from feeling helpless in the traffic jam to regaining control by entering the fastest-moving lane. Then you can test whether this lane is consistently the fastest to get you out of the heavy traffic: looking for correlation.

3. Discovering serenity in the middle of turbulence reduces anxiety. Looking for a relaxed driver in congested traffic connects you with someone who remains serene in the middle of turbulence. This unique observation offers an invitation to bond with serenity. Reducing anxiety increases your sense of direction.

4. Seeking additional novelty increases your sense of adventure. Stopping at a pleasant place gives you opportunities for discovery under more serene conditions: finding better routes, taking time to enjoy your surroundings, and so on. Also, since engaging novelty increases creativity, it can bring you closer to discovering ways to exit complex turbulence.

5. Evidence of mastery (overcoming a challenge) shifts a mind-set of helplessness to empowerment consciousness. Finding your way to your destination on your own provides evidence that contradicts your belief that you're bad with directions.

These deceptively simple strategies have significant mindbody consequences. As you move from the anxiety of turbulence to the empowerment of mastery, your biology shifts from triggering stress hormones that suppress your immune system to releasing anti-inflammatory and antibody molecules that strengthen your immunological protection. When you read the "Cultural Brain" chapter, you will learn how these changes take place.

Now you may be able to see why the complexity compass points to the inherent novelty in complex turbulence. Next time you panic when your objectives are radically derailed, shift your focus from looking for old tools from the past to discovering new strategies in the present.

CHALLENGING THE CULTURAL BELIEFS YOU WERE TAUGHT TO ACCEPT

When you venture beyond the pale, some of your within-the-pale beliefs will be challenged, but I caution that appealing to reason is not sufficient to change well-established perceptions coauthored and sustained by your cultural editors. Returning to the driving example, once you have evidence that you can be good with directions, you will find that the old scripts that supported the limiting myth need to be confronted and modified when replayed by your cultural editors. I suggest that when you dismiss your old scripts, you should give your coauthors permission to not like your new strategies, and, in some cases, to not accept your new beliefs. Remember, your evidence of mastery should be used to change your self-perception rather than to change the perceptions others have of you.

One of the most effective ways to strengthen your new beliefs is to share them with friends and family who are willing to coauthor excellence with you. It's also helpful to recognize moments when you defy your old image and when you celebrate your new assertiveness.

We are cultural beings who require social acceptance in order to thrive and build worthiness. The good news is that you can choose the social circles that promote your personal development. This requires carefully selecting the coauthors you choose to share your personal journey.

DISCOVERING THE ARCHITECTS OF YOUR LIMITATIONS

We're born with propensities to express our causes of health, our empathy, and our unique excellence. And although not all within-the-pale lessons are bad, it's important to discover how we learn the limitations that stifle our potential for abundance of wellness, love, and success. But your discoveries should not lead to blaming those who taught you to undervalue who you are. Instead, when you recognize that you were exposed to dysfunctional lessons from teachers who imposed their limitations "for your own good," it can free you from another myth: *You are a slave of your genetics.* Your DNA cannot be changed, but how your genes are expressed is mostly controlled by the cultural beliefs you share with your tribe. This correlation elevates mindbody science to a place of hope grounded in robust evidence that longevity is learned, the causes of health are inherited, and your ceiling of success is determined by your worthiness. And although this book is not meant to provide a quick fix for complex problems, the mindbody methods I teach are powerful antidotes for the learned despair you may be inadvertently imposing on yourself and those you choose to love.

Most life lessons are learned by observation. In fact, what your parents and other cultural editors teach you with words is not as powerful as what you learn from observing their actions. Let's suppose you saw your father succeed in his career at the price of hating his job and anesthetizing his pain with alcohol. His verbal lesson to you might have been that you should do what you love; your observed lesson was more likely that success requires deprivation and struggle. The significant conflict in assimilating your dad's positive lessons is that the symbol of success you witnessed is associated with a journey of pain. Later, you reason that your dad's way is not for you, and that you will succeed without having to pay his price. Everything goes well because you're purposely following a different path. Surprisingly, the turbulence comes when you reach the success you want—*without* suffering major struggles and planned deprivation. Why the turbulence? Because reaching your objective is based on your deliberate actions to be different, but maintaining your success is influenced by your embodied cultural beliefs. The goal is based on reason, and the outcome is tainted with the negative embodied evidence you witnessed from your dad.

This incompatibility between your dad's journey and yours can cause a very subtle, but powerful, conflict. Your internal dialogue could go something like this: "I did better than my dad. I succeeded without having to pay his price." Then what may happen is that you begin to look for ways to compensate for the "inequity." Some counterproductive reactions to your perceived inequity could be to let guilt for your joy sabotage your success; to resent your dad for not living up to your expectations; or to mask your internal conflict with behaviors of excess (alcohol, drugs, gambling). These self-defeating patterns can trigger gene expressions that compromise your immune system and allow illness to be the price you pay for your success. If this sounds like dynamics limited to psychiatric disorders, look around you to see how some psychologically "normal" people you know sabotage their success with devastating financial decisions or by contracting an illness at the peak of their success.

I argue that although psychiatric disorders can lead to the deep conflicts I am illustrating here, many people who are psychologically sound suffer from sociocultural disharmonies that mimic mental illness. I want to be clear that I am not implying that health professionals impose their treatments on healthy people. Instead, I am suggesting that some dysfunctions that stem from violating cultural agreements are diagnosed and treated as pathology rather than as normal life challenges.

FROM COLLECTIVIST TO INDIVIDUALIST PERCEPTION

Although our early perceptions are grounded in culturally learned collectivist premises, our development also requires individuation. What does this mean? While we mostly function tightly connected with tribal objectives, to develop a sense of who we are as individuals requires making decisions that mostly serve our unique needs. Some of these decisions can place us in direct opposition to the collective goals of our tribe. At this point of our journey we're faced with two choices: developing our personal identity or surrendering to a diffused self that is mostly defined by tribal rules. Many are willing to pay the price of a collectivist identity for the sake of belongingness and safety.

Fortunately, there are outliers who defy their cultural restraints and move on to self-discovery. These rebels bypass the stigma of family illnesses: They refuse to be defined by their age, they maintain their sense of humor, and they look surprisingly younger than their chronological age. The primary characteristic that defines outliers is their ability to avoid the cultural portals that determine their progression through life. When you enter a culturally established portal, you surrender to the expectations of the portal. Since our biology is influenced by our cultural beliefs, our mindbody conforms to what we are expected to be in each portal. The moment you capitulate to the expectations of cultural portals, you become one with the constraints of the portal. For example, the moment you enter the culturally defined *retirement portal*, you embrace the limitations of the portal: You acquire a retirement consciousness that admonishes against falling in love again, starting a new career, making plans beyond the actuarial tables that predict how long you're going to live, defying notions of how you should look your age, and so on.

NAVIGATING THE CULTURAL PORTALS

We generally develop our identity through the cultural portals of our tribes. This apparently seamless process shifts from one set of portal expectations to another. The newborn, child, teenage, young adult, middle-aged, and elderly portals have designated identities and limits. But most important, attributions and expectations change from portal to portal. Additionally, rather than being universal, portals differ from culture to culture. For instance, if you go to a doctor with pain in your elbow without knowing the cause, the attribution is strongly influenced by the cultural portal you're in. In the child portal, the pain may be attributed to a fall, but if you are in the elderly portal, it could be attributed to your age. The child is told to run more carefully to avoid falling; the elderly patient is asked, "What do you expect at your age?" In the U.S., the cause of a migraine is mainly attributed to vascular/hormonal disturbance; in France, to liver symptoms; and in the U.K., to gastrointestinal irregularities. Although migraines have multiple causes, medical science is not exempt from cultural influence.

Armed with these anthropological principles, you can look into which cultural portal is presently defining who you are. Based on your culture, once you recognize the portal you're in, you can begin to explore beyond-the-pale paths that can lead to your individuation.

When you identify what you need as an individual versus accepting the constraints determined by your cultural portals, you can decide what is beneficial in your present portal, and what stifles you within the pale. If you recall what was most significant in each of the portals you've lived, you will find the labels and identities you coauthored. For example, in the childhood portal you were identified as intelligent, in the adolescent as wild, in the young adult as ambitious, in the middle-aged as responsible, and so on. Some of the labels could be accurate, but if you take them as fixed personality traits, you will continue to be vulnerable to additional branding that ignores contextual influences. I'll explain: Intelligence, wildness, responsibility, and any other portal label does not consider the contexts that branded a part of you as all of you.

The good news is that if you explore the conditions (contexts) that triggered each of the portal identities you coauthored, you can begin to enhance what served you well, dismiss what is no longer functional, and move forward knowing you can design contexts that promote your worthiness. But I caution that the recontextualizing process requires more than reasoning your way in and out of portals. In each of the cultural portals you learn a powerful mindbody language requiring experiential tools that I will introduce in the applications section at the end of the chapter.

THE INTIMATE LANGUAGE OF YOUR CULTURAL SELF

Now you know that cultural portals influence your identity and that unwittingly you coauthor the process. Gradually, you begin to communicate an intimate language that expresses a convergence of your labels from previous portals and the expectations of your present portal. Following the branding examples above: You assimilated labels of intelligent, wild, and responsible. But what you did not learn is that these labels are contextual, and if you use them in favorable conditions, they serve you well, but when you express them out of context, they lose their beneficial value and become dysfunctional. Perhaps the intelligent identity worked well because you had inspiring teachers who coauthored the best in you, and the wild identity in the adolescence portal came from abusing drugs that coauthored the worst in you. But as you worked your way out of the drug culture, you began to coauthor responsibility with your spouse and children, who need you.

So who are you now? You are all and you are none of the identities you acquired in your cultural portals. This answer may sound like a Zen koan (riddle), but instead, it's a proposal that you are what you coauthor with your contexts. This does not mean, however, that you are a puppet controlled by cultural portals. But you could be, if you don't question the subtle cultural lessons you received from your tribe as you traveled its portals.

Your cultural self retains some of the rituals and archetypes that you learn across cultural portals. Although some of these stable characteristics will be challenged in some portals, the challenge could be an opportunity to evaluate what to uphold or dismiss in the process. I believe that cultures mold helplessness or empowerment. Helplessness engulfs your cultural self when you conclude that you're not willing to set limits with your cultural editors for fear of losing the belongingness and safety they provide. Empowerment, however, is embraced when you decide that the belongingness and safety you have are not worth the price of losing your identity. Helplessness confuses belongingness with ownership, and safety with dependence.

I'll use relationships with partners or groups to explain what I am proposing. Belonging *with* a partner/group is very different than belonging *to* a partner/group. I am certain you've known people who are in relationships or groups in which one person functions as if they own their partner or the other group members. They control the decisions their partner and group members make, and they are unwilling to recognize the ownership price their partner or group members are paying.

In the case of safety, an implicit agreement is made where one partner or group leader becomes the "protector." Of course, the price for the protection is relinquishing control. As you can see, dysfunctional belongingness and safety have different psychological processes, but both require relinquishing control—one to feel emotionally connected, the other to feel protected.

Each of the cultural portals can enhance or diminish healthy belongingness and safety, consequently leading to helplessness or empowerment.

Operational Definitions:

Helplessness is a condition where resources are not sufficient or available to overcome a challenge.

Empowerment is a condition where you have sufficient access to resources that can overcome a challenge.

Take time to assess the following:

- What is your present portal mostly demanding of you?

- Are you paying a price for your belongingness?

- Are you paying a price for your safety?

- How did previous portals contribute to your helplessness?

- How did previous portals contribute to your empowerment?

I hope you're appreciating the power that cultures have to mold your perception in very subtle ways. But more important, as you discover how you become what you coauthor, you can begin to change what no longer is in your best interest. At the end of the chapter, I'll share methods you can use to resolve any conflicts you detect after answering the questions above.

CULTURAL EDITORS AND ARCHETYPES

Cultures develop their identity slowly through trial-and-error strategies that are passed on from one generation to the next. When the needs of the tribe reach a point where they're no longer functioning for you, you face the dichotomy of choosing to acquiesce or rebel. Although one can enslave you and the other can set you free, both options have consequences because change, whether good or bad, causes turbulence. As you may recall, cultural editors are chosen by the tribes and are given authority to promote and maintain a within-the-pale consciousness. Although their authority is contextually defined, the effects are not readily discerned from portal to portal. Some examples of cultural editors and their assigned contexts of authority are: parents at home, teachers in classrooms, doctors in hospitals, clergy members in places of worship.

In addition to the cultural editors who define the social structure of a culture, there are universal constructs called archetypes that are found in every culture. The intriguing aspect of archetypes is that although they are found in every culture, they are also influenced by the collective rules of the tribe. The archetypes evolve from the function they have in each culture. Some examples of archetypes are: mother, father, warrior, healer, teacher, student, visionary, hero, and so on. I purposely did not use the traditionally female *heroine* label as archetype because heroism has no gender. Also, using *hero* to mean both genders rescues the term from its male-imposed exclusivity.

43

But just as cultural editors coauthor your cultural self, archetypes coauthor their universal function with their culture. The father archetype in Eastern cultures has a different image and function than its counterpart in Western cultures. The father archetype's mission to coauthor the development of the child is the same in all cultures, but how the mission is accomplished is culturally interpreted. For example, the mother archetype in one culture may be more authoritarian, nourishing, and essential than in another culture: The archetype co-emerges with the implicit rules of the culture.

So far on our Indiana Jones journey we've identified cultural editors, cultural portals, and archetypes. By now, I hope you appreciate the complexity of developing your cultural self. But use this awareness to embrace curiosity, rather than to avoid challenges. Explore with trust or be overwhelmed with fear.

You enter cultural portals with set expectations dictated by cultural editors of what you should be at each stage of your journey. Eventually, you also embrace archetypes that reflect the collective consciousness of your culture. If you were an intelligent child, a rebellious teenager, and a responsible mother, you have some clues about what you coauthored in each portal on your journey toward *individuation* (ultimate selfhood).

At this point you may wonder what the difference is between cultural editors and archetypes. They appear to serve a similar coauthoring function in your development. The cultural editor is given authority limited to a context. For example, a chef has more cultural influence in the kitchen of her restaurant than a doctor who orders dinner at the restaurant. But the chef and the doctor may assimilate the same teacher archetype in the development of their respective cultural selves. One teaches the art of cooking and the other teaches the technology of healing. The cultural editor is the weather and the archetype is the climate. To further differentiate, cultural editors lose authority outside of their designated contexts, but the archetype that you assimilate influences how you function across contexts and cultural portals. The archetype you embrace becomes your strategy to engage the world and your universal identity. If, for example, you embrace the hero archetype, your implicit mission is to save the world; the mother archetype, to nourish the world; and so on.

Some possible scenarios could be a teacher in the classroom (cultural editor) who conveys his lessons in the father or hero archetype, and a mother at home who cares for her children in the healer archetype. But I must caution that although archetypes are universal, they can be dysfunctional if overused across contexts. For instance, if you embrace the teacher archetype, it excels in the classroom and in rearing children, but if overdone with partners, lessons become pontifications that will eventually be resented. The journey of the mindbody self requires finding *the middle way* in every lesson.

The distinctions will gain significance as I explain how cultural editors and archetypes can influence your health and longevity. Everything that we do is contextual for a reason. To make sense of your world and to function at your best, you have to be coherent with your context. A clown will find it difficult to preach a sermon that would be second nature to a clergy member, and vice versa. But a clergy cultural editor who has a clown archetype could entertain and make the parishioners laugh while delivering the sermon. You see?

Cultural editors convey the different segments of wisdom of a culture: how and what to learn in each portal, how to heal, rites of passage, views on aging, and all the other essential learning required to identify with the tribe. Archetypes are more universal because they tap into what Swiss psychiatrist Carl Jung called the *collective unconscious*.

With the recent advances in cultural neuroscience, we now have a better understanding of how the brain learns within a culture, as well as how far a culture can influence the brain. In other words, because of its makeup, there are universal components of the human brain that remain fairly stable across cultures: the prefrontal lobe of each brain handles our planning and abstracting, the hippocampus archives the context of our memories. And although there's much brain plasticity (parts of the brain can change functions based on trauma or context), all members of all cultures share the potential and limits of their brains.

THE HORIZONS OF CULTURAL EDITORS AND ARCHETYPES

As human beings we develop strategies to make sense of our world. Our brains are designed to determine meaning based on the contextual conditions involved. Someone approaching you with a knife in an alley alerts your brain to interpret potential danger. But if you want to purchase a knife at a department store, when the salesperson approaches you with a knife, your brain makes a benign interpretation. Similarly, cultural editors function within their respective contexts to maximize the teaching of tribal rules at different stages of your life: The most efficient context for a teacher is the classroom, the hospital for a doctor, and the home for a parent. The unique contribution that I propose throughout this book is that our biology also works best when our function is coherent with its context. When there's incoherence between function and context, our actions become dysfunctional and can lead to illnesses.

The lover archetype works well in an intimate context with a partner, but if the lover stays in this archetype in a context with children, not only does it violate the law by committing incest, but also creates a mindbody dysfunction with serious consequences for the lover and the child. Why? Because our biology adjusts to the demands of the context in order to maximize mindbody coherence. If you're a successful CEO running a global company, the leader archetype is the most effective to run the organization, but this archetype loses its ultimate function if you use it in your personal relationships that require a partner, mother, or sibling archetype. Returning to the tools analogy, if you use the handle of a screwdriver to hammer a nail, you will damage a tool that was made for a context of screws.

What happens when cultural editors and archetypes go beyond their contexts? Cultural editors lose their contextual authority, resulting in disempowerment. Archetypal transgressions, however, have more serious consequences. Archetypes are universal constructs with deeper meaning and function. The best way I know to explain transgressions is by giving examples.

The authority context of the teacher as cultural editor is limited to the classroom and learning materials in the tribe, but the context of the teacher as archetype has universal symbolism and transcends the parameters of its culture of origin. Nelson Mandela was an attorney from South African culture and a member of the Xhosa tribe. Martin Luther King, Jr., was a pastor from Southern Baptist and African American culture. And Mahatma Gandhi was an attorney from Indian Hindu culture. All had different cultural-editor identities (professions) and came from different cultures, but all three inspired the world (transcultural) with their visionary archetype.

Tribal members become cultural editors through their professions, vocations, and assigned responsibilities, but archetypes are defined by the symbolic identity they occupy in their cultures and beyond. Cultural editors are given responsibilities and authority limited to their contextual space, but archetypes emerge to represent universal symbols of the best and the worst in our human species: Mother Teresa versus Adolf Hitler.

Then, how can going beyond the set tribal horizons cause illness? The loss of function is clearly noted when cultural editors go beyond their contextual domain: they lose their authority. But how archetypes affect health is more difficult to illustrate because the problem stems from the interaction between cultural editors and archetypes. Before going further, I want to clarify that we are all cultural editors but very few of us embrace archetypes.

Let's explore the process using another example: You embrace the visionary archetype and you're designated the cultural editorship of leader for a large company. As long as you're functioning within the visionary/leader parameters, your mindbody thrives: Your cultural editorship and archetype are cohesive in a business context. But let's suppose that you take your visionary/leader function home where the family context requires you to coauthor partner and parent rather than visionary/leader. The transgression of context triggers a dysfunctional coauthoring between you and your family because what served you well at work is incompatible with the needs of a home context.

The *loss of authority* of the leader and the *loss of meaning* of the visionary are two of the main ingredients that can lead to illness. After many years as a consultant for global companies, I found that rather than stress, responsibility without authority and work without meaning are the two strongest contributing factors to chronic illness. I'll explain how illnesses can be triggered when loss of authority and meaningless behavior take hold of your life.

Loss of authority is another way of describing loss of resources to overcome a challenge; loss of meaning equals loss of purpose. When we humans—as well as any other living system—are unable to access resources to overcome a challenge, we go into a state of physiological helplessness that weakens the immune system's ability to the fight pathogens that wait patiently for opportunities to compromise our health. Additionally, tasks void of meaning negatively affect the overall purpose for living. Living without purpose leads to a meaningless existence that can also compromise immune function and, consequently, health and longevity. People who retire without meaningful purpose live an average of six years beyond retirement. Why? Because watching sunsets in lovely settings is not sufficient to maintain optimal health. Some may ask, "How could something that I worked hard for many years to obtain be detrimental?" The key to the riddle is that, in many cases, "working hard" implies delaying present joy for a future with little meaning. If you're not convinced, I ask you to withhold final judgment until you finish this book. You may be pleasantly surprised when you read the "Growing Older versus Cultural Aging" chapter.

Tools to Navigate beyond the Pale

Now I'll teach you practical methods to make sustainable mindbody changes. But as you've gathered from the previous chapter, these changes have to be embodied with a new felt meaning. This means you have to reexperience how and under what conditions you learned the behavior you want to recontextualize. I cannot overemphasize that biocognitive techniques are different from cognitive behavioral therapy. That is, we're not intellectually replacing one behavior with another. Instead, we are changing the experiential meaning of the behavior and the context where it was assimilated. In order to achieve lasting change, the techniques are introduced after you deliberately enter a contemplative mode, rather than under hypnosis. As I noted in the "Coauthoring the MindBody Self" chapter, the suggested method of winding down your mind is a bit different in each chapter, so you can find the way that works best for you.

Discovering Novelty and Setting Benign Boundaries

- Go to your favorite place where you can take time to practice contemplative techniques without distractions. Sit quietly and pay attention to what you're thinking, feeling, and sensing in your mindbody field as if you were watching the patterns and movements of clouds.

- Scan your body for areas of tension and observe its manifestations without trying to release them. The mindbody language for releasing is passive *observation*, rather than active intention.

- As you observe without judgment, notice any novelty in your scanning. For example, you may be observing patterns of thoughts, sensations, images, and emotions that keep reappearing in your field of internal awareness. Notice when a new pattern surfaces. Pay attention without attachment to these novelty percepts, and let them pass on. Do this process for a few minutes. This exercise helps you tune in to your internal novelty so you can then look for the novelty in your external world. Knowing how to tune in to novelty is one of the ingredients for healthy longevity. It also prepares you to assimilate new lessons faster and more effectively.

- Now you can proceed from discovering novelty to calibrating your benign boundaries when setting limits.

- Bring to your field of internal awareness (your mind's eye) a situation where you think you need firmer limits with someone in your life. Decide if you want to merely set limits or fully exclude that person from your life.

- If you decide to maintain the relationship, determine the area where you want to set limits. For example: frequency or duration of visits with someone who is not supportive; avoiding conditions in which you feel manipulated; determining what you require to keep someone in your life.

- In your continued state of contemplation, bring the person and what you want to limit into your internal field of awareness.

- Determine the extremes of your limits before trying to calibrate your benign boundary. For example, if you want to cut the frequency and duration of visits with that person, determine what would be too much and too little. Perhaps one extreme might be three times a week for five hours per visit; the other extreme, once every three months for one hour per visit.

- Test each limit using two emotions: resentment and guilt. If you do too much, you will feel resentment; if you don't do enough, you will feel guilt.

- Move back and forth from one extreme and its corresponding emotion (guilt or resentment) to the other until you sense your benign boundary: a place where you feel no guilt and no resentment. It may take more practice to calibrate your benign boundary if you tend to frequently feel guilty or resentful in your interactions with others.

- While doing the extremes shifting, notice where you embody the felt meaning. In other words, what are the sensations, thoughts, images, and emotions you experience when you go to each extreme? Experiencing the unique mindbody cluster generated by each extreme will also help you recognize any time when you're in a guilt or resentment mode. For example, feeling tension in your stomach, heat around your neck, and sadness when you're in the guilt mode; feeling tension in your chest, pressure in your head, and anger when you're in the resentment mode. The felt meaning clusters vary from culture to culture and person to person. Anytime you recognize either felt meaning cluster, you will also know if you're doing too much or not enough in a specific context. You can stop this exercise when you're ready and try the next one later, or you can return to the state of contemplation you learned above and continue to the next exercise.

Resolving Panic during Turbulent Conditions

Panic is the extreme expression of fear. It can be triggered by dangerous conditions, loss of control, and anticipation of punishment. Identifying the characteristics of panic will let you know how to navigate it and shortcut its intensity and duration. Now let's go to the tools.

- After reaching your desired state of contemplation, bring back a memory of a situation where you felt extreme fear. Elaborate the panic scenario in your internal field of awareness.

- Allow the cluster of felt meaning generated by the memory to manifest as much as you can safely experience. If the cluster of felt meaning feels like more than you can handle at this time, either stop the exercise or choose a memory with less intensity. It could be fear without reaching panic intensity. *If you suffer from panic attacks or other anxiety disorders, consult your mental health professional before attempting this exercise.*

- After you identify the cluster of felt meaning (shallow breathing, tight chest, fear, negative images, etc.), determine the salient characteristic of the fear/panic memory: loss of control, danger, or anticipation of punishment?

- For the *loss of control factor*: Recall a time when you felt in control; elaborate the conditions in your field of internal awareness and embody the cluster of felt meaning (proud, pleasant, warm, relieved). For the *dangerous factor*: Follow the same recalling and embodying procedure, but this time use a memory of a time when you were faced with danger and acted in a way that was courageous or wise (or empowered, strong, accomplished, resilient, relieved). For the *punishment anticipation factor*: Follow the same recalling and embodying procedure, but this time use a memory of a time when you faced punishment and endured the emotional and/or physical pain. Think about how it added to your emotional strength (serenity, resourcefulness, relief).

- This is the most important part of the exercise: Shift from the felt meaning cluster of the source of panic to the antidotal felt meaning cluster. As you shift from one to the other, notice how the negative cluster begins to subside when juxtaposed with the positive cluster. Do the shifting until you begin to sense a transition from helplessness to empowerment. Commit to celebrating your mastery of this technique with one of your coauthors of wellness.

Debriefing

Now let's unpack the dynamics of these exercises.

Both exercises included embodying the clusters of felt meaning. Why? Because, unlike most *cognitive* methods that replace one behavior with another, *biocognitive* tools recontextualize the felt meaning of the targeted behavior. The former modifies behavior with mind strategies, whereas the latter redefines the cluster of felt meanings with mindbody experiences. Similarly, both exercises included the *relief factor*. Why? The felt meaning of relief is the closure phase of fear and panic: a shift from the end of helplessness to the beginning of empowerment. The repeated shifting from one felt meaning cluster to another allows a meeting of horizons where most mindbody change takes place. In the "Entering the Biosymbolic World" chapter, I explain in greater detail how and why change happens between horizons of felt meaning clusters.

I am purposely using biocognitive terminology to help you expand your interpretations from the reductionist worldview model most of us learned to the mindbody model that views the world as an inseparable living field of information (bioinformation) that finds meaning in culturally constructed contexts. These practical exercises are designed based on your needs for desired change, and they should be practiced in the safety of your internal awareness field, under deep contemplation, before you try them in actual circumstances in your life. I also recommend that you gradually practice the exercises that interest you in this book until they become second-nature tools for times of turbulence or to change what no longer serves you well.

chapter 3

Entering the Biosymbolic World

Most of us can agree that mind and body communicate with each other, but when it comes to explaining how the communication takes place, theories go from esoteric word gymnastics to reductionist mechanics. They lack the substance to be convincing. But why is it so difficult to explain what seems self-evident? I believe the main obstacle is that the life sciences continue to alternate between two opposing premises: It's either mind over matter or matter over mind. In my opinion, there are two major considerations missing:

1. Mind and body communication *co-emerges* as inseparable oneness rather than one emerging from the other: replacing mind-body with *mindbody*.

2. The co-emergence is contextually and culturally influenced. Sentient beings do not communicate in a vacuum: replacing mind-body with *mindbody* in a culturally influenced context.

I'll expand on my two proposals to avoid word spinning that could put you to sleep.

FROM SYMBOL TO BIOSYMBOL

After years of discarding theories that added to the confusion, I found how the domain of mind (word, thought, sign, gesture, memory, image) co-emerges with the domain of body (emotion, sensation, feeling, mood) to coauthor symbols. For example, a dweller of the Amazonian rain forest sees a stop sign, and although curiosity about the novel object will trigger physiological reactions (pupil dilation, dopamine release, and so on), the sign does not have the meaning given to it by a dweller of the developed world. To one, it arouses curiosity; to the other, it gives instructions to stop. The process to recognize here is that whether they cause curiosity or convey instructions, *symbols are interpretations rather than representations of our world*. This subtle contrast differentiates *biocognitive* (mindbodyculture) theory from *cognitive* (mind) theories that argue that symbols are mere representation of our environment. But for now, let's move on with further clarifications. The reason I used the example of curiosity versus instruction is because it will make it easier for me to explain how culture is interwoven with the interpretation of symbols and how symbols affect our biology as they transition to biosymbols. In other words, since the Amazonian rain forest culture does not include stop signs in its symbols domain, its members will perceive a red octagonal object with white markings. Anticipating your question—"Is the Amazonian interpreting anything?"—the answer is yes. Let me suggest why. To perceive that an object is not part of their cultural perception requires *interpreting* that it does not belong to their domain. Hopefully, as you learn more about biocognition you'll agree with my proposal that *culture is a collectively learned propensity for how to perceive the world*.

Cultural Perception

If perhaps you're finding this too theoretical for your taste, I assure you that if you stick with me, you will understand why and how biosymbols can facilitate your healing or make you sick. Remember, we're not into the quick-fix or sound-bite mentality that leads to disappointing results. Instead, when you learn how something works, you know what to do when it breaks.

If we can agree that symbols are culturally interpreted with different degrees of mindbody registry, then we can propose that perception is culturally learned. In other words, our culture submits the meaning of our experience. I argue that symbols are actually *biosymbols* (embodied interpretations) that we experience even before we have a language to describe them. For example, a newborn *feels* physical discomfort when hungry, and comfort after feeding. Yet the words *hunger, breast, milk, mother,* and *bottle* are absent until the baby acquires a language. But, although at that early developmental stage there's no language to interpret what the infant perceives, there is physiology that registers the conditions that transition from the discomfort to the comfort experience. And since nourishment is essential for survival, we're predisposed to pay profound attention to the people and contexts we learn to associate with our preservation. Of course, the associations are prelinguistic interpretations of what we register somatically and cognitively.

But like any other biosymbolic learning, breastfeeding can vary culturally: Following childbirth, a mother from Ecuador is taught to remain indoors for 42 days; a traditional Korean family prohibits people other than the parents from seeing the newborn for the first 100 days; Lebanese culture discourages breastfeeding; in the U.K. and France, the old tradition of hiring wet nurses to breastfeed is gaining popularity. Once again, these examples illustrate how interpretations of our mindbody experiences vary across cultural contexts.

THE MINDBODY ARCHIVES

In the "Life beyond the Pale" chapter, you learned that cultural editors strongly influence the molding of your beliefs because of the contextual authority given them by the tribe. The power is strongest in the designated context of the cultural editor: doctor in hospital, parent at home, teacher in classroom, chef in restaurant, clergy member in place of worship, and so on. Now we can go deeper and see *how* our beliefs are transduced to our biology. Initially, the implicit mindbody language we learn is designed to meet our basic needs for survival. But when we discover awareness of selfhood (15 to 18 months old), contextual meaning becomes the driving force of our existence. As soon as toddlers learn a new word, they start testing it in different contexts to differentiate the meaning—a way of deepening the interpretation. For example, the word *mother* is initially interpreted as a symbol for all females, but when the child discovers that only one female is the mother, the contextual meaning also changes: A female who does not breastfeed is not mother, but perhaps nourishes the child with a formula bottle at daycare.

The reason I am illustrating this obvious developmental process is because as the child learns to differentiate symbols determined by contexts, there is also a corresponding biology taking place. The nervous, immune, and endocrine systems' reactions during the experience are archived (registered in memory) as mindbody culturally *interpreted clusters* rather than mental representations. In other words, the memory of the event includes the mental activity as well as how each of the biological systems responded to the experience. As we continue to explore the mindbody self, I hope you will gradually embrace the brilliance and complexity that has been refining for more than 150,000 years the person you become.

INTERPRETATION CLUSTERS

Computers process data as representations of the world, but humans interpret experiences to bring meaning to their world. But what is this "meaning" that I am so passionately inviting you to value? The human body has 336 reflexes: Some respond to internal body signals (coronary reflex), others to external stimuli (knee-jerk reflex), and some can be conditioned (salivation). Everything else is learned within culturally influenced contexts. This is good news because anything you learn can be unlearned. But here is where meaning comes in: You can *ostensibly* replace one behavior with another without assigning meaning to the change. For example, replacing smoking with chewing gum. Then where's the rub? Although the replacement is done without looking for the *implicate meaning* of smoking, there's *explicate meaning* in wanting to improve the smoker's health. Identifying the surface meaning of smoking serves to modify the smoking behavior but fails to address the deeper meaning—that it's a dysfunctional distraction rationalized as pleasure, need, addiction, habit, or social status. And here's the bomb I am dropping: All dysfunctional distractions are avoidances of personal turbulence or self-worthiness. I strongly argue that unless the implicate meaning of an unwanted behavior is recontextualized, the dysfunctional distractions will surface somewhere else. In the case of smoking: Eating, drinking, gambling, and other behaviors of excess are the usual suspects.

I am guiding you to understand why conduct that does not serve your best interest is so difficult to change. It has little to do with lack of willpower and a lot to do with using the wrong tools. Since we assimilate biosymbols as mindbody clusters interpreted in cultural contexts, we need more than reasoning to change their operational meaning. The clusters are more than mental images and physiology. They are the totality of the interpretations ascribed to symbols—from your cognition to every cell in your body. This does not mean, however, that symbols originate at the cellular level (reductionism) or the mental level (cognitivism). Instead, they *co-emerge* as coauthors of holisms that are greater than their parts.

Now we can land all this theoretical information on practicality. For example, you have a friend who shames you when you make a mistake. You feel embarrassed, devalued, chastised. But since you have to interpret your friend's words (symbols) as shaming before you respond with embarrassment, your physiology also has to make the interpretation to coauthor the biosymbol (embodied words) you experience as shaming. Your immune system secretes inflammatory molecules (tumor necrosis factor, interleukin 1); your nervous system increases your heart rate, galvanic skin response, and blood pressure; your endocrine system secretes cortisol, epinephrine, norepinephrine, and so on: A constellation of mindbody responses takes place based on a cultural interpretation of words with the label *shame*.

But are these mindbody responses the same worldwide? It depends on the culture making the interpretation. The mindbody response to individual shaming that I outlined above happens more if you're from an individualist culture (U.S., Australia, U.K.); if you're from a collectivist culture (Japan, China, Indonesia), the shame response is triggered more intensely if interpreted as shaming the family or group, rather than the individual. Once again, symbols are culturally interpreted as mindbody clusters. In the "Cultural Brain" chapter, I'll show you how to resolve shame with what I call the *healing field of honor*.

AGENTS OF CHANGE

What are the conditions that facilitate desirable change?

1. Changing unwanted behavior requires more than reasoning. A logical mental act does not impact the totality of the mindbody interpretation cluster (biosymbol) that maintains the unwanted behavior.

2. To implement change you cannot wait for your coauthor to change with you.

3. When you implement change you must give your coauthor permission not to like your new behavior.

4. Lasting change takes place when the interpretation cluster shifts its contextual meaning (biosymbolic).

These four steps must be incorporated when attempting to change what no longer serves you well. The first step requires *embodying* the biosymbolic meaning of the unwanted behavior in order to experience how it manifests in your thoughts, emotions, and sensations. For example, if you want to stop sabotaging your success, you have to identify the thoughts, emotions, and sensations evoked when you recall memories of how you obstruct your good fortune. This first step of change reveals the mindbody signature of the biosymbolic cluster. In the experiential section I'll have more to say about how to apply all four agents of change.

The second step involves identifying the coauthors of your unwanted behavior. Remember, nothing is learned in a vacuum. The coauthors could be persons, circumstances, or memories. And just because you're ready to grow, it does not mean that your coauthors are going to support you or that you're willing to confront unpleasant memories that obstruct your growth.

The third step has to do with setting limits and allowing your coauthors to not like them. If you set limits without allowance for disapproval, you might recant in order to be liked again.

The fourth step is the most important because it is where change takes place. In other words, the first three steps set the conditions for the fourth step to implement the shift in contextual meaning. Using the example of setting limits, the felt meaning that you're being aggressive or contrary when you set healthy limits is recontextualized (mindbody reinterpretation) to mean that you're being self-caring when you establish emotional boundaries.

CULTURAL MANDATES AND THEIR VIOLATIONS

Let's define biosymbols as the embodied language of a culture. This implies that what is communicated includes the mental and physiological expressions of the communicators. Symbols are no longer viewed as disembodied mental activity. We're redefining them as biosymbols expressed and archived as mindbody interpretation clusters: Now words can hurt you as much as sticks and stones, as well as empower you more than any pharmaceutical concoction. However, this paradigm shift *does not* mean replacing reductionist health sciences with your positive *thoughts*. Instead, it encourages integrating functional health sciences with your positive *actions*. I cannot overemphasize that biocognitive science is integrative rather than divisive.

Now, we can look at how cultures set boundaries and enforce them. More important, since cultural communication is biosymbolic, we can look at how rules and their violations affect the relationships, success, well-being, and longevity of the mindbody self. This means you and me—because we did not come to life and develop in a cultural vacuum!

While knowledge is power, wisdom is empowering. And there is no better formula for healthy longevity than an empowered cultural self. But before learning how to transcend the suffocating aspects of cultures, let's look at how they stifle your growth.

By now you know that cultural editors are the architects of their respective domains. They define the parameters of aesthetics, ethics, religion, health, and relationships, as well as the consequences for digressing from their rules. Consequently, the embodied beliefs will strongly influence the development of your worthiness, wellness, success, and longevity.

I am not suggesting Big Brother or conspiracy theory scenarios. Instead, I propose that each of the cultural domains was established and refined during millennia of trial and error with the relentless objective of protecting the tribe. Of course, in the process of "protecting" the tribe, members dehumanized and abused those who were excluded. No race, nationality, or ethnicity has a monopoly on infamy: Romans enslaved Britons, Britons enslaved Africans, Africans enslaved other Africans, Americans enslaved Africans and conquered Native Americans, and so on. My point? Cultures develop degrees of empowering and disempowering collective consciousness and pass them on through their cultural editors with powerful effects on their members. I indulged in this digression to emphasize the historical vicissitudes of the mindbody self, but more important, its legacy of commitments to bring meaning to challenges and celebration to triumphs over evil.

HORIZON CODES

Paradigm shifts introduce new concepts with a unique language to define their function. Often old terms are expanded rather than replaced when the shifts occur. For example, *horsepower*, a remnant from horse-drawn carriages that became a unit to measure the rate of energy released from engines; *candlepower* for the luminosity units of lightbulbs; *nautical miles* from ships to airplanes. These are but a few illustrations of how old concepts resist change. The paradigm shift I propose challenges established principles that ignore how cultural beliefs teach us to perceive our internal and external world.

I introduce the *horizon code* concept to explain how the functional rules of cultural domains work, as well as how to recontextualize them when they no longer work for you. In other words, how the cultural domains of aesthetics, ethics, health, religion, and relationships are learned with rules that define their limits, enforcements, and novelty.

In my theory of the mindbody self, there are three horizon codes that govern the domains: *internal horizon, regulator horizon,* and *explorer horizon.*

The internal horizon defines the extent of the domain's established principles: What is beauty in the domain of aesthetics, what is morality in the domain of ethics, what is deity in the domain of religion, and so on. The internal horizon governs the cultural identity of the domain.

The regulator horizon activates when there's a challenge or violation of the established identity of the domain. It determines what to accept or reject and how to admonish transgressions. The regulator horizon governs the enforcement on the domains.

The explorer horizon seeks novelty to expand the extent of the domain. Paradigm shifts generate conflict between the explorer and regulator horizons because new information challenges established principles of the domain.

A balance of the three horizon codes is necessary in each of the domains for a culture as well as for its members: Without the internal horizon there's no identity, without the regulator horizon there's anarchy, and without the explorer horizon there's no new learning. Cultures implicitly establish the parameters to navigate each of their domains through the horizon codes. For example, how you're taught to identify who you are: intelligent, decent, religious, or their opposites. How you're taught to deal with transgressions: loving, patient, fair, tolerant, or their opposites. How you're taught to respond to novelty: curious, flexible, hopeful, creative, or their opposites. In the experiential section, I'll show you how to manage the three horizon codes and make desired changes.

The concept of horizon codes allows you to assess how your culture taught you to perceive the identity, flexibility, and novelty of each domain. For example, some cultures teach very rigid horizon codes for the religion domain: The identity is so narrow, the punishment so harsh, and the novelty so prohibited that the horizons of the domain become impenetrable boundaries. Consequently, when horizons are replaced with inflexible boundaries, it leads to cultural subversion that eventually *forces* paradigm shifts—some peacefully and others violently.

The Meeting of Biosymbolic Horizons

Although you're learning how the mindbody self co-emerges, the power of cultural editors, and many other biocognitive concepts, you may still wonder: *How does the mindbody self find identity with multicultural biosymbolic contexts?* Let's suppose you were born in the U.S., have an African American Protestant father and a Japanese Buddhist mother. Your very reasonable question might be, "How does my mindbody self develop in this biosymbolically mixed environment?" Well, let's decipher a phenomenon that's becoming increasingly common in globalized societies.

Initially, when we're confronted with alternative cultural belief systems, the choices seem limited to either rejection or acceptance. But since we want to clarify the underlying complexity of the mindbody self, I will introduce three anthropological concepts that can help us understand how we assimilate cultural diversity in the form of biosymbols: *enculturation, acculturation,* and *hegemony.* I promise you're going to end up loving biocognitive science. But let's get to the point.

Enculturation is the learning of established behaviors from your own culture. **Acculturation** is the learning of established behaviors of a host culture. And **hegemony** is sustained domination by another culture. History is replete with all three conditions. Just as cultures go through these transformations when they meet, relationships are also exposed to these three assimilation pathways. The changes range from a wife taking her husband's family name to an entire culture imposing its religion on another by force. One of the key issues to note here is that once a belief gains cultural meaning, it is embodied in our biology—from symbol to biosymbol.

Let's put these new concepts to use with the biracial relationship example above. The father brings to the relationship enculturated African American behaviors and acculturated as well as hegemonized American behaviors. In other words, the American-born father learned established behaviors from his African American subculture (enculturation), learned established behaviors from predominantly white American culture (acculturation), and his ancestors were forced to live in another land and to change their religion and social value (hegemony). He is the product of all three processes.

The mother migrated to the U.S. with her Japanese culture and Buddhist religion. When she married her African American husband, she and he were already enculturated in their respective cultures, but they acculturated to each other's. For example, they decided to expose you to both the Protestant and Buddhist religions, and allowed you to choose your religious path when you were old enough; your mother taught you Japanese; your paternal grandmother taught your mother to cook delicious soul food (West African cuisine); and so on. Then who is your mind-body self? You are a fortunate individual who developed within a hybrid family from two beautiful cultures. And when you look around your world, you will find that most of us are a hybrid self from culturally diverse backgrounds with an embodied history of enculturation, acculturation, and hegemony. Of course, you can add to the recipe all the other cultural editors who come your way: teachers, doctors, clergy, and so on.

Tools to Identify and Change
Unwanted Aspects of Your Cultural Self

Let's move from the theoretical to the practical. We'll start with the four agents of change.

The Four Agents of Change

1. Changing unwanted behavior requires more than reasoning. A logical mental act does not impact the totality of the mindbody interpretation cluster (biosymbol) that maintains the unwanted behavior.

A biosymbol is a cluster of learned thoughts, emotions, sensations, memories, and context interpreted to make sense of our experiences. For example, when you see or think of a stop sign, you can understand the sign (symbol) because you interpreted a set of factors (cluster) to make sense of the sign—what it means to stop, what happens if you don't stop, red being associated with danger, memories of a previous fine for not stopping, and so on.

2. To implement change, you cannot wait for your coauthor to change with you.

We often withhold personal change until we convince others to agree with our objectives. But it's important to understand that our need to change may not be the same as those who disagree with our actions toward wellness.

3. When you implement change you must give your coauthor(s) permission not to like your decision.

Assertiveness requires setting limits, and allowing others to disapprove of or dislike our new boundaries. In the process of healthy change, accepting disapproval from coauthors is essential.

4. Lasting change takes place when the interpretation cluster shifts its contextual meaning (biosymbolic).

All the components that maintain a belief or behavior must change their meaning (interpretation cluster). For example, if the meaning for obedience (interpretation cluster) was learned in the context of an abusive parent, the fearful emotions, sense of helplessness, and all other associations with the experience need to shift their meaning in order to achieve lasting change. This is why some people believe (thought) they have forgiven a perpetrator but negative emotions (affect) continue to surface anytime the experience comes to mind.

Putting the Agents of Change to Work

Now that you understand how the mindbody self learns from family, cultural editors, and cultural diversity, identify the behavior that is no longer serving you well. For example: Are you not setting limits? Are you self-sabotaging? Are you having a problem in a relationship?

- Once you identify what you want to change, bring to mind the first agent: *Changing unwanted behavior requires more than reasoning. A logical mental act does not impact the totality of the mindbody interpretation cluster (biosymbol) that maintains the unwanted behavior.*

- The best way to access mindbody archives is by sitting in a quiet place, slowing your breathing, and paying attention to your sensations, emotions, and memories as they pass your awareness. In other words, notice the *mindbody* manifestations of what you're visualizing. Observe them without judgment and allow them to pass. You can do this exercise with your eyes open until you can perform the procedure with your eyes closed.

- Bring to your awareness what you want to change and embody the experience. For example, setting limits with a friend who ignores your needs. Whatever you experience when you bring to awareness the desired change, observe without judgment, then proceed to the second agent: *To implement change you cannot wait for your coauthor to change with you.*

- Bring to awareness whoever is related to the mindbody behavior you wish to change (coauthors from the past and present). For example, the person who does not respect your limits.

- Embody the experience when you bring the coauthors to your awareness. That is, where do you manifest in your body what you feel, think, and sense?

- Whatever you experience, observe it without judgment until it subsides, then proceed to the third agent: *When you implement change you must give your coauthor(s) permission not to like your decision.*

- Play out in your mindbody a scenario telling your coauthor what you are changing. See yourself playing out the change in that condition and giving your coauthor permission not to like your new behavior. For example, visualize your friend not liking the limit you set.

- Whatever you experience when you bring to awareness the desired change, observe it without judgment until it subsides, then proceed to the fourth agent: *Lasting change takes place when the interpretation cluster shifts its contextual meaning (biosymbolic).*

- Bring to awareness the behavior you want to change. See yourself in a situation where you're experiencing the unwanted behavior. For example, letting your friend ignore your wishes. Embody the experience (what are the mindbody manifestations?).

- Now bring to awareness the new behavior and play it out. Pay attention to how the new behavior is manifesting in your mindbody.

- Notice the difference in mindbody manifestations between the old behavior and the new. How does not setting limits feel versus setting limits? How does it feel when your coauthor likes or dislikes your limits? Observe both situations without judging the content.

- Start shifting between the old and the new behavior. Do it several times and experience how the shifting is taking place. For example, go back and forth from not setting limits to setting limits and be aware of the mindbody shifting experience.

- Now go back and forth from setting the limits with approval from your coauthor and setting the limits with disapproval from your coauthor. Be aware of the difference. Keep shifting until the disapproval loses intensity.

- Bring awareness to your stomach, count from one to five, then open your eyes. Sit quietly for a few minutes and recall what you experienced without trying to interpret what happened during the exercise. The shift in the interpretation cluster has already taken place without you having to intervene. Remember this is not an intellectual process: it's mindbody communication at work.

- Practice the exercise within the next few days, and begin incorporating safe amounts of the new behavior in your life. For example, if it's self-sabotage, take gradual steps to increase worthiness with evidence. Do things that confirm you're worthy. Treat yourself to something that makes you feel good, without waiting for a reason or using it as a reward.

- When you try the new behavior, always embody how you experience it. If old scripts of fear intrude, take a deep breath and bring back the pleasure you experienced when you tried the new behavior before.

Debriefing

This apparently simple exercise incorporates essential components of lasting mindbody change. By bringing the *unwanted* behavior to awareness and embodying its manifestations, you identify the biosymbols that your mindbody interpreted. Then when you bring the *wanted* behavior to awareness and embody its biosymbols, you present a competing alternative that gradually recontextualizes (changes the felt meaning) of the unwanted behavior during the juxtaposing of the two horizons: a teetering of the old and the new. Think of it as something akin to shifting back and forth between tasting a known mediocre wine and an unknown superior wine until your mindbody experiences the difference and changes preference without you having to intellectualize the change. The old wine did not disappear. Instead, the felt meaning of what constitutes a good wine was recontextualized. But I remind you this process is not a behavior-modification technique that replaces one behavior for the other. Nor is it desensitizing the negative effect by repeated exposure. It is a change of the contextual meaning that maintains the unwanted behavior. As you learn more biocognitive science, it will become increasingly clear that it is not behaviorism. The recontextualizing changes the mindbody meaning by reinterpreting the biosymbol that maintains the behavior. If, for example, the unwanted behavior was difficulty with setting limits, its biosymbol, learned from cultural editors, interpreted assertiveness as something to avoid. Consequently, your mindbody *learned* to experience "setting limits" as disturbing and, in some cases, foreboding.

The Horizon Codes

Cultures teach you propensities for how to perceive the world, and the horizon codes are the rules to contain, regulate, and expand what you learn about the world. It could be your perception of a particular behavior (setting limits, intimacy) or a cultural domain (religion, aesthetics). After you sit in a quiet and comfortable place, scan your mindbody and observe, without interfering or interpreting the thoughts, sensations, feelings, and memories that come to your awareness.

- Take a deep breath and let your mindbody slow down by not engaging whatever enters your awareness. View all of your body inhaling and exhaling in unison by gradually expanding the area where you feel the breathing (chest, stomach, nostrils) to the rest of your body. Imagine all of your body expanding when you inhale and contracting when you exhale. Do this breathing imagery for a couple of minutes before moving on to the next step.

- Choose a cultural construct to explore what you learned about the three horizons. For example, if you choose abundance, how do you define it for your life (internal horizon), what happens when you go beyond your definition (regulator horizon), and how do you expand your definition (explorer horizon)? Do you define abundance in terms of health, wealth, love, or all three?

- Pick one of the three that you consider in need of improvement. For example, if you choose wealth, how do you personally define it: having enough money to pay your bills?; maintaining a certain standard of living?; accumulating as much money as you can?

- What did your cultural editors (parents, relatives) teach you at home about wealth? Examples: Is it only for the wealthy? Is it your birthright? Is it achieved exclusively by hard work?

- What is the difference between what they taught you verbally about wealth and how they lived it? Perhaps your father *told* you wealth was available to everyone but you *saw* that he barely made enough money to pay the bills.

- Bring to awareness your actual financial condition and determine if it resembles what you were *told* about wealth or what you *saw* from your cultural editors about wealth. Are you just paying the bills as you observed, or did you break from that model and create wealth? Perhaps you're between the two models? Embody what you experience when you compare the differences. How do they manifest in your mindbody (thoughts, emotions, sensations)?

- If you found a difference in what you saw and what you were told, what horizon could be maintaining the difference? For example, you embraced what you saw rather than what you were told (internal horizon). You were afraid to surpass your cultural editor's accomplishments (regulator horizon). You did not learn the necessary skills to embrace what you were told (explorer horizon).

- If you choose to change your wealth concept (domain), which horizon will you need to resolve? Do you need to redefine your wealth concept (interior horizon)? Do you need to confront the fear, guilt, and doubt that may be stopping you (regulator horizon)? How far do you want to expand your new wealth concept (explorer horizon)?

- After you choose the horizon you want to work on, bring to awareness making the changes and embody the experience. Is it joy, fear, doubt, guilt?

- Now comes the teetering between the scenario you're presently living and the one you want to embrace. Embody the experience of one and switch to embody the experience of the alternative you chose. Notice what you experience in each of the two conditions and observe them without judging, interpreting, or choosing. Let your experiential teetering do the work.

- Take a deep, slow breath, and after the count to five, open your eyes and reorient yourself before getting up. If you did the exercise with your eyes open, follow the same procedure of giving yourself time to get up.

- Whichever domain and horizon you chose, commit to exploring new behaviors that will give you evidence that you're making desired changes. For example, if you found the regulator horizon responsible for keeping you within the pale for wealth, determine what you need to do (gradually) beyond the pale. Also, be patient with the coauthors of your wealth domain so they can assimilate your changes at their own speed. If the coauthors don't like your changes, give them permission to disapprove, and time to assimilate that they also need to change how they relate to you.

Debriefing

This experiential method allowed you to identify the cultural learning that led to how you are living your unwanted behaviors and the mindbody biosymbols that maintain them. You can apply what you learned about how to recontextualize horizons to any behavior you want to change. Earlier in the chapter you learned the four agents that are the necessary conditions for change to take place. You also learned how the three horizon codes govern what you're trying to change. More important, the two experiential exercises show you how to apply what you learned.

You noticed that both exercises accomplish change by teetering what you want to give up with what you want to incorporate in your life. As you practice variations of this *embodied teetering* (experiencing the commuting of opposing horizons), you will begin to trust that experiential change occurs at the meeting of horizons rather than by intellectualizing the merits of why the change should take place. A juxtaposing of unwanted and wanted behavior leads to recontextualizing what no longer serves you well. And the power of the biocognitive method is that mindbody changes take place seamlessly when you get out of the way. You set the stage with the right conditions for your mindbody to accomplish optimal change.

chapter 4

Permanence, Control, and Other Illusions

As we continue to develop the biocognitive language, I want to identify what I consider illusions that, if not challenged, can derail our progress. In my judgment, these illusions are so culturally embedded that we give them the status of reality, and then we are perplexed when they fail to materialize. For example, if you believe you can control others, you will be sorely disappointed when they assert their independence.

As we go through this chapter, I'll systematically address each of the illusions. First, though, I will use fictional narrative to explain how we create them to avoid our primal fears.

Permanence

In my psychological novel *The Man from Autumn*, I brought literary fiction and cutting-edge science together to explain complex mindbody concepts using creative narrative rather than dry academic lessons. I was fascinated with how ideas can gain clarity when the messenger has freedom to convey the message. The format is a novel within a novel in which the main character, Breogan, teaches the author, Enrique, how to develop the story. This allowed me to express my ideas in a dialogue between the writer and the main character he was creating. But the most revealing part of this literary experiment was when Enrique (the author) explained my biocognitive theory as if he were learning it from an unnamed "psychologist friend." Although the identity was never revealed in the book, I was the informant.

As I was gathering my notes for this chapter, it occurred to me that although I have been teaching my theory of permanence and existential dread for many years, I have never explained it as clearly as I did in the novel. In other words, through the *voice* of the unnamed psychologist in the novel, I was able to articulate what remained unexpressed in my head. So, I will explain how the concepts I proposed in *The Man from Autumn* about existential dread and its resolution apply to the mindbody self.

An Antidote for Existential Dread

There is a compelling force ready to propel us out of disillusionment when we can extract wisdom from our anguish. Some welcome the chance to abandon misery, whereas others retain their disparaging scripts and seem surprised when the obvious pain remains. Those who engage their toxic reruns are aware of their position and can be very incisive about what enslaves them, while somehow remaining stuck. The reluctance to give up self-destructive patterns ranging from addictions to abusive relationships has been attributed to unworthiness, passive control, lack of will, masochism, and other counterproductive labels.

Although these defeatist behaviors are certainly identifiable in those who live in misery, they merely reflect distractions, not causes. Just like obsessions and compulsions are strategies to avoid anxiety-producing thoughts and emotions, self-destructive behaviors are paradoxical efforts to deny our mortality. Every act of self-destructiveness is a futile attempt to defy the inevitable end we dread: a choice of piecemeal suicide to circumvent the realization that the Grim Reaper does not break appointments. In my research I find that most phobias can be reduced to a fear of death, and all underlying motives to maintain the phobic condition are the product of embracing a fatalistic life.

But if someone fears dying, how can they engage in acts that can hasten death? The heavy smoker and the cocaine abuser are certainly aware they are shortening the lives they fear losing. So there has to be a hidden logic operating these self-defeating codes.

I propose that there are *three* implicit distracters born in fear that maintain the drive to unwittingly self-destruct. This *fear triad* serves to avoid confronting death-anxiety, to engage in behaviors that challenge death, and to control the manner in which death will arrive. The smoker uses nicotine to be distracted from death-anxiety, to challenge the limitations of lung function, and to choose cancer or emphysema as the most likely way to end life. Similarly, the battered spouse colludes with the abuser to be distracted from the same death-anxiety, to challenge the limits of how much trauma the body can take, and to choose fatal injury as the destructive end. However, I want to clarify that colluding with the abuser is not an agreement to participate in demeaning behavior. It is, rather, being present for the abuse to take place. Thus, rather than willful acts of self-destruction, the fear triad illustrates how disconnecting from our self-worth leads to dysfunctional distractions. I propose that when we feel worthy, we can confront our existential fears without personal damage. When we don't, the self-defeating strategies remain hidden while their respective distractions reach consciousness with masked causes. And although the masks may have some legitimacy, they serve to hide the real culprit. Examples: "I smoke because I am addicted"; "I let my partner abuse me because I am committed to the relationship"; "I know my hobby is very dangerous but I love the thrill."

The fear triad offers *avoidance, defiance,* and *control*—a dismal deception for the mindbody self at the service of dread. But if the practitioner of misery could access existential depth, the real enemy would materialize to be defeated by reckoning that the solution is choosing *how* to live, rather than *how* to die: trusting that the end of our physical existence is the beginning of another phase on the eternal journey of our soul. Likewise, for those who do not believe anything follows after physical death, trusting that the end comes peacefully after living a good life. Although these propositions may be construed as comforting platitudes, the choice to make peace with our mortality frees us to embrace the abundance of life rather than to die a thousand deaths before our time on earth is over.

The confrontation of the fear triad is the foremost milestone of our journey. We can ignore it with our demands for evidence and live in terror, or we can let faith guide us to trust what we cannot verify with our puny senses. But the faith I am suggesting is not about religious beliefs. It is rather a commitment without evidence that the outcome will be *the most propitious in the long run*. Rather than expecting a desired outcome, it's a resolution, without regrets, to allow sufficient time for the *best fit* to unfold. For example, a desired relationship ends with deep anguish, but if given enough time for the best fit to reach its ultimate function, what appeared to be a curse transforms into a blessing. However, this is not the same as passively accepting that things will turn out for the best. Passivity assumes that undesired things happen and one must capitulate to fate. What I am proposing is existentially different—that it is your underlying wisdom coauthoring with the pathways of destiny to activate the best fit in the long run. Thus the faith is really in your creativity to navigate the future. Fate is surrender—destiny is opportunity.

The fear triad is a colossal deception, but the self-defeating codes that support it can be exposed for what they are. Avoidance serves to maintain distance from reconciling our mortality, defiance encourages action to test limits of our mortality, and control determines how we hasten our self-determined mortality. Given that fear is the most primitive of our emotions, it can only yield inadequate solutions for our existential predicaments. But if we are reminded that compassion is the supreme expression of love, it provides impetus to face our dread with courageous tools.

When we engage the wisdom of self-compassion to confront our death-anguish, trust the power of our creativity, and relinquish the obsession to know our end, it can deliver us from a life of terror. Fear cannot live in the house of love. But before advancing to the practical applications, I'll explain the psychology of our existential struggle. We're given a period of time and space to live with the knowledge that there is an end. The dread of this awareness of being mortal comes from the dilemmas it poses. We have to surrender a body that we have dedicated our lives to nourishing, we have to leave those we choose to love, and we have to question whether we end in nothingness or transcend to something ness. So, there are two basic predicaments: to disengage and to confront.

Disengaging from our cultural self and others requires a farewell to physical love, whereas confronting a beyond-life dimension summons mystery. Two psychological directives are operating here: releasing the known and facing the unknown. When we explore the roots of our dread, struggle with decisions to let go, and welcome what is best for us, it sensitizes us to judge others with greater compassion because we realize we share a universal human challenge. But these ostensibly simple questions can be overwhelming because their solutions involve disengaging and confronting what we dread to death.

One of the greatest obstacles to resolving our transcendental dread is our categorical reluctance to live our love and our life as one. Why? Because when we attempt to avoid, defy, and control our death, we apply the same dreadful criteria to loving others and ourselves. But if we accept love unconditionally does it not make it more difficult to let it go when our end arrives? This line of reasoning assumes that love is an emotion we own rather than an expression we live. We mourn the absence of what we possess, not what we live. Just as we cannot possess love, we cannot own our existence. The illusion of ownership enslaves us with dread. But living love and life as one, rather than existing them separately, liberates us from the fear triad. We no longer have to avoid, defy, or control what does not belong to us.

In biocognitive theory, I contrast the grossly misunderstood Eastern concept of attachment with the Western version of ownership. In particular, Buddhist philosophers view attachment as the root of suffering. They teach that attachment encompasses craving, ignorance, and avoidance. Attachment endorses craving the delusion of permanence, perfection, and substance in the world; ignorance or not wanting to see the direct experience of reality because we interpret the world as illusions that conform to our personal beliefs; and avoidance of our pain by giving hatred power. Buddha taught that hatred was synonymous with clinging because it gives our causes of pain substance and permanence. In other words, releasing hatred requires moving on to love again.

The Buddhist concept of attachment can help us explore the element of control in the Western model of suffering. We can make the infamous claim that Western cultures contribute their own cause of suffering by endorsing the illusion that control is synonymous with ownership. The differences between Eastern attachment and Western ownership are subtle, but culturally significant. The East emphasizes spirit at the expense of the physical, while the West sacrifices the transcendental for material gains. Both approaches beg convergence. For instance, as members of the human community we cannot afford to meditate our lives away while children die of hunger and illnesses. But just as imminent, for believers, abundance of wealth loses meaning without spiritual depth, and for nonbelievers, material gains without secular humanism feed existential emptiness.

I propose that the operational advances in Western biocognitive science can offer new ways to explore the Eastern philosophies of suffering. With this ambitious claim, we can begin to demystify transcendental dread and hopefully find its antidote. Considering that believing is one of our most powerful cognitive tools, we can choose to embrace whatever empowers us to encounter our existential and transcendental challenges. Since love is the most advanced emotion we have been able to develop as a species, we can *choose* to believe that love is the antidote to our greatest fear. Although we cannot take attachments or ownerships beyond our end, we can choose to wake up from our deceptive nightmare, reclaim our abandoned inspirations, and discover the power of love. And what is the deception? Although knowing permanence is not real, living as if it were.

In biocognitive theory, we redirect our course to confront our dread and to discover the true obstacles to its resolution.

Lamenting how we lived our lives is the greatest contributor to fearing our end. There is substantial evidence from research in hospices showing that lamenting is the biggest obstacle to dying peacefully. We have evolutionary mechanisms that expel the amniotic fluid from our lungs when we are born and turn off our breathing when we expire. We cry when we are born, not out of anguish but to expel fluids and inhale our first breath of air. Yet we give our first life-enhancing mechanism sinister interpretations: entering a cruel world, leaving the safety of the womb, and so on. This same tainting of a natural process is applied to our end when we cease to breathe.

While these breathing transitions are inherent and involuntary, we have no biological equivalence when we exercise our freedom of choice. Our biocognitive fabric provides coping devices to begin and end our lives without our consent, but our design does not include predetermined interpretations for actions that we have to learn. Instead of interpreting our first cry with anguish and our last breath with terror, we can gain existential insight by accessing our most exalted emotions (love-based) to investigate our transcendental dread. Without denying the Eastern ingredients of attachment and the Western craving for control, we can acknowledge that our transcendental dread stems more from lamenting what we fail to do while we live than from our fear of the unknown when we die. If instead of avoiding our fear of dying we empower our passions, we can diminish our lamenting and learn how to face our end gracefully. This existential shift resolves transcendental dread in several ways: We can move from avoiding death to approaching our neglected dreams, from defying death to accepting our joy, and from trying to control how we die to choosing how we live. Then we no longer need to crave the illusion of permanence, avoid with hatred, or remain ignorant of the reality we could live. Fear is our venom and love is our antidote. Although I believe control is an illusion we create to increase predictability, we're not passive victims of randomness.

Control

"Everybody relax, nothing is under control." – Gandhi

Just as we build things and bond with people as if we had permanent residence on earth, we tend to overestimate the control we have over some events in our lives. My colleague Ellen Langer is a brilliant social psychology professor at Harvard. She was the first female professor to be tenured in the psychology department at that university. Dr. Langer conducted research showing how contexts can age you or reverse the effects of aging, as well as many other intriguing studies. But her pioneering contribution to social psychology was a series of studies that consistently showed how people overestimate their perception of control in conditions where there is little or no actual control. For example, gamblers believe they have some control in winning despite losing fortunes in their efforts to win. They tend to throw the dice harder when they want high numbers and much softer when they want lower numbers. Dr. Langer introduced the term *control illusion* to explain the overestimating effect. One of the strongest pieces of evidence for the control illusion is how revenue from gamblers' losses made it possible to build the opulent city of Las Vegas in the middle of a desert.

Although most of the research on the control illusion was limited to conditions where there is little or no actual control, later studies looked at how individuals respond when they have more actual control. Participants underestimated their perception of personal control when actual control was increased. In other words, when given little actual control on a designated task, people tend to overestimate their control, but when the actual control is increased, they underestimate their personal control. Thus there's a general tendency for people to misestimate control. Of course, in conditions where there's 100 percent control, the estimates are precisely on target.

When depressed individuals were asked to estimate their perceived control, however, the results were not what the researchers predicted. Researchers expected that since depressives perceive themselves to have less control over their actions than nondepressives, depressives should underestimate their perceived control in both low and high actual control conditions. Instead, researchers found that depressives were accurate in perceiving uncontrollable tasks and inaccurate in perceiving controllable tasks. In other words, by having a mind-set of being out of control, depressives can identify conditions in which there's actually little control but not those in which control is high.

Since depression reduces the perception of personal control, trying to convince depressives that they have control over their lives is not productive. To help people with depression regain their sense of personal control, I give them tasks where they have 100 percent actual control, and then have them pay mindbody attention to the moment they complete the task—embodying the experience of control.

Cultural Influences on the Control Illusion

As you may recall from the "Coauthoring the MindBody Self" chapter, cultures influence perception. Studies have found that Japanese men and women (collectivist culture) overestimate their ability to control their outcomes collectively compared to individually. They overestimate their personal control in groups more than as individuals. As expected, American men (individualist culture) show the opposite effect. American men overestimate their ability to control outcomes as individuals more than when they are in groups. American women, similar to the Japanese, tend to be more optimistic about obtaining a favorable outcome in groups. This research indicates that the psychology of control is influenced by culture as well as how some cultures influence gender.

In addition to the individualist and collectivist factors, cultures also influence the control illusion by how we perceive figure and background. It's intriguing how the philosophy of a culture influences self-perception and perception of our world. Western cultures are mostly influenced by ancient Greek philosophy that viewed the world as separate objects and individuals with attributes. In contrast, Chinese and other ancient Eastern philosophies focused on the relationship with objects and individuals in the world. To understand control, Western mind-set tends to focus on the individual attributes of people and objects, whereas Eastern mind-set tends to focus on the relationships of people and objects.

Studies that evaluate how these cultural biases affect the control illusion find that Chinese participants perceive more control when they find relationships between figure and background, whereas American participants perceive more control when they find attributes of the figure. For example, if given a task where you have to find the relationship with objects or with individuals, Chinese perceive more control than Americans, but if the task involves finding characteristics of individuals or of objects, Americans perceive more control than the Chinese. I will have much more to say about this in the "Cultural Brain" chapter.

The control illusion research shows us how we tend to misjudge the control we have when actual control is low or high, but just as important, how cultural biases influence our misjudgment based on Eastern or Western perceptual mind-sets. In general, Eastern perceptual bias tends to place more value on cooperation than on control. Conversely, Westerners place greater value on having individual control than on cooperating in groups. But keep in mind that these differences can also vary within cultures because we learn our perception from many sources that cut across cultures. Also, as you can conclude from this section, the illusion of control refers to how we misjudge our sense of control based on external factors, rather than denying that control exists. I propose that *cultural perception of control* is a more accurate term to describe how we misread our influence on the outcome of our actions based on what cultures teach us to see. In other words, control is a cultural interpretation of how much power we perceive we have on the outcome of our intentions.

But when we look at the results of these studies, it seems that they show the opposite of what we would reasonably conclude. For example, why would people underestimate their perceived control with tasks that have actual high control? If you do something that works most of the time, your confidence in what you're doing should increase rather than decrease the estimate of the control you have. So why does the research show these unexpected results? Well, because the illusion of control has little to do with confidence. If this were the case, in the face of consistent losses gamblers would lose confidence in what they're doing and conclude that they have little control. But as you know, the opposite is true: The more losses, the greater their illusion of control. What is really going on?

Intention and *outcome* are the main factors that affect the illusion of control. Now we can make sense of what the research shows about the control illusion. And here's the formula to keep in mind when I give you practical examples: When intention for desired outcome is far from actual outcome (gambling), we tend to overestimate our perception of personal control. In other words, we keep going in the face of failure because we believe that if we try harder (overestimate control) we will get the outcome we want. On the other hand, when intention for desired outcome comes closer to actual outcome, we tend to underestimate our personal control. The gambler example clearly explains the condition of overestimating control when there's very little actual control. But the underestimation of control when there's higher actual control is going to require a less obvious example. An executive of a global company gets a large bonus *some* of the time. But although the executive's intended and actual results come closer than the gambler's, it's still not 100 percent. Instead of overestimating personal control when the frequently reached desired outcome does not materialize, the executive underestimates personal control. In other words, if reaching the desired outcome is *highly infrequent*, the gambler assumes more control is needed (overestimates the effect of personal control). But if the desired outcome is *highly frequent*, when it does not happen the executive assumes no amount of control is enough (underestimates the effect of personal control). And this range of uncertainty between 0 and 100 percent is what guides the direction of the control illusion.

I've taken you through this psychological quicksand because the control illusion is alive and well in our daily lives. If you understand its dynamics, you will be able to break the control illusion and find reasonable middle ground between the gambler and the executive. Other studies that are more interested in why people misjudge their estimates of control show that your personal expectation of how much control you're *going to have* in a task will influence how you perceive your personal control during and after the task. This seems obvious until you ask yourself how often you consciously estimate your success before doing a task. Also, most of the studies on the illusion of control are done with artificial scenarios that are different from real conditions you face at work and at home: actions such as deciding to push a button to get a light to show up on a screen. But rather than dismissing the lab results because they do not resemble actual life conditions, let's take them as human tendencies that we should consider when we make important decisions in our lives. In the practical tools section at the end of the chapter, I'll show you how to minimize the tendency to miscalculate your personal control.

OTHER ILLUSIONS

The Law of Attraction

From a neuropsychologist's perspective, I propose that there's no scientific evidence to support the existence of the "law of attraction." But before I embark on my reasons as a scientist, I am going to discuss the limitations of science.

The two extremes of science are unwavering disbelief and arrogant overconfidence. As it relates to evidence, the life sciences study averages at the expense of individual differences: average lifespan, average response to medication, average side effects, average morbidity, average symptoms, and so on. If you fall within the average on the bell curve, science can most likely offer answers, but if you're an *outlier* (on either tail of the curve), you will get answers such as "stress-related," "age-related," "all in your head," and "genetics" before you get the "idiopathic" label. In scientific jargon, *idiopathic* means "unknown origin or cause." In common language it means, "We don't know what the hell is going on." Although there are theories that cannot be confirmed because they are false, there are conditions that cannot be measured because science does not have the right instruments. For example, some of Einstein's theories had to wait years before precise instruments were invented that could test them. Also, most of the life sciences are not very interested in exploring the mindbody components of intuition, spontaneous healing, stigmata, placebo, nocebo, and the healing power of love.

So as a scientist I am an open skeptic willing to consider the evidence and to pose what we call *empirical questions*: looking for clearly defined answers from collected data. You may be a scientist, healer, mystic, psychic, teacher, mentor, or layperson looking for ways to understand yourself and improve your life. Independent of your background, I want to propose a way to approach the subject at hand. As I lay out my reasoning for disbelieving there's a law of attraction, join me as an open skeptic of what *you* believe. Question your own beliefs (for or against) without fear of what you may find. What I promise you is that I will discuss my views without know-it-all arrogance.

The New Age concept of the law of attraction comes from the New Thought philosophy of Phineas Quinby, who was a 19th-century American healer, inventor, and philosopher. Quinby had little formal education and learned mesmerism (an old term for hypnosis) from the French mesmerist Charles Poyen. Quinby suffered from tuberculosis and was treated with calomel, which was the conventional medication at the time. Calomel is a compound of mercury chloride—a highly toxic chemical that, in addition to not curing his tuberculosis, rotted his teeth. Quinby decided (wisely) to look for alternative ways to heal his illness, and found hypnosis, magnetics, and other methods that worked for him and for some of the people he treated who could not be helped by physicians in those days.

Quinby believed thoughts have energy that can heal or cause illness, and that this energy is universally present and transmittable. Thus the law of attraction originated from Quinby's New Thought movement. As with most well-intended ideas, there are benefits to believing in the law of attraction—but not for the reasons believers think. I propose that rather than attracting anything, it gives you hope, replaces negative thinking, and allows you to be more empathic and recognize you're not alone in the world. The real benefits, however, are due to the positive response from your immune, nervous, and endocrine systems when you believe in something empathic and act accordingly.

The word *attraction* is very telling. You can be attractive, things can attract you, and you can attract others without the law of attraction. What happens in each of the conditions I mentioned is that you are doing something to fulfill an unmet need that someone has. If you make yourself more "attractive," someone who needs an attractive person will come to you *if* they know you exist. This *if* factor is very important in what I am trying to convey. You have to do something that someone wants or needs— but it can only work if you make yourself available. There's a need factor and an exposure factor.

Here's a simple experiment to disprove the law of attraction: One hundred people sit at home for six months having thoughts and wishes about attracting wealth or someone to love. It's highly unlikely that the experiment will result in anyone knocking at their door with a fat check or a marriage proposal. Why? Because if there were a law of attraction in which thoughts are energy that could travel universally, most of the 100 people in our experiment would already have their wishes granted. Making yourself attractive does not attract anyone unless they see you and they need your attractiveness. It has nothing to do with energy. In fact, you could make yourself very attractive without wanting to attract anyone and if someone likes you, they will be attracted to you. Did you attract, or did you meet a need?

When you read the "Causes of Health" chapter you will understand why good thoughts without healthy self-esteem have little effect on changing behavior. In other words, having good thoughts to attract an abundance of love, health, and wealth will have positive effects only if you feel worthy when your good fortune arrives. Without having to attract anything, high self-esteem allows good thoughts to enhance your health.

But you don't have to believe in the law of attraction to find what you want in your life.

Let me give you another example of how what I am proposing works. My dear friend Dr. Christiane Northrup told me a beautiful story about the founder of a large privately owned publishing company. Dr. Northrup related that when the founder started her company in her late 50s and with little capital, one of her greatest joys was writing the royalty checks for the few authors she had. This mind-set has powerful implications. It assumes a sense of abundance (joy rather than fear for sharing wealth), and the self-esteem necessary to turn positive mindfulness into proactive action. Taking the joy of sharing wealth to a practical example, let's assume you engage positive thoughts and emotions when you pay your monthly bills. Your bills will continue as long as you have living expenses, but your empathic approach to paying them will have several incidental benefits: 1. Since you take the negativity out of the task, you will most likely pay your bills without procrastinating until the due date or beyond; 2. Awareness of your empathic approach may increase your appreciation for the services you're getting or the loan you were trusted to pay back; 3. Since pleasant tasks increase curiosity, you may discover you're living beyond your means and consequently adjust your budget to reduce unnecessary expenses; 4. Most important, by removing negativity associated with paying bills, you replace stress hormones with immune-enhancing emotions. You gain all these benefits without attracting anything.

But if you still choose to believe in the law of attraction, now you can do so with greater joy, knowing the incidental benefits that empathic beliefs can have on your well-being. In the practical applications section, I'll show you ways to reach your objectives independent of believing in the law of attraction.

The Universe Conspires to Fulfill Our Wishes

I figured that since I am already treading on New Age waters, I should dive into another illusion. This time, I'll tackle why the universe *does not* conspire to fulfill our wishes.

Again, I ask you to join me with an open mind. The concept that our universe conspires to support our happiness is poetically pleasing and mystically enticing. But sometimes what looks good and sounds great is not the best path to take. The most obvious argument against this "attractive" notion is that it's highly unlikely that supernovas, planets, meteors, galaxies, and black holes are going to take time away from their infinite expansion to support our earthly needs. As you know, we did not exist when the Big Bang started the perpetual path of celestial bodies into deep space. But you know what? If you believe that we're one with the universe and that mental energy travels light-years, then although you have no cosmological evidence, my argument will not have any impact on your beliefs. And if that is the case, stay with me and enjoy the exploration. There's more to come.

One of the indirect benefits of believing that the universe conspires with you is that it promotes a sense of interconnectedness. The experience of *feeling* connected, with or without the universe's support, is good for our health. It reduces our sense of alienation and the consequent existential anxiety. Feeling connected, whether we are or not, is immune-system enhancing because our need for social bonding is being met. Just as there are indirect benefits of believing in the law of attraction, believing in the universe as a granting entity has health benefits—but again, for the wrong reasons. Unfortunately, the gained tranquility that is good for your health will vanish when you find that these beliefs do not materialize your expectations. So one suggestion is that if I can show you how to reach your objectives without having to wait for the law of attraction to find you or for the universe to assist you, then I will be able to do my job without having to change your beliefs. Fair enough? Of course, if you agree that we should demand more evidence for our beliefs and from those who teach them, I am preaching to the choir.

Tools to Relinquish Self-Entrapping Illusions

There are paths to liberate us from false beliefs that lead to self-entrapment. Faith in our creativity to navigate the future resolves dread of the unknown, and turning old laments into new commitments resolves dread of our mortality. But these lofty claims need the right tools to make them worthy of your consideration. If you approach this section with a curious mind, you will learn empowering methods to relinquish the existential dread that robs you of fearlessly loving yourself and others. I will also show you how to frame your intentions in ways that minimize your tendency to miscalculate the control you have over your actions.

Dreading the Unknown

Since the future is not foreseeable, we can only estimate what could happen. If the expected outcome is positively or negatively charged, we feel what's known in psychology as *anticipatory anxiety*. In other words, the anticipation of what you wish or dread is what causes the anxiety. For example, expecting promotion or dismissal at work releases the same stress hormones because our mindbody is responding to the unknown component of the future. Although planning for as many outcomes as you can imagine may reduce anticipatory anxiety, it does not resolve it. Why? Because the preparations take place in a present based on an imagined future. You're better prepared but the unknown remains a mystery. In addition to preparing for what could happen in the future, you need a time-travel tool from the present—something you have in the present that does not change in the future. So, rather than predicting what could happen, you use a tool that can deal with whatever happens. You already own this tool. It's your *creativity*: a strategy to find novelty in turbulence. Imagine your creativity as a compass that points to what unfolds in the future that you did not anticipate in the present. This shifting of awareness takes you from dreading the unknown to welcoming how your creativity will navigate what you dread. Before showing you how to access and develop your creativity during turbulence, I'll share some examples. You anticipate your boss is going to fire you, so you prepare for the worst: you discuss with your family how unemployment is going to affect your budget, you update your résumé, you look for job opportunities in your area of expertise, and so on.

But although all these strategies are practical, you can't count on any of them because they are options without certainty.

The future arrives and your boss tells you the company is downsizing and they can only offer you a half-time position. No amount of planning prepared you for this outcome. If you use the solutions you planned based on what you expected was going to happen, you would focus on how to explain to future employers that you're coming from a part-time job, how to adjust your budget to a part-time salary, and so on. But this is not the creativity I am proposing. Although you're asking practical questions, you're using anticipated strategies to solve what you did not anticipate, rather than finding novelty (creativity) in what actually happened. Here are some examples of looking for novelty in the unanticipated outcome: What is the advantage of having a part-time job? How can you create new revenue from something you love to do but are unable to do with a full-time job? What did you dislike about working full time at your job? How can you find another half-time job that you would enjoy? These questions seek novelty in the unexpected, instead of imposing solutions based on what did not happen. Let's apply the antidote to dread of the unknown.

Learning Curiosity

- Sit quietly when you have uninterrupted time to explore your creativity. The objective is to learn how to be creative during calm times so you can apply the strategies during unexpected turbulence.

- Choose a routine at work, at home, or in social settings that you can use to practice creativity. For example, what you usually do before going to work, coming home, and so on. You might decide to get up a half-hour earlier to meditate and have a cup of tea. But whatever you decide, do it differently than before. For example, instead of drinking coffee while watching the news, sit quietly and enjoy a cup of jasmine tea.

- Throughout the day look for ways to do your work more creatively. Find new (novelty) strategies to break from established routines. You can improve the quality of what you do when you find more innovative ways to do it. Nobody forces you to do things in ways that bore you.

- When you go to new places, discover details that you would usually overlook.

- Engage your creative mind when you're bored.

- Practice innovation on a daily basis. Turn the mundane into discovery. For example, people eat an average of just 12 different types of meals throughout their lives. If your eating is routine—pasta on Wednesday, fish on Friday—vary it. Next time you go to the supermarket, buy something to eat that you have never tried.

Accessing Creativity during Unexpected Times

The first set of exercises prepared you to ease access to your creativity. Now we can apply the training to dealing with anticipatory anxiety: dread of the unknown.

Find a situation you're dreading to confront. You can use either an actual condition or an imagined one to practice this next set of exercises.

- After you identify the real or imagined condition, record possible strategies to deal with each expected outcome. Identify how your mindbody responds to each scenario and observe without judgment.

- Review all the strategies and embody the experience. Observe without judgment.

- Imagine the most dreaded scenario and review the strategy you plan to use. Check your mindbody reaction without intervening.

- Go from focusing on what strategies to use for the dreaded condition to finding novelty in what was not expected. For example, a medical checkup shows unexpected high cholesterol in addition to the expected chronic pain. You have a strategy for the expected outcome (medication and meditation) but no specific strategy for the unexpected high cholesterol. There's nothing creative about the medication and meditation. They are the planned strategy rather than the creativity that the unexpected condition can provide.

- Now comes the time to rely on your creativity for any unexpected outcome: In this example, high cholesterol.

- You research 10 foods and two activities that can reduce your high cholesterol. You find delicious ways to cook the foods you choose, and you identify one of the two activities that you would most enjoy doing. For example, roasted salmon with almond and walnut sauce on Mondays, avocado dip with garbanzo chips on Tuesdays, qigong or biking on Wednesdays, Fridays, and Saturdays. You replaced the dread of an unexpected outcome with an opportunity to create joyful and healthy strategies in your life. Trust that your creativity will unfold in the future to handle *any* outcome.

- As you learn to use your creativity as an antidote for the unknown, dread gradually transitions to anticipatory joy. By the way, although the same hormones are involved in negative and positive anticipation, your mindbody interpretation will either trigger detrimental gene expression or access the causes of health. In the "Cultural Brain" chapter, I'll explain how these psychoneuroimmunological interpretations work.

Dreading Our Mortality

I developed a method to confront the dread of mortality by drawing from my own existential concerns and clinical observations as well as from philosophers and psychologists who brought me greater clarity when I reconciled their ideas with my fear triad theory. Although it may appear that this dread of our physical end would only interest those who are approaching their own end, I strongly encourage you, regardless of your age and health status, to consider my method when addressing your own mortality challenges. Even if you are not interested in philosophy, I invite you to stay with me, because if you do, it could liberate you from a dread you may not know is limiting your potential to live a full life.

From the philosophical side, Søren Kierkegaard set the stage for modern psychologists, anthropologists, and sociologists to study our fear of death. The lessons from this 19th-century Danish philosopher, considered the "father of existentialism," were powerful incentives for me to explore how we can reconcile our inevitable physical end. For Kierkegaard, dread is *unfocused fear*. When we fear, we can identify the source of our fear: heights, failure, public speaking, snakes, and so on. But dread is the unfocused fear we experience *before the abyss of uncertainty*: We fear the known and dread the unknown. There's no better example of uncertainty than the mystery surrounding death. But don't get depressed—I am not going to leave you in suspense.

According to their terror management theory (TMT), social psychologists Jeff Greenberg, Sheldon Solomon, and Tom Pyszczynski propose that cultures are symbolic systems that provide life with meaning and value to manage the terror of death. In other words, cultural values are portals to find meaning in your existence. These cultural values include literal immortality (beliefs in afterlife, religion) as well as symbolic immortality (national identity, posterity).

But, although the TMT brings culture to compensate for the dread of uncertainty, it does not offer ways to confront Kierkegaard's abyss. For example, what happens when the cultural buffers fail to resolve existential dread for those who do not believe in afterlife, or when meaning is not sufficient to bring serenity when confronting physical end? Here is where my approach to reverse the fear triad can provide an alternative. Rather than cultural distractions from dread, I propose jumping into the abyss with methods to resolve the dread of uncertainty. Analogous to pilots trusting their navigational instruments when they enter a storm, it's a decision that allows you to confront uncertainty with tools you can learn to trust. And when you do, your tendency to avoid the unknowable gradually decreases until it vanishes.

Earlier in the chapter, I explained how the fear triad provides avoidance, defiance, and control to compensate for the helplessness imposed by the great unknown. Addictions, risky lifestyle, and self-sabotage are examples of the fear triad at work. The good news is that although the fear triad offers a dismal deception to the mindbody self, its opposite path provides a way to confront our existential despair. Instead of avoiding, defying, and controlling our end, we can confront, accept, and control how we want to live. I agree with Kierkegaard's concept of unfocused fear, and with TMT's explanation of how cultures provide meaning to manage terror. But the difference in the solution I propose reflects how I define dread. As I mentioned earlier in the chapter, we have natural mechanisms to enter and leave life that work flawlessly if we don't interfere with the process. In fact, Tibetan Buddhist lamas understand the concept well. They practice a meditation called *phowa* to recognize the signs of impending death so they can allow their end to come peacefully.

Cultures teach us to avoid, manage, or enter the abyss peacefully. This means that the fear of death is not universal, and that there are ways to make peace with our end without cultural management to avoid dread. Finally, I can introduce you to the reclamation triad. But before applying the method, I want you to understand its principles.

1. Dread of death is culturally learned. Kierkegaard was a Lutheran Dane reconciling his philosophy with a Western god.

2. Existential truth is found by making a decision, not by reasoning. Existential truth is known to a personal self and is discovered in a crisis. Knowledge of our mortality compels us to consciously or subconsciously decide how to approach or avoid the challenge.

3. Cultures that teach how to manage dread of death misunderstand the hidden cause. They assume dread comes from facing our mortality. I propose that dread of death comes from lamenting missed opportunities to meet essential needs.

4. As death draws near, the accumulated lamentations (bygone options) increase dread. Lamenting increases helplessness by focusing on what life could have been rather than what it can be.

5. Lamentations of what did not happen are disempowering *thoughts*. Reclaiming what can be done is empowering *action*.

6. The reclamation triad is an antidote for the fear triad; it replaces dysfunctional distractions from the abyss with life choices that allow us to peacefully enter the abyss.

7. Coming to the end of a lamented life is what causes dread. As lamentations increase in the face of impending mortality, dread turns to terror.

8. Lamentations are missed opportunities to live a fulfilling life.

Reconciling your dread (unfocused fear) is one of the most important self-loving steps you can take toward embracing a joyful life. But I am not proposing a technique or change of behavior. That would only put a Band-Aid on the existential challenge posed by the dread. Instead, the reclamation triad offers a change of consciousness, a perceptual shift that allows you to view yourself in the world through a different lens. It's a life project with gradual gains and celebrations.

Replacing unresolved lamentations with empowering actions reduces the intensity of the abyss and leads to reclamation consciousness: *rescuing love from dread*. But if the process overwhelms you, seek professional help to support your project. Like most biocognitive methods, the reclamation triad seems deceptively simple. Although the procedure is fairly uncomplicated, its effects are profound. By reclaiming your essential needs, you fill the void created by missed opportunities. You no longer have to *avoid* your essential needs, *defy* how much you can neglect your essential needs, and *control* the ways you neglect your essential needs. As you practice identifying the essential needs embedded in your lamentations, you will find a short list that will keep surfacing: admiration, autonomy, competence, social connection, trust, honor, commitment, loyalty. Although fewer than expected, the essential needs are the foundation for a meaningful and loving existence. The reclamation consciousness (empowered perception) gradually prepares you to approach the abyss of uncertainty with courage, and to enter the great unknown with the serenity gained by replacing lamentations with the essential needs of life. The most important mystery solved here is that by reclaiming your joyful life, you incidentally learn to access your innate capacity to let go when you must. As I mentioned earlier, it's a process well known to Tibetan Buddhist lamas.

Although I am not suggesting that confronting our dread is something to take lightly, we have inherent mechanisms to guide us through our greatest turbulence if we allow them to do their job. The objective is to frequently clean out lamentations from your existential bin.

The Method

- Create a digital file on your laptop or buy an attractive notebook to journal your reclaiming experiences. Give the notebook a meaningful title: *Resolving Dread*, *Reclaiming Joy*, *Freedom from the Fear Triad*, and so on. Keep it private to avoid contaminating your process with the fear of others. Your journal will house the recorded evidence that you're experientially ending the accumulating damage of lamentations.

- Write a small, medium, and large lamentation in your life that you want to resolve. For example, missing a live performance no longer available in your area (small), ruining a vacation by arguing with your partner (medium), not finishing college (large).

- Start with the small lamentations: Find the *essential need* hidden in what you're lamenting. For example, you missed your favorite concert. But the essential need you're lamenting is more than not seeing the performer. Instead, you were deprived of an essential need to experience admiration. Always look for the essential need embedded in your lamentations.

- Bring back the memory of how you felt when you missed the opportunity to experience what you're lamenting. Embody the feelings, thoughts, and sensations. Allow the experience to enter and exit your mindbody awareness. Take a deep, slow breath and allow your awareness to return to the present.

- Take action that allows you to reclaim your essential need to experience admiration. It does not have to be the same situation. The source of the lamentation is the loss of an essential need projected to a person or situation. For example, you can watch a video of a person you highly admire, go to another concert, or take any other action that allows you to experience strong admiration. When you feel the admiration (warm feeling), stay with it until it leaves your awareness.

- Follow the same procedure for all other lamentations. Some of the reclamations require more involved commitments, but when you find the neglected essential needs that you're lamenting, your creativity will blossom.

- Keep journaling your experiences. Revisit your journal as needed, and celebrate your reclamations. Also journal your comments and insights. You're recording the private journey of your reclamation consciousness.

Debriefing

The reclamation triad method you learned here is based on evidence from dying patients and the observations of health-care professionals working in hospices. Although the terror management theory and other theoretical models offer valuable information about how people culturally manage their fear of death, most of their studies use college students from Western cultures. I argue that young individuals in college have not accumulated much lamenting in their lives to test the effect it has on the fear of death. Also, as I propose throughout this book, Eastern cultures have profoundly different views of how to approach death. Some of the studies that investigate older populations find that while college students rely on self-esteem to buffer fear of death, their older counterparts rely more on religion. Additionally, some Eastern cultures do not have dread issues regarding death. As far as I know, my lamentation theory is unique and should be thoroughly researched across cultures. I am currently conducting ethnographic studies with healthy centenarians, and find that my theory holds well across cultures—especially with cultures that teach management of dread. I have little to teach Tibetan Buddhist lamas about how to die. In fact, my Tibetan lama mentor died a few years ago very peacefully using the *phowa* meditation I described earlier.

Beyond the Illusion of Control

Independent of questioning the law of attraction, the conspiring universe, or how much control you have in your life, there are practical methods to improve your strategies to reach desired outcomes. You learned how we tend to overestimate personal control when actual control is low, and to underestimate when actual control is high. Also, one of the ways to minimize these miscalculations is to consciously define your intentions and estimate how much control you expect to have before embarking on a particular task. Finally, rather than *waiting* for external forces to attract or grant what you wish, *determine* what you can offer others that will satisfy your needs by meeting theirs. But just as important, determine how you can make others know that you're available to *transact* rather than *attract* the exchange. In other words, you're creating need and exposure versus wishing for the fulfillment of needs from mysterious sources.

- As with all the methods in this book, find a quiet space to practice without interruptions and distractions. Make time for yourself because you're worth the investment.

- Find three tasks that you want to accomplish and estimate their level of difficulty. For example, starting daily walks to increase your physical activities and health habits are your intentions. Upon further reflection, you also find that your other intentions are to lose weight and look more attractive to yourself and your partner.

- Based on your past attempts, seasonal climate, available time, and level of fitness, you assign the task a medium level of difficulty and high level of personal control.

- After a few days of doing the activity, identify the self-created obstacles and external constraints. Self-created obstacles could be procrastination, longer working hours, choosing unlikely times for the activity to take place (too early or too late in your day), and so on. External constraints could be inclement weather, illness, fatigue, emergencies, and unavoidable commitments.

- Adjust your initial estimates of intention and control to actual outcome. For example, you find that longer working hours and scheduling your walks too late in the day are stronger obstacles than initially estimated. You also find that the external obstacles are fewer than you expected. Perhaps the weather was better than predicted and you did not have any external derailing (no emergencies).

- After readjusting estimates, you can continue the commitments with greater probability of success.

Frequent readjustments decrease uncertainty of outcome.

- When you overcome an obstacle using a creative strategy, notice how you experience the success in your mindbody. For example, you changed your task from late afternoon (low success rate) to early morning (higher success rate). How does awareness of your successful change manifest as sensations, feelings, and thoughts?

- Be mindful of how you increase your internal control by changing self-imposed obstacles. By paying attention to how you can change self-imposed obstacles, your perception of internal control increases.

- Practice this method of reevaluating estimated control and actual control when you overcome or are unable to control an obstacle.

Debriefing

These simple procedures take you from all-or-none success to frequent adjustments of your estimates of difficulty level and internal versus external control of the task. As you frequently reevaluate your internal expectations with actual conditions, your tendency to misestimate process and outcome decreases and your probability of success increases. You can use the same method when you want something from others. For example, when you practice the transaction versus the attraction approach, you also determine intention, estimated internal and external control, as well as the need you want to transact with another person or condition. If you want to make more money, estimate the level of difficulty, the level of internal and external control, and what you must do to transact the outcome. Determine what you can offer others that will satisfy their need when they meet yours. What does your employer or market need that you could offer in order to get what you need? Better skills, more training, new market, different department, new job? Again, these are transactional strategies that take you out of waiting to attract or have the universe conspire to meet your needs.

chapter 5

An Anthropology of Self-Esteem

The concept of self-valuation has been studied extensively in American psychology, but like most other research in Western life sciences, the cultural influence on how we assign value has been ignored until recently. Fortunately, I am going to remedy the gap.

VALUATION OF THE MINDBODY SELF

Self-esteem is the common term used to determine the degree of self-valuation: a way of knowing how much you like yourself. I purposely used the word *like* because, as we will explore in this chapter, we have to like what we're valuing before we can value ourselves. It's very difficult to value a characteristic we dislike about ourselves. Of course, sociopaths are an exception because they like everything, good or bad, about themselves. But let's go deeper to truly understand the relationship between *like* and *value*. Let's assume that you're gifted in math, but you learned to dislike your gift because your schoolmates thought you were an egghead. When not accepted by your peers, the capacity to understand the complexity of math transformed your gift to a burden. Many potential Einsteins fail to unfold their excellence because they never accept the value of what they dislike.

Recent studies of how self-esteem is derived in different countries show how much cultural contexts influence the outcome. The studies also illustrate that some factors are found in some cultures and others in all cultures. This confirms the central theme of this book: Although the brain learns to perceive based on the culture, certain propensities are found in all cultures. These studies show that people derive most of their self-esteem from what they identify that best fulfills the values of their culture. Cultures that value self-direction and having a stimulating life (U.S., Western Europe, and some countries in South America) derive their self-esteem from a sense of control over their lives. In contrast, cultures that place greater value on conformity, tradition, and security (Middle East, Asia, and Africa) tend to derive their self-esteem from doing their duty. The importance in these findings is that self-valuation is strongly related to the values that people assimilate to bond with their culture. We are social beings who place greater value on cooperative connection than competitive alienation.

The Three Pillars of Self-Esteem

Some of the inconsistent results in cross-cultural research are due to measuring self-valuation without including the cultural context, and assuming self-valuation is the only component of self-esteem. Valuing yourself is necessary but not sufficient for healthy self-esteem because it does not include valuing what you do and the people you value. In addition to including cultural contexts, I propose that in order to fully understand how the mindbody self derives personal value, we need to consider three components: worthiness, competence, and affiliation.

Worthiness self-esteem includes what you value about yourself and how deserving you feel about the good fortune that comes your way. Although cultures influence how you value yourself, contradictory evidence from personal experiences can challenge what you are taught to value. For example, although your culture may teach you to value tradition, you find some self-directed behaviors (nontraditional) that give you a sense of pride and accomplishment.

Competence self-esteem has to do with how good you are at what you do in life: home, work, relationships. In the development of self-concept, cultures have specific definitions for what constitutes excellence in each of your roles. For example, a culture can value or devalue motherhood based on whether the woman chooses a career or stays home to raise her children. Although it may seem quite obvious that it is not an either-or decision to be a competent mother, some cultures prohibit women from working outside the home. Unfortunately, not all cultures share a sense of gender equity.

Affiliation self-esteem reflects the quality of people you choose to bring into your life to share your journey. Cultures will give you their prescription for how to select and what obligations you should have to the people you choose, but like anything else in human endeavor, it's a matter of what you *should* do versus what you *choose* to do. Cultural lessons can be wise or oppressive.

Considering the three components of self-esteem can help you assess and develop each of the areas rather than assuming self-valuation is one-dimensional. For example, someone could be a highly effective manager (competence self-esteem), unable to accept personal worthiness (valuation self-esteem), and with no close family or friends (affiliation self-esteem).

WHO LOVES YOU?

Your cultural self acquires a set of values that determine how to position yourself in different social settings. Depending on the setting and based on your self-esteem, you could feel loved, hated, accepted, rejected. Your positioning in social settings is much more complex than liking yourself. It involves the three pillars of self-esteem I propose: how much you value yourself (worthiness), how good you are at what you do (competence), and how much you value others (affiliation). Let's say you're presenting a project in an office meeting with your best intentions, but your social positioning will most likely influence your delivery and level of satisfaction with your performance. Did you feel you contributed something valuable? The answer to this straightforward question depends on how you assessed yourself in the three areas of self-esteem: how worthy you felt in the meeting, how knowledgeable you were with the subject presented compared to your co-workers, and how well you think of those co-workers. This assessment takes place without conscious planning. It's a positioning style that you take to professional and social settings. Although you can sense whether your presentation was liked or not, the intensity of your reaction to the feedback will be mostly determined by your social positioning in the setting.

Self-Valuation in Times of Adversity

All meaningful relationships experience occasional disruptions caused by not feeling understood or validated. During these challenging periods resentment trumps generosity and goodwill becomes a scarce commodity. The implicit quid pro quo (I give you this, you give me that) in relationships ceases, and selfishness gets confused with self-caring. It makes sense to focus on self-caring when outside nourishment is not available. However, if you're in a relationship worthy of your love, solely self-caring during adversity turns to selfishness. But how can my proposal make sense? Should we neglect ourselves when those we love neglect us? This is a legitimate question that I hope to answer to your satisfaction. When caring is based on quid pro quo, it fosters a fragile harmony in the relationship. The exchange is recorded in an emotional ledger to keep score. You give expecting to receive, and receive expecting to give back—a bookkeeping nightmare. Some examples: "Look at all I've done for you." "I invest more in this relationship than you do." "When are you going to start giving back?" All the effort of keeping score confuses what each person actually needs. In quid pro quo relationships, when your partner stops giving, you stop giving back. The neglecting becomes an invitation to neglect back.

Self-caring during adversity in relationships is only half of the formula to navigate the challenge. In addition to giving up quid pro quo relationships, I introduce another Latin term to replace it. You know that *quid pro quo* is a Latin phrase that literally means "something for something." I propose *aliquid nihil*: "something for nothing back."

Aliquid nihil is what I call my method to navigate adversity in meaningful relationships. When you go into a period of giving without expecting anything back, you enter a consciousness of generosity that comes from self-sufficiency. This does not mean self-deprivation. It's a way of nourishing yourself while offering nourishment to your partner. You suspend quid pro quo when you stop expecting anything back. But more important, since you continue to give in the spirit of aliquid nihil, you refuse your partner's invitation to neglect back. During your commitment to give without expecting anything back, you can increase your self-sufficiency in the following ways:

- Look for what you can do for yourself that no one else can do for you. This is a very effective way of self-caring without being a martyr or victim.

- View your period of aliquid nihil as honorable conduct, and allow your mindbody to absorb the emotional benefit of this elevated cognition.

- Reinstate abandoned interests, passions, and rituals to your aliquid nihil phase. This shifts you from neglecting your partner to recovering your neglected joy.

- When your partner is ready to nourish you again, celebrate the moment and commit to replacing quid pro quo with aliquid nihil. This means the new model of giving without expectations is not restricted to times of adversity in the relationship: Aliquid nihil becomes the operational mode. In my experience, dropping the emotional ledger increases goodwill and appreciation in relationships during adversity as well as good times.

When you incorporate the aliquid nihil method in relationships that are worthy of your love, you prevent wallowing in self-pity, gain self-sufficiency, give your partner room to discon-nect from dysfunctional scripts, avoid resentment and retaliation, learn to access internal resources when external nourishment is not available, and your fear of emotional abandonment subsides.

Caveat: This method does not work with sociopaths and pathological abusers. If the period of aliquid nihil continues for longer than you consider reasonable, have a discussion with your partner to determine if the relationship can move forward with mutual generosity. If not, whatever you decide is best for you will be free of guilt for not having tried your best.

The question of who loves you depends on how much you're willing to love yourself. I learned from the centenarians I studied worldwide that they don't wait for others to love them before they value themselves. In contrast, much of the self-destructiveness in celebrities who are widely loved is rooted in their inability to accept their own worthiness. Love is assimilated only when you can exis-tentially conclude that you are worth being loved. Considering that self-esteem has three components, we can better understand how some public figures are self-destructive. For example, an idolized singer may have high competence self-esteem (great voice), but if worthiness self-esteem is low, no amount of love from fans will be sufficient to accept the idolizing. Due to imbalance between worthiness and competence self-esteem, these insecure celebrities reason that if their loyal followers *really* knew them, their adora-tion would end. It's interesting to note that the self-destruction is most likely to happen when they reach their peak popularity and when they begin to descend. Paradoxically, their popularity is both blessing and curse.

Beyond the Cultural Constraints of Self-Valuation

Three Principles of Freedom from Oppressive Cultural Lessons

Just because your culture may teach rules that you find unfair, prejudicial, and intolerant, it does not mean you have to blindly accept them. Some of these impositions are learned so early in life that you're not aware of the limitations they impose on your personal development. You encounter an additional hurdle when you awaken from the collective dream and find that people around you are unable to validate your discovery. Suddenly you feel as if you're from another planet. At these crucial moments, you face a crossroad: relinquish your discovery or suffer cultural alienation. I find that when people choose to squelch their option for cultural liberation, they enter a state of helplessness that suppresses one of the most essential causes of health—hope for change. But it's not all gloom and doom. The cultural crossroads have a hidden path: finding people who are willing to confirm and support your newly discovered liberation. They feel the threat of cultural alienation just as much as you do. I am not implying, however, that you should suspend your decision to break away from cultural oppression until you find external validation. Instead, I am suggesting that once you shift your cultural beliefs, your selective perception will detect kindred qualities in others that are off the radar when you comply with cultural impositions. There are three steps to evaluate cultural impositions:

1. **Assessment:** Cultures are powerful contributing architects to your reality, but you are the coauthor of their influence. Determine the power of the cultural imposition you're evaluating. How much does it influence your daily activities and relationships? Whom or what will you have to confront? What is the price to pay?

2. **Disconnection:** Negative coauthorship ends when your new actions no longer engage the toxic dance. How will you fill the void created by your disconnection from oppressive people or activities? What will the new freedom mean to you?

3. **Defiance:** Embracing your excellence in defiance of the cultural editors who coerced you to believe that you *are* your mistakes. How will you validate what others are not willing to confirm? How will you deal

with alienation? Who will support your defiance?
How much are you willing to lose?

These three areas cover the conditions you have to navigate when you discover hidden oppressions or when you're ready to change their impositions. The process should be gradual and prudent to avoid premature decisions. Also, it's always wise to consider implicit values in the cultural impositions and their intended function. For example, there are cultures where women are not allowed to leave home until they marry. Although this cultural condition limits a woman's financial potential, its initial function was to assure economic security in a culture where women did not have access to the marketplace. My clarification is not meant to rationalize the oppression; its purpose is to recognize that what was initially well intended became oppressive when it lost its function. Interestingly, most cultural oppressions are maintained by reluctance to welcome options that were not available when the rules were made. Using the gender oppression example above, although jobs are now available to women in most economies, some cultures (male-dominated) remain oblivious to the liberating options. From my personal global consulting experience, I can tell you that companies that practice gender equality perform significantly better than those that continue to exclude women from leadership positions.

JOY AND ITS PERILS

Toward Healthy Self-Valuation

If you ever feel unworthy of your good fortune, it's mostly because your cultural editors taught you to minimize your laudable actions. Next time something good happens to you, shift from asking what you did to deserve it to identifying what you did to make it happen. You can detect in everyday language the limitations cultures place on self-valuation. Individualist cultures

(U.S., Western Europe) use the word *lucky* when things are going well or when praised for exceptional achievements. But since collectivist cultures (Japan, China, Korea) place greater value on the group than the individual, they replace the word *lucky* with the word *duty*. Although globalization is eroding cultural differences, the area of how self-valuation is determined continues to resist change.

When I teach my model of cultural empowerment in different countries, I make a simple request of my audiences: "Please raise your hand if you think you're bright." In the U.S. and Australia, most raise their hands without hesitation, but audiences in Korea and the Philippines will cautiously look around to see how others are going to respond. Fortunately, I am finding that when I work with young executives from companies in some collectivist cultures, they do not hesitate to raise their hand when I ask them to express their self-valuation. I frequently discuss how most cultures teach you what I call *pseudo-humility*: minimizing, rationalizing, or denying compliments and achievements. Some examples:

- "I love your shirt." "It's just an old shirt."
- "You really did well with your presentation." "Ah, it was okay."
- "I like your new car." "The old one was falling apart."
- "You have a beautiful smile." "You can thank my orthodontist for that."

These dialogues are not news to anyone. We've all heard them. My interest is in the psychology of why cultures teach us to disown our excellence, attributes, and abundance.

Reluctantly Great

In my previous book, I wrote extensively on our reluctance to accept personal greatness. Now I am going to show how the mindbody self learns to be dubious of highly ambitious goals. We have religions teaching meekness and detachment from material goods; parents teaching their children to excel and avoid boasting; peers praising social popularity and ridiculing academic achievement; employers hiring new talent and ignoring old experience. Most cultural lessons are based on mixed messages: "Go far, but not too far." "Be great, but deny your greatness." "Admire your heroes, but find their faults." Think about how it's much more comfortable and acceptable to say you're honest, faithful, and responsible than to proclaim you're great. But let me tell you how a centenarian (a 102-year-old woman) responded when I told her she was great: "Yes, I know. Thank you for your kindness." After talking to her for two hours, there was no other way to describe her, and she accepted my compliment with gratitude. Conceited? I'd say she's damn refreshing!

There's an old Irish joke about how you're popular at the pub if you're talking about writing a book, but when you actually write it, you are soon ignored. This is a great example of how most cultures, one way or another, place more value on the struggle than on the achievement. Why? There are several reasons for this most unique cultural trait. As long as you're struggling people can identify with your effort, perseverance, and challenges; it's a way of confirming that you're imperfect and a mere mortal like the rest of the tribe. But when you achieve the improbable, the identification ends. Now you're in a class of your own, leaving others with two choices: to admire or envy you.

Most Western and Eastern mythologies attribute supernatural powers to their immortal gods and superhuman powers to their mortal heroes. But only the gods can excel without reproach. Mortals have to remain imperfect and willing to have their feet of clay exposed when they remind us of our unattainable dreams. The jump from science to mythology is useful because we can visit the origins of our cultural realities and perhaps understand why we hold on so steadfastly to our peculiar beliefs. Then mindbody science can help untangle the mindbody self from what no longer saves the day.

The Cultural Faces of Self-Esteem

In my search for the mindbody self I had to ask a basic question: "From what culture?" Selfhood is the entity we create within cultural portals to identify us in relation to others. Western psychology has developed personality theories and tests assuming that one self fits all. Of course, most of these psychological tests are adapted for different populations, but until recently there was little interest in exploring how the cultural construction of selfhood affects how we perceive the world and the emotions we generate. The cultural construction also includes how we learn to value ourselves. For example, whereas Western cultures value individual self-esteem, most Eastern cultures place value on the relationship with others: I call the Eastern concept *group-esteem*. In the "Cultural Brain" chapter, I discuss how different parts of the brain are activated depending on how the individual perceives self and the relationship with others.

The lessons are subtle and start early. In the U.S., parents tell their kids to eat their food because children in Bangladesh are starving, but Japanese parents tell their children that the farmer who worked so hard to produce the food would feel bad if they don't eat the meal. Americans use guilt to differentiate between individuals, and Japanese to interconnect with individuals. (I remember when I was a kid the "starving children in India" were my source of guilt during meals.) A motivational coach in the U.S. would encourage clients to look at themselves in the mirror and say that they are beautiful, but a coach in Korea would ask clients to tell others that they are beautiful. The self-esteem versus group-esteem difference gains significance in the area of health care. Substantial research evidence shows that poor health is related to low self-worth, but since cultures determine how you value yourself, health-care professionals need to know whether to focus on building self-esteem or group-esteem.

Cultural Construction of Self-Valuation

Cultural psychology and research show that although the formation of self-valuation is complex, there are some patterns that seem to predict how cultures affect the process. Across cultures, four universal values can strongly influence self-evaluation: *controlling one's life, doing one's duty, benefiting others*, and *achieving social status*. But there are different degrees of compliance based on the collectivist or individualist orientation of a culture. For example, individualist cultures like the U.S. and Australia tend to place more value on controlling one's life and achieving social status than collectivist cultures like Japan and the Philippines, which place greater value on benefiting others and doing one's duty. Of course, these are general trends rather than absolute characteristics. For example, in situations of emergencies and natural disasters most cultures increase the value of benefiting others from a sense of duty and compassion.

Since cultural values are so ingrained in every aspect of life, we exist and measure our self-worth by them. When these cultural values are taken to extremes, they can affect our well-being. Let's look at ways that cultural values become problematic. For example, in a culture that values benefiting others as ideal, if taken to extremes, caring for others gains priority over self-caring. This is what happens with caretakers who derive their worthiness from taking care of others while neglecting their own personal needs. Eventually, self-neglect takes its toll and the caretaker's health deteriorates. Clinicians are very familiar with the dynamics of people who are not aware of how they are ruining their health by neglecting their personal needs. Caretakers have difficulty setting emotional limits because they fear not being loved or appreciated. But I propose that more than psychological pathology, excessive caretaking is a learned sociocultural dysfunction. In my clinical psychology practice, I found that unless the caretaker is able to readjust the cultural value that is imbalanced, most therapeutic interventions lose their effectiveness. For caretakers, it's a matter of finding balance between two cultural sources of self-valuation: benefiting others and controlling one's life.

Achieving social status is one of the most abused cultural values in economies that transition quickly from poverty to wealth. Fierce competition becomes a way of life at school and work. Countless sacrifices are made to gain wealth and social status. Only the most ambitious and relentless seekers of social status by way of wealth and power are able to rise to the top. Cultural rituals (family meals, worthy affiliations) that add to the quality of life and health are replaced with long working hours, and success becomes a moving target that is never sufficient. In the past 30 years, South Korea advanced from a poverty-stricken, underdeveloped economy to one with an annual GDP (gross domestic product) of more than a trillion dollars. Worldwide, South Korea ranks third in number of patents, has the highest educational enrollment rate, and pays higher salaries than Japan, among many other impressive statistics. What is the price for all these achievements? Number one in suicide rate for schoolchildren and working adults, one of the highest gender gaps in the workplace, highest number of smokers among Asian countries, one of the highest incidences of lung cancer, and so on. Why? The obvious reason is that anything in excess is harmful. But since we are exploring the mind-body self, there's another more compelling reason.

It takes cultures thousands of years to develop values that support the causes of their health. Each culture has its own particular way to maintain balance within its value system. Our biology adjusts to the combinations that support health and break down when the balance is disrupted. Evaluate how well your culture and family are balancing the four universal values (controlling one's life, doing one's duty, benefiting others, and achieving social status).

Cultural Outliers

The bright side of our quest for the best qualities in a cultural self is that not all members of cultures are doomed to suffer the damage of living within portal impositions (middle age, retirement) and imbalances of cross-cultural human values (controlling one's life versus benefiting others). Outlier individuals and families are able to step out of the collective beliefs that are detrimental to their health and longevity. I have dedicated my professional life to studying these cultural rebels from five different continents. I can attest that rather than genetically gifted, outliers have the ability to detect collective beliefs that don't serve them well. And as you know by now, anything positive that comes naturally to some can be learned by all. A few will choose to disregard the gradual damage of surrendering to helplessness because they fear the responsibilities of personal empowerment. But if you choose to learn from cultural outliers, I strongly recommend that you remain empathic with those who will not join your liberating path. Existential choices need to be honored after inviting others to go your way. It's not easy to see how those you love remain loyal to their misery. But the best you can do to help them is to commit to your empowered journey because, in addition to self-caring, you will live alternatives that they may eventually accept.

Tools to Build Balanced Self-Esteem

Now you have a better understanding of how self-valuation is a coauthorship with your culture. I suggest you approach the key concepts outlined below like a menu to pick and choose what you want to work on. As your needs change, you can return to the tools section of any chapter to help you solve new challenges.

The Three Pillars of Self-Esteem

- Worthiness – Self-caring action
- Competence – Capability in what you do
- Affiliation – Quality of relationships

Cross-Cultural Values

- Controlling one's life
- Doing one's duty
- Benefiting others
- Achieving social status

Process to Resolve Cultural Impositions

- Assessment – Identifying the imposition
- Disconnection – Detaching from the imposition
- Defiance – Rebelling against the imposition

Applications

- As usual, go to your favorite quiet place to learn the tools from this chapter.
- Choose topics you want to explore from the outlined areas above—especially something that you believe needs attention.
- Determine if you're overidentifying or neglecting any of the topics, such as affiliation self-esteem, cultural imposition, or achieving social status. In your biocognitive journal or a digital document, note the topics you choose to address. Don't take on more than you can realistically handle. You have all your life to make desired changes; it's a journey of gradual gains rather than a rush to reach a goal.
- Identify how the topics are interconnected. There's always some relationship. For example, low affiliation

self-esteem related to over-identifying with social status (all work, no friends) or low worthiness self-esteem related to neglecting control of your life (letting others abuse your kindness).

- *Assessment*: How did you learn to connect your issue with the cultural imposition? For example, you were taught that it's your duty to take care of others before attending to your self-caring needs. You learn these cultural impositions from what you see as you're growing up and from the values you are verbally taught. Sometimes what you observe and what you're taught are in opposition, such as a workaholic father who tells you that work needs to be balanced with family time.

- *Disconnection*: Identify how you need to disconnect from the cultural imposition. For example, you want to set limits with those who disregard your needs. In order to achieve your goal, you have to find balance between two cross-cultural values: control over your life and benefiting others. In the disconnection stage, you readjust cultural values to find balance between your individual needs and the cultural values you learned.

- *Defiance*: Whom will you have to disappoint and what conditions must you confront to achieve balance? The defiance stage should be approached prudently. It does not have to be aggressive. It is resistance and replacement of what no longer works for you. The replacement has to be well planned before implementing the change. Defying without offering alternatives weakens your position. In other words, the plan is to approach what you need, and discard what ceases to be functional for the worthy self. Fear of not being loved is the enemy of positive change.

- After you identify what you want to change and the imbalances that maintain the unwanted condition, practice what you decide to do using the biocognitive contemplative methods you learned in the "Coauthoring the MindBody Self" chapter. Then, after you embody the different experiences (challenges, insights) in contemplative method, gradually turn intention to action. In other words, first, rehearse the condition in the safety of your mindbody contemplative scenario to build the necessary skill and identify how you experience the rebellion. Then, after you gain some mastery, you begin to gradually implement what you learned.

Debriefing

I cannot overemphasize the importance of identifying the imbalances in your cultural values before trying to improve self-esteem. The mindbody self needs to discover the lessons that create hidden value disparities responsible for blocking self-valuation. When you want to improve a component of your self-esteem (worthiness, competence, affiliation) you have to find the cultural value you were taught to prioritize: Too much of one value at the expense of another.

When you begin to view imbalances in cultural values as your blocks to positive change, you'll find the right tools to see the world beyond hammer and nails.

chapter 6

The Causes of Health

In this chapter we'll identify the causes of health and how to facilitate their expression. Contrary to most conventional health-science theories, I contend that we inherit millennia of wisdom on how to achieve optimal health. Rather than mechanical products of our genes, we are the coauthors of their expression. With few exceptions, illnesses are only genetic propensities, not inevitable disruptions waiting for their time to unfold. But although we inherit the causes of health, we need to engage the right contexts to let them thrive.

In the conventional paradigm, we are led to believe in a science of mechanical forces that combat illness and maintain health. The key to understanding the limits of this reductionist science lies in the language it teaches us to take for granted: *mechanical forces*, *combat*, *maintain health*. This model conceptualizes battlefields that destroy the enemy rather than conditions that disrupt the expression of wellness. And yes, I chose the word *wellness* to differentiate it from the established concept of *health*: the absence of illness. Wellness goes beyond battlefields where illness is defeated, to *healing fields* where we find meaning in our existence and celebration in the love we share. And if these views seem like New Age naïveté or pseudoscience claims, wait until you read the "Cultural Brain" chapter to relieve your concerns.

BEYOND THE ABSENCE OF ILLNESS

Notice the pattern of answers most people give when asked how they're doing. "Can't complain." "I'm okay." "Same old, same old." "Not bad . . ." These responses reflect how most cultures teach us to be complacent with our lives and satisfied with the absence of illness. Am I asking too much? Well, the average person might think so. But if you're reading this book, you're far from average. Thus, you're more willing to venture beyond living in the absence of illness and the blandness of capitulating to the impositions of cultural editors. Blandness is void of passion and capitulation stifles curiosity. I'll have more to say later about passion and curiosity.

If I am encouraging you to go beyond complacency with your living conditions and satisfaction with the absence of illness, where do you look and how do you manage what you find? First, answer the following two questions:

1. *Who taught you compliance?* For example, if you respond to being asked how you're doing with answers like "I can't complain," where and from whom did you hear these words when you were growing up? Sometimes it's not the words, but rather the repeated helplessness you observe from your cultural editors.

2. *How did you learn to be content with health as the absence of illness?* For example, diabetes runs in your family and your concept of health is the absence of diabetes.

These cultural subtleties that gradually sneak up confine you to conceptual tribal boundaries. And if you dare to question their impositions, you might be called a charlatan or naïve. I propose that we should be revolutionists who venture beyond the pale to assert our abundance birthright of health, love, and wealth.

This revolution, however, is based on change by example rather than by imposition. It entails recontextualizing your beliefs and how they are expressed, without expectations that others will join you or be pleased with your transition to personal excellence. It can be lonely at times, but I assure you that if those you love are *ever* going to change, it will mostly happen by consistently speaking your new language and experiencing your new life.

Setting the Terrain for the Causes of Health

Let's conceptualize *health* as genetic propensity and *wellness* as its optimal cultural expression. In other words, you're born with a gift but your culture teaches you how much to express and benefit from the endowment. It can go from not knowing or denying that you inherit the causes of health, to not feeling capable or worthy of accepting your inheritance. These clarifications may help you understand why I propose we inherit the *causes* of health, rather than health itself. We need to find what causes our health as well as to determine how much we are willing to gracefully accept what we discover. Once again, I ask you to withhold judgment on the relevance I assign to cultural beliefs in gene expression until you read the "Cultural Brain" chapter.

We need to prepare a terrain that can express the causes of health: a coauthorship of script and player in a cultural scenario. For example, to express your brilliance at finding directions (endowment), you need relevant conditions (context) such as searching for an address, driving in a foreign country, and so on. This obvious illustration of endowment and context coauthorship becomes less self-evident when we deal with the causes of health. Why?

1. Because the *causes of health* concept is not as established as the *causes of illness* mind-set. New paradigms go through three stages: *disdain, doubt,* and *acceptance.* It takes repeated exposure for the subtleties of novel constructs to become obvious.

2. A "healthy" lifestyle is not the same as expressing the causes of health. For example, eating organic food, exercising, and meditating have limited benefits if the causes of health are missing.

If you're still wondering why I insist that healthy living is not enough, let's dig deeper. When we do things to be healthy we may be inadvertently seeking the absence of illness. But if you learn the conditions that trigger the causes of health, then you purposely enter wellness. Just as healing is superior to curing, wellness is the optimal expression of health.

So, what is the terrain that can express the causes of health?

1. A commitment to view your mindbody as a self-organizing entity that integrates culturally driven contexts with personal experiences to develop a cultural self. Your worldview is a convergence of how your culture teaches you to perceive and what you discover from your personal experiences.

2. A commitment to challenge genetic sentencing in family illnesses. In addition to propensities for some illnesses to run in families, our heredity also includes the causes of health that can prevent pathological genetic expression.

3. A commitment to learn worthiness. Whereas health in the conventional view is defined as the absence of illness, in the biocognitive paradigm, health is only one of the three components of wellness: abundance of health, love, and wealth. And yes, for those who see wealth as undesirable materialism, my definition goes beyond monetary accumulation. Let me give you examples. I have interviewed many healthy centenarians (100 years or older) worldwide, and when I ask them to define personal wealth, their usual answers are: the number of good friends they keep, their creativity, their passion for life, their capacity to feel gratitude, and so on. By the way, I see honestly gained monetary wealth as evidence for others to break from their self-imposed helplessness. I say "self-imposed" because people in profoundly impoverished countries suffer from endemic poverty rather than self-imposed disempowerment.

4. A commitment to avoid people who live in "illness consciousness." I am certain you know people whose

illnesses define their identity, and their existence revolves around their medication schedules and their visits to health professionals. We should differentiate, however, between having an illness and becoming your illness. For example, some people discuss their illnesses with as much enthusiasm as if planning a vacation to Tahiti, while others, like one of my mentors, confined to a wheelchair by muscular dystrophy, was one of the most inspiring individuals I've known.

5. A commitment to relinquish personal power gained from having an illness: using illness to avoid what you dislike or to sabotage what you like. With avoidance you manipulate others; with sabotage you manipulate yourself.

The terrain is built on commitments that challenge the conventional views we learn from our cultural editors about the attainment and maintenance of health. In addition to preventing and treating illness, we need to embrace an abundance mindfulness not considered in the usual pursuit of health: moving from the absence of illness to the presence of wellness.

Pathways to the Causes of Health

Preparing the terrain to engage the causes of health does not happen overnight. It requires concerted effort to shift from conventional thinking to abundance mindfulness. But you don't have to wait until you master all five commitments to start practicing the causes of health. In the "Coauthoring the MindBody Self" chapter, I promised to expand on my concept of *universal propensities*. But first a quick clarification: Some anthropologists propose that there are traits found in all cultures (anthropological universals), and some psychologists claim there are universal human needs (hierarchy of needs). The debates are endless because they entail the question of nature versus nurture. Fortunately, my concept of universals is different. Rather than universal traits or universal needs, I propose we have universal propensities to express our causes of health. And although these propensities are expressed with cultural interpretations, they serve to bring contextual relevance to our actions, which indirectly maximize the conditions for optimal health: wellness.

Our human fabric is woven with predispositions *to belong, to be understood*, and *to be valued*. These predispositions function as pathways to find existential meaning and learn the language of love: *Who am I? What am I doing here? Who cares?* I contend that these essential questions relate to the causes of health, and when we find worthy answers, we incidentally invoke our wellness and venture beyond the absence of illness.

The answers to these three questions set the horizons (perceived limits) for the three propensities. Yes, this is a loaded statement, but I hope to unravel it to your satisfaction. You need *identity* to belong, *purpose* to be understood, and *affiliation* to be valued. When you determine each of the answers, you implicitly set the horizons (fluid parameters) for the respective propensities. Put simply: the extent of your identity, purpose, and value.

Now we can identify the long-awaited causes of health and their pathways. I had to show you the scenario in order to make sense of the path to wellness. I'll delineate how each of the propensities unfolds its respective causes of health.

To Belong: Who Am I?

We have to conceptualize our cultural self before we can experience belongingness. The coauthoring includes differentiating self from non-self. We then need to set boundaries to protect our identity. But what happens if we fail to set clear boundaries? The most obvious example is that if you feed others and neglect your own nourishment, you eventually die of starvation. Although this is an extreme illustration, the same dynamics operate when you neglect your emotional needs. A classic example is the caretakers who give to others until their health breaks down. Let me introduce you to the causes of health related to identity.

Setting Benign Limits: Having difficulties setting protective boundaries for fear of being disliked or feeling guilty for not doing enough is one of the main characteristics of the so-called Type C personality. Although the Type C personality is strongly associated with cancer, the letter *C* does not actually stand for *cancer,* it stands for another category alongside Type A and Type B personalities. And I want to emphatically clarify that this set of behaviors is a correlation with rather than a cause of cancer. What I can say with more certainty is that people who have difficulties setting limits are not in their best mindbody wellness.

Righteous Anger: The capacity and justification to express anger when warranted is healthy; suppression of righteous anger is unhealthy. But I should point out that if the anger is taken out of context, it could become chronic and lose its health benefits. In fact, chronic anger is one of the causes of stress that contributes to illnesses ranging from hypertension to cardiovascular disorders. Examples of righteous anger include: protecting innocence, responding to injustice, protecting against violence.

Forgiveness: When the mindbody self establishes identity and boundaries, what happens when they are violated with assaults to self-worthiness? Most of these transgressions are resolved amicably, especially when there's no malicious intent. But when we are abandoned, shamed, and betrayed by those we love and trust, the damage can be devastating. Although these *archetypal wounds* (found in most cultures) have corresponding healing fields— commitment for abandonment, honor for shame, and loyalty for betrayal—forgiveness needs to be enacted before the healing can take place. The forgiveness I am addressing here is much more than an intellectual act of resolution. The process has more to do with liberation from self-entrapment than with empathy or reconciliation with the perpetrator. Mindbody forgiveness is complex, but there are powerful tools to get the job done. I will not go into it here because I dedicate a full chapter in my previous book, *The*

MindBody Code, to why forgiving is so difficult and how it can be accomplished with biocognitive methods.

To Be Understood: What Am I Doing Here?

Meaning: As we learn about who we are, being understood becomes vital in our social and cultural communication. Recall what you feel when you're arguing a point or expressing an intention that gets misunderstood. You may feel frustrated, and even worse, helpless, when you find others are not getting the message. Having others understand the *meaning* of our actions and intentions is one of the causes of health. Neuroscientists have been able to use functional magnetic resonance imaging (fMRI) to detect how a part of the brain related to rewards and pleasure (middle insula) is activated the moment a person feels understood, whereas not feeling understood registers in an area of the brain related to negative emotions (anterior insula). These brain-scan studies also show how subjects reported lowered self-esteem when they felt misunderstood. But let's not mechanistically conclude that we try to be understood to seek reward from the brain's pleasure areas. We're not like monkeys performing for food. Our need for meaning goes deeper than seeking pleasure. Fortunately, there's other research that shows how our immune system responds positively to pleasure with pro-social meaning and negatively to hedonistic pleasure (pleasure for the sake of pleasure). I will explain in greater detail in the "Cultural Brain" chapter.

Passion: A strong sense of enthusiasm or excitement for what you do. The passion you experience in your work, vocation, relationships, and other endeavors enhances health. It's worth noting that many people who retire without meaning lose their passion, and within four to five years develop major illnesses and die. They disengage from two robust causes of health: passion and meaning. I have asked many centenarians why they continue to work, and after giving me a confounded look, they tell me it makes no sense to retire from what you love. That passion for what they do contributes more to their healthy longevity than their family genetics.

To Be Valued: Who Cares?

Inclusivity: The mindbody self finds valuation internally and seeks to be valued externally. Before anyone can care, they have to be given permission. They have to be included in the caring coauthorship. Inclusivity increases affiliation self-esteem: the degree of quality people whom you choose to share your joy and good fortune. There's much medical anthropology evidence illustrating the deleterious health effects of marginalizing, excluding, banning, and exiling people. Conversely, strong family ties and highly inclusive subcultures living in poverty have better health than their higher socioeconomic neighbors. Thus, better health care, education, and living conditions may not be as contributory to well-being as cultural inclusivity. It's important to understand that I am arguing for the power of inclusivity as one of the causes of health, rather than denying the value of good health care and education.

Bonding: Inclusivity embraces; bonding solidifies relationships. There are factors in common as well as unique features in these two causes of health. Both inclusivity and bonding require openness and tolerance to connect with others. Bonding, however, is dependent on the triumphs and tribulations that a group experiences. You can see these dynamics at play in classrooms, sports teams, army platoons, and other group conditions where people are brought together with a shared objective. The necessity to coexist as well as to experience fortunes and misfortunes as a group increases kinship. Another indicator of group bonding is the resistance to accepting new members; and when they do, the newbies have to gain the trust and respect of the group.

Curiosity: The main characteristics of curious people are their inquisitive interest in others and their seeking novelty. When the life sciences look for factors that contribute to sustainable excitement in relationships, healthy longevity, recovery from trauma, creativity, and success, *curiosity* surfaces with greater significance than intelligence, education, and other traits ordinarily attributed to human resilience and excellence. I propose that curiosity is one of the most powerful causes of health for several reasons: Curiosity is highly correlated with positive growth in people suffering from post-traumatic stress disorder (PTSD); healthy centenarians score high on novelty-seeking scales; people with high self-esteem exhibit more curiosity than the average; clinically depressed patients experience less curiosity than people with most other psychiatric disorders. Curiosity is an antidote to wallowing in misery, rerunning failure, and fear of exploration.

Rituals: The meaningful actions that define who we are in our culture. Rituals keep us grounded during turbulence, have a rewarding effect when we engage them, transmit cultural identity from one generation to another, function as rites of passage, and carry other culturally venerated symbolism. Some research shows that maintaining family rituals provides a protective factor for children of alcoholics. Most important family rituals include mealtimes (without digital distractions), vacations, holidays, and traveling to places that hold special meaning for the family. Marriages, funerals, anthems, dances, and religious rites are other examples of more expansive cultural rituals. Interestingly, when I ask centenarians for their secret to longevity, they frequently point to their rituals: a cigar before bedtime, a shot of rum at night, a special prayer, a morning walk. But you should note that although some drink and smoke, they never do it excessively. Unlike addictions, rituals are self-validating behaviors rather than dysfunctional distractions.

I hope I've persuaded you to see that healthy endeavor is not the same as healthy life. Health is more than absence of illness, and wellness is much more than health. If you prepare the terrain, engage the dispositions of our human fabric (to belong, to be understood, to be valued), and find existential meaning (know who you are, know what you're doing here, know who cares), then you will incidentally enact your causes of health. But remember, the journey of the mindbody self is contextual. One of the main reasons why some of the great existential philosophers suffered from despair is that *they looked for an absolute self void of context and culture*, asking, "Who am I in all circumstances and all cultures?" rather than "Who am I as a Chinese father, American mother, African professional, French student?" and so on. The questions should be archetypal in context and cultural in nature.

Tools to Access the Causes of Health

The most effective way to implement what you've learned is to use the chapter as a consulting manual to help you set the conditions that enact the causes of health. It's important to view the learning process as a gradual shift of consciousness rather than a set of quick-fix techniques. The chapters are resources to review as you refine the strategies for your journey. I'll outline the basic components to transition from the conventional focus on how the body breaks down to how the mindbody heals and achieves wellness.

Principle: The Causes of Health Are Inherited

The Commitments

1. View your mindbody as a self-organizing entity that integrates culturally driven contexts with personal experiences to develop a cultural self.
2. Challenge the genetic sentencing in family illnesses.
3. Learn worthiness.
4. Avoid people who live in illness consciousness.
5. Relinquish personal power gained from having an illness.

The Predispositions

1. To belong.
2. To be understood.
3. To be valued.

*The Existential Questions**

1. Who am I?
2. What am I doing here?
3. Who cares?

*Remember to ask the questions in contexts: for example, as they relate to father, mother, student, husband, wife, partner, and so on.

The Causes of Health

1. Setting limits
2. Righteous anger
3. Forgiveness
4. Meaning
5. Passion
6. Inclusivity
7. Bonding
8. Curiosity
9. Rituals
10. Self-love

Putting the Principle into Practice

- Review the five commitments and choose one that you believe needs the most work. For example, *learning worthiness.* Pay attention to how you are coauthoring what is not serving you well. This is done to identify how you may be participating in blocking the commitment rather than to place blame.

- Identify if the blocked commitment is affecting one of the three predispositions. For example, you're not committing to *learn worthiness* because you *feel misunderstood.*

- Identify if the blocked commitment is related to one of the three existential questions. For example, is not committing to worthiness related to the question of *who cares?*

- Now you have identified the interconnection of commitment, predisposition, and existential question. If you're finding it difficult to find interconnections, give yourself time to practice. The connections will surface if you close your eyes for a few minutes and evaluate the possible connections in different contexts—at home, at work, with friends, and so on. If you only find two out of three, work with them, and the third will co-emerge if it's relevant.

- Whether you have two or three connections, move to the next step.

- Now look at one of the 10 causes of health to find the best fit: one that could clear the block and begin to find solutions. Perhaps you decide that *setting limits* will help you *learn worthiness* and *feel understood.* Setting limits will free you to commit to worthiness and be better understood and appreciated.

- Begin setting limits by going from easier to more difficult situations. The limits could also apply to you. For example, setting limits in how much you may be over-informing others so you can feel worthy and understood.

Debriefing

This exercise has several objectives:

- To experience how the commitments, predispositions, and existential questions are interrelated. They affect each depending on context. For example, feeling worthy, understood, and loved at home as a mother, but feeling unworthy, misunderstood, and unappreciated as a professional at work.

- To experience how blocked commitments preclude setting the terrain for the universal propensities to unfold: the cause of health.

- To understand how choosing one of the causes of health as a possible solution can also guide you toward wellness: more than health as absence of illness.

- To recognize that a healthy lifestyle is necessary but not sufficient to experience wellness.

Anticipating Difficult Conditions

Let's suppose you try these experiential tools and find that others are not responding or are making it difficult for you to keep your commitments. What can you do? Well, celebrate that you recognize how your coauthors may not be ready to dance wellness with you. And after the celebration, try the following:

1. Look for a different commitment that needs work and coauthors who are more willing to support your new behavior: alternative goal with new players.

2. Apply the process to yourself independent of your coauthors. This may trigger a clever question: Given that according to biocognitive principles nothing happens in a vacuum, what do you engage if there are no coauthors? The answer? You engage yourself. There's external coauthorship with people and conditions in your world, and internal coauthorship with yourself. In other words, staying with the example you practiced, you commit to learning worthiness based on your own actions, to better understand yourself, and to better care for yourself. Most important, use the chosen cause of health to set limits with yourself. The good news is that it works equally well coauthoring with others or with you alone. In fact, if you experience the process with yourself first, you will have a better understanding of what to do when you try it with others. Also, after you succeed with yourself, succeeding with others will be icing on the cake. Always remember—you are the cake!

The concepts introduced in this chapter need to be assimilated and implemented gradually to better extract and support the causes of health. I suggest that rather than taking on too much at once, you experiment with each of the concepts until you are comfortable to make a connection and move on to the next. For example, you can choose one of the commitments (challenge genetic sentencing in family illness) and explore how your family bought into the concept; find family members who do not fit the pattern of having the illness and determine what is different about how they live.

After having a good understanding of how your chosen commitment unfolds, you can move on to one of the predispositions that you determine may be related to the commitment. For example, a commitment (challenge genetic family illness) and a predisposition (to belong). In this example, you may discover that in order to make the commitment, you can no longer "belong" to the collective belief that you're sentenced by your family illness.

But remember, this is not just an intellectual shift in beliefs. You have to experience belongingness in a different way, perhaps by connecting with relatives who do not fit the pattern of your family's illness.

The next step is to identify the existential question most affected when you relate it to your chosen commitment and predisposition. For example, you may find that the question *Who am I?* is the most relevant because if you commit to challenge family genetic sentencing, you may have to redefine who you are in the context of family illness.

Finally, you can choose the cause of health most helpful to shift out of the consciousness that identifies you with family illness as inevitable. Following the example above, you could choose *inclusion* as the cause of health you want to explore. I suggest inclusion since belongingness and *Who am I?* need to be recontextualized when you commit to challenge the family illness. Then, as you find inclusion somewhere else (like-minded friends and colleagues in the context of wellness), you indirectly trigger one of the causes of health.

Although the process of making the connections between the terrain and the other concepts may initially appear daunting, you may be pleased to know that all of these concepts are already part of your inherent wisdom—150,000 years of fine-tuning the terrain for the causes of health to thrive. Take your time and become a skillful navigator of your causes of health. Oh, yes, one more thing . . . did you wonder why I chose *self-love* rather than *love* as one of the causes of health? Because the other causes of health listed are expressions of self-love that can expand to love others. But if you focus too much on loving others while neglecting yourself, the love you give is most likely to be loved back rather than to simply *love*. I argue that loving others becomes a powerful health enhancer after you learn to love yourself.

chapter 7

From Presenteeism to Embodied Present

Although *presenteeism* is commonly defined as "the act of attending work while sick," in this chapter we are going to look at another interpretation unrelated to being sick that is gaining interest in organizational science. If you're absent at work, there's no confusion about whether you're there or not, and if you go to work when you should be home mending your health, it's based on a conscious decision. But if you're at your job in a state of presenteeism *without* being sick, you are still only physically there. Your thoughts are elsewhere—planning your next vacation, paying bills, rerunning an argument with your partner—along with their corresponding emotions: happy for vacation planning, annoyed for paying bills, and angry for arguing with partner. For many, presenteeism also includes preoccupation with having their cell phones readily accessible. Unfortunately, this type of presenteeism is not limited to work; it is also well entrenched in relationships and other life endeavors. This mindbody disconnection makes you more accident-prone and reduces your productivity at work as well as your emotional availability at home. The presenteeism I am describing is not the occasional tuning out we all do when preoccupied or bored. It's much more than that. It is a pattern of distractibility from what you have to do that lacks passion and meaning; it's another form of disembodied cognition that does not support maximum health.

Interestingly, this lifestyle is slowly becoming the norm in the wealthy and fast-developing countries. Recent studies show that the socioeconomic gains in China have not led to increased happiness. Higher income improves how we evaluate life, but not our emotional well-being. Adding to the complexity of understanding well-being, other studies show that happiness predicts future socioeconomic improvement. In other words, the happier you are, the greater your probability of improving your standard of living. But how does this make sense in light of studies that indicate higher socioeconomic status does not increase happiness? Rather than trying to confuse you, I want to show you why the results of these apparently opposite findings make sense.

Being happy facilitates access to what could improve your standard of living, but increasing your standard of living does not make you happier. Why? Because happiness is not based on how much money you make. And here's the lesson for the mindbody self: If you're happy, you have a better chance of improving your standard of living. But if you're improving your standard of living to be happy, it won't work.

The iSelf

The gradual disconnection from experiencing the embodied present is aided by the digital culture I describe in the "Coauthoring the MindBody Self" chapter. A study showed that when participants were not allowed to answer their cell phones while performing a task, their physiological markers of stress (increased heart rate, muscle tension, blood pressure) went up significantly. This emotional attachment is also evident in restaurants and other public places where some people are unable to have a meal or sit quietly without doing something with their cell phones. Persistent preoccupation with e-mails, calls, photos, games, and texts makes the cell phone an intimate need for the user—resulting in what psychologists call the "extended self." Some cellular users are so identified with their digital companions that their extended self becomes an "iSelf." If you think I am exaggerating, consider that there's a new term in psychology to describe a fear of being out of mobile-phone contact: *nomophobia*. Although not a phobia in the clinical sense, there are several studies that show participants experience considerable anxiety when deprived of their precious cell phones.

Another explanation offered by cognitive scientists for the emotional attachment to cell phones is a fear of missing out (FoMO)—on conversations, events, and experiences shared across social circles. The cell phone becomes the link to remain connected with what's happening of value around the user. Tom Hanks brilliantly illustrates in the film *Cast Away* the emotional attachment to objects. After surviving a plane crash, Hanks's character, Chuck, finds himself alone on a deserted island. To deal with his isolation, he paints a face on a Wilson volleyball he discovers amid the wreckage. He names his sole companion "Wilson" and carries on conversations with the ball as if it were a person. The emotional connection is so strong that when Wilson is dislodged while Chuck is attempting to leave the island on a raft, Chuck jumps into the rough waters at his own peril in an attempt to retrieve his valued friend.

Although it's generally not played out as intensely as in the film, what I like to call the "Wilson effect" seems to be widely afflicting the digital culture.

The Wilson Effect

The scenario in *Cast Away* illustrates how objects are humanized to cope with isolation. But I want to show how the Wilson effect can help us understand presenteeism. Could isolation also be the cause for workers to detach from their jobs, and users to attach to their cell phones? I propose that isolation can be a cause *or* effect for the extended self.

Our human propensity to socialize is thwarted when there's no one to satisfy the need. Here, isolation is the clear cause. Isolation as the effect, however, takes place when we emotionally engage objects that *cause* isolation. In other words, by consistently replacing people with cell phones, digital games, and the Internet, we isolate ourselves from people: objects become the cause and isolation the effect. When we allow objects to isolate us from people, we seek less human interaction and more engagement with the digital world.

When the iSelf goes to work, more people interaction is required, and there's less time permitted to interact with digital companions. Most important, in addition to disconnecting from face-to-face interactions, the iSelf uses entertaining objects to avoid *mindbody reflection*. Avoidance leads to disconnecting from experiencing the embodied present: learned distractibility. You may recall that passion and meaning in what you do are two of the most important causes of health. But distractibility does not allow for the sustained attention needed to discover passion and meaning in your tasks at work and your relationships at home. I am certainly not suggesting we stand in the way of digital progress. Instead, we should make technology our servant rather than our enslaver. When given a chance, face-to-face human experiences are profoundly more interesting than Wilson's face.

RETIREMENT CONSCIOUSNESS

Now we understand how we create isolation when disconnecting from others by turning to objects (iPhones) as well as how forced isolation causes us to connect emotionally with objects (like Chuck's Wilson volleyball). Both conditions extend the mindbody self to include objects in its emotional space. But what causes presenteeism at work when isolation is not involved? Cultures determine when to enter the portal of *retirement consciousness*: the age or time in your life when retirement becomes a preoccupation. This is not the same as planning for your retirement. The preoccupation is centered on looking forward to retirement many years before it's time. For those of you who might think you're too young to benefit from this section, I suggest you pay attention because some cultures determine you should start winding down while still relatively young. It's not difficult to understand why the average retirement age for professional football players is 28. The physical demands plus the wear and tear of the sport shorten the professional life of the player. What I am going to illustrate, however, is the subtle ways retirement consciousness surfaces in the workplace much earlier than retirement age.

In my work with global corporations, I find retirement consciousness is influenced by the organizational culture of the business and the culture in which the organization conducts business. Countries have different compulsory retirement ages, ranging from 45 in Turkey to 70 in Australia. But if you lack meaning and passion in the work you do, retirement consciousness leads to presenteeism at any age. For example, I've interviewed workers in predatory organizations that view employees as "production units," and workers in companies that value their employees. Not surprisingly, the incidence of retirement consciousness is significantly higher in the predatory organizations because the workers are emotionally disconnected from what they do. In fact, a 24-year-old worker from a predatory company told me his motivation to go to work was imagining what he was going to do when he retired! You can bet this unfortunate employee is a member of the presenteeism crowd: Lack of meaning and passion are the culprits. Rather than frustration for not having access to a cell phone, the young man tuned out from a work environment void of intrinsic value.

I also found that when managers and executives are in retirement consciousness, their creativity, productivity, and leadership are hampered by their lack of interest in their job and the inordinate amount of time they spend fantasizing about what they're going to do when they retire. Even worse, when employees offer innovative ideas, the retirement-conscious managers dismiss them to avoid "rocking the boat" for the remainder of their uninspiring tenure.

DISEMPOWERMENT AT WORK

Some authors argue that going to work has nothing to do with personal meaning and that you should just do your job and stop complaining. In other words, you're getting paid for what you produce rather than to feel good about yourself. This mindset made sense in the early-20th-century sweatshops when little was known about the relationship between productivity and wellness. We now know that having meaning and passion for the work you do increases productivity and creativity as well as decreases absenteeism, presenteeism, and visits to health-care professionals. The World Economic Forum (WEF) estimates that the cost of chronic illnesses could reach $47 trillion by the year 2030. Considering that most of these illnesses are related to working in toxic environments and in predatory organizational cultures, it makes financial sense to see workers' health as the greatest asset. But it's not just about safe environments, attractive offices, gyms, and decent salaries. I find that all these conditions are necessary but not sufficient to maximize productivity and wellness. Disempowerment in the workplace is the main contributor to chronic illnesses. There are two conditions that lead to disempowerment: responsibility without authority and jobs without meaning. Both create helplessness associated with chronic illnesses. Just as helplessness is a major contributing factor to illness, empowerment is an essential component of health. *Empowerment* is a popular buzzword in the corporate world, but there's little agreement on what it entails. I define empowerment as "access to the necessary resources to overcome a challenge." This means responsibility with authority.

Studies consistently show that assigning tasks without access to solutions increases helplessness and decreases meaning: Both outcomes are interrelated and have negative effects on health. I will have more to say about this in the "Cultural Brain" chapter.

OTHER DISEMPOWERING ENVIRONMENTS

Family, Friends, and Lovers

It's important to note that what causes helplessness and sets the terrain for poor health is not limited to work environments. The same conditions can exist at home and in any other relationship. Although you may not have a disempowering boss, your family, partners, and friends can disempower you by consistently ignoring your attempts to bring meaning and validation to your relationship with them. Instead of not having access to resources needed to overcome a challenge at work, coauthors of helplessness in any environment deny you their participation to empower the relationship: using illness to control you, devaluing your goodwill, and any other conduct that obstructs your personal development. This happens because, inadvertently, they're committed to coauthor helplessness. But remember, coauthoring is an invitation, not an obligation.

Government

Populist governments are notorious for teaching helplessness to the masses by praising the nobility of poverty and condemning the evil of wealth. By blaming the rich for the plight of the poor, governments can conveniently disown their incompetence and promote their populism. But before you begin to see my comments as apologies for the rich, hear me out. There's no doubt that some use their wealth to abuse the less fortunate. My argument here is psychological rather than political. To some extent, all governments and political parties gain their power by manipulating their electorate. My concern here is how disempowerment raises its ugly head in the political arena.

The class-envy manipulation that I am describing has stealth consequences. If the poor are noble and the wealthy are evil,

145

who would want to transition from pride to shame? Additionally, rewarding poverty and punishing wealth makes it easier to maintain business as usual. The poor are contained in their dependence on government, and the wealthy are compelled to pay taxes that punish expansion (creating new jobs) and incentive (creating new products). So, independent of your ideological affiliation, consider how governments maintain dependence for the poor and live off contributions from the wealthy. The disempowering message from populist governments is that if you remain poor you are noble and will pay lower taxes, but if you remain wealthy you are evil and will pay higher taxes. Both positions disempower incentives for socioeconomic growth.

Religion

Religion is one of the most emotionally charged topics because it involves faith in the continuation of our existence beyond physical death of the mindbody self. Having faith in answers to what transcends our physical presence is beneficial whether the end is Paradise or fertilizer for Mother Earth. Let's not forget that to believe in god or in its nonexistence are acts of faith: belief without evidence. And as much as atheists would like science to prove the nonexistence of god, and believers for religion to confirm its existence, neither camp is able to win the argument. The essence of the arguments continues to be a matter of where to place your faith. But the psychological need to know has been a major concern since the beginning of human existence. The health benefit of faith in the existence or nonexistence of god is that it brings resolution to one of the three existential questions I propose in the "Causes of Health" chapter: *What am I doing here?*

Why? Because when you answer what you're doing with your life, it begs the question: *What happens when my life ends?* Until this question is addressed and resolved, there's a persistent existential anguish that creeps up at the most inopportune moments in our lives. Although we make our final decision based on what we choose to believe, there's a lingering need to confirm with science the randomness of our creation or to validate with our religion that we are the outcome of intelligent design. I choose to believe we're not Darwinian accidents, but since either argument can be refuted, I will simply tell you that I *chose*, without evidence to convince others. The key to existential resolution is to be at peace with *your* transcendental decision without forcing it on the opposition. Consider that neither side has a monopoly on compassion. I have seen atheists live with the benevolence of saints, and heinous crimes against innocence perpetrated in the name of religion. Although unresolved questions about religion or its absence promote presenteeism to avoid existential anguish, the moment you decide what to believe, serenity will entice you to live in the embodied present.

EMBODIED PRESENT

We looked at how presenteeism disrupts living your passion and celebrating your meaningful actions. Knowing the conditions that support your disconnections can help you determine if you want to change what no longer serves you. Perhaps at some point in your life disconnecting from painful experiences and haunting memories had a protective function. But when disconnection becomes a way of life, it replaces mindbody in the *here and now* with mind *somewhere else*, other than the body. So how do you begin the shift from being *out there* to being present in mind and body? All biocognitive processes are explored in culturally constructed contexts. To fully connect with the present requires looking at where you experience most of your presenteeism. Does it mostly happen at work, home, in social commitments, or in other relationships? To illustrate the process, let's assume it happens mostly at work and at home.

You find that your job has little meaning and you cannot bring passion to your assignments. You spend most of your day at work on automatic pilot (presenteeism) to deal with the lack of challenge. You leave work, and as soon as you get home you engage your digital companions instead of connecting with your family. But why would you choose the disconnection? Does it mean your family is also not challenging or interesting enough to engage you? The most obvious solution is to try to make your job more challenging and your family more interesting. But if it were that simple, there would be no need for this book.

So let's find the real reasons for the disconnections and decide what to do about them. As you already know, presenteeism can be the cause or effect of isolation, but perhaps you're not considering what happens when isolation also takes you away from mindbody reflection. When you get home from a full day of presenteeism void of introspection, the last thing you want to do is connect with others. But instead of taking time for yourself, you continue presenteeism by engaging your digital companions (laptop, TV, cell phone, video games). Some would argue that taking time for yourself includes enjoying your digital companions. The difference is that mindbody reflection means observing what is going on with your inner self rather than entertaining yourself with interesting technology. For example, enjoying your internal observations in your living room, or communing with nature during a walk in the park.

But here's how cultures derail your objective to experience the embodied present. If you ask for more creative challenges and greater control over what you do at work, you will most likely be told you're getting paid for doing your assigned tasks and nothing else. At home, if you say you want to spend some time alone, you may find it easier to go directly to your laptop than convince others that you are not avoiding them. But most likely your family is already engaged with their digital partners as well.

Our modern societies, both Eastern and Western, are slowly replacing cultural *rituals* of wellness with escapism *routines*. And this, my friend, is not a good formula to engage the causes of health. I am not suggesting becoming a monk in the asphalt jungle to introspect your life away. My concern is that we're not giving ourselves the necessary time to assimilate the challenges of our daily lives. At the end of each day, we have an assortment of half-baked emotions, incomplete interpretations, fragmented ideas, and preoccupations that carry over to the next day without giving them their required attention. Think of a baby crying because of a soiled diaper, rash, or hunger. Instead of attending to the cry, you ignore it. Eventually the baby stops crying and finds entertainment with a toy in the room, but the damage from ignoring the baby's needs intensifies.

In a less graphic way, this is what happens when you ignore a cry for mindbody reflection. It does not mean that by reflecting you will solve every challenge of the day. Instead, it's an acknowledgment that you're worth the time to consider your issues and soothe your apprehensions.

MindBody Reflection

Before moving forward with possible solutions, I want you to understand what mindbody reflection really is. It is more than relaxation, meditation, mindfulness, and introspection. In addition to reducing tension, attending to the immediate present, and self-observation, mindbody reflection *embodies* the internal experiences and external surroundings that enter your awareness. You do the contemplation with eyes open and purposely observe how your body is manifesting your experiences. By contrast, meditation and mindfulness methods done with eyes closed exclude experiencing your external space. They teach observation of your *internal here and now*. Additionally, when these methods are done with eyes open, external awareness is limited to what's in front of your visual field. Understandably, meditation and mindfulness have a different purpose: to quiet your mind and allow unencumbered observation. However, none of these contemplative methods includes intentional observation of how your body responds and manifests your inner and outer here and now. And why is this important? Because our frequent disconnections to avoid apprehensions and unresolved needs desensitize our physical reactions, eventually creating a mind-body split.

Typical examples:

"How do you **feel** *about how your boss treated you?" "I* **think** *he was very unfair."*

"How do you **think** *we should handle the situation?" "I* **feel** *we should proceed slowly."*

Although language mostly reflects how we perceive the world, cultures teach us how to express what we perceive. For example, Eastern cultures perceive holistically, rather than analytically as Western cultures do. Interestingly, studies show that American liberals think like Western cultures, whereas American conservatives think more like Eastern cultures. Analytical thinkers tend to focus on the parts and how they come together toward the whole. In contrast, holistic thinkers tend to see the totality of the situation rather than its parts individually. Of course, these are generalizations to show propensities rather than rigid labels.

Embodiment

The embodiment concept must be clearly understood before practicing mindbody reflection. The philosophy that makes embodiment such an important component of my work proposes that rather than perception being *about* the body, it should be *from* the body. The difference is subtle and profound. Embodied and disembodied perceptions differ in how we determine the boundaries we set, the separateness we feel, and the disconnections we make. Embodiment embraces subjects; disembodiment separates objects. I argue that due to these differences, disembodiment has a profoundly negative effect on our relationships, health, and longevity.

I implore you to consider my proposal as much more than a topic for armchair philosophizing. In the "Cultural Brain" chapter, I'll provide evidence to support what I am teaching about the health benefits of embodiment. But now, let's look at the effects of perception *about* the body rather than *from* the body. In the medical field you're treated like a mechanical object to fix *from outside* with chemistry or surgery. In the workplace you're a production unit to motivate *from outside* with money. In politics you are a voter to manipulate *from outside* with enticing promises. In religion, you are a parishioner to learn faith *from outside* with heavenly rewards or punishments. But rather than sinister institutional agendas, the culprit is the implicit mind-set that objectifies the body and views the subject from an outside world. Disembodiment separates mind from body and person from world. Of course, when I mention the body I am referring to the totality of the mindbody self. Medical anthropologist Thomas Csordas argues very convincingly that the body is not an object to be studied in relation to culture. Instead, the body must be considered as the subject of culture: the existential ground of culture.

In mindbody reflection, embodiment involves more than experiencing from the mindbody self in the world. It also includes how your perception of your inner and outer world is expressed and manifested. In other words, how does perceiving from the mindbody in the world affect the body? As obvious as this inclusion appears, to my knowledge no other method combines both components of embodiment as I do in the mindbody reflection.

Illness as the Embodiment of Adversity

Some medical anthropologists correctly propose that the experience of illness can be studied as the embodiment of generalized adversity. In other words, looking at how distress is embodied as perceived turmoil in the external world. Then we can evaluate how the embodiment of external adversity is expressed differently across gender, socioeconomics, race, and ethnicity. But I caution that the objective should be to identify how each group interprets illness, without concluding that it's due to genetic differences. Why? Because just as reductionist science attributes genetics as the main cause of family illness, it also concludes that illnesses categorized by gender, ethnicity, and race are genetically specific to the group. For example, African Americans genetically predisposed to hypertension, women to rheumatoid arthritis, Hispanics to diabetes, without considering the cultural and socioeconomic conditions embodied by each group. Oppression and prejudice, rather than genes, are the major contributors to illnesses prevalent in minority groups. What I am arguing here is based on research in cultural neuroscience, functional medicine, cultural psychoneuroimmunology, neuroanthropology, narrative medicine, and other disciplines that are looking beyond genetics to provide alternatives to the marketing of illness.

I want to emphasize that I don't deny genetic predisposition for noncommunicable illnesses or illnesses caused by genetic abnormalities. My profound concern is the emphasis placed on genetic predisposition without much interest in the cultural factors that trigger the predispositions. In the "Cultural Brain" chapter, I have much more to say about how medicine as a subculture diagnoses disease, and how the culture in which the diagnosis is made conceives illness.

Preparing to Embody the Present

The concept of embodiment is not easy to convey and assimilate. You may still have questions about how to apply it to your life. I believe when you begin to practice the tools in this section, you will get a sense of where and how embodiment can be beneficial in your daily activities. There are many philosophical and existential theories to conceptualize the *lived* body, but for our purpose let's look at two of the most relevant. For sociologist Chris Shilling, the body is an ongoing "project" that is worked on and transformed as a central part of self-identity. We can see evidence for his theory in how much time and money we spend on gyms, health food, vitamins, cosmetics, fashion, plastic surgery, and other ways to improve (transform) our self-identity through our body. In contrast, physician-philosopher Drew Leder proposes that the body has a tendency to remain in the background until physical (illness, pain) or social (embarrassment, fears) adversities cause it to appear. Leder uses the term *dys-appear* to define appearance when something goes wrong.

Shilling's and Leder's theories are useful because rather than choosing one over the other, they illustrate two different body images that you can explore with my method. For example, with the mindbody reflection method you can experience Shilling's ongoing transformations for self-identity as well as connect with Leder's hidden body without waiting for adversity to make it surface. In other words, you can embody outside experiences as well as the hidden body that remains unnoticed until something goes wrong.

Most of us don't have the option to devote our lives to introspection. Even nuns and monks have assigned responsibilities that take them out of their self-reflection. Although some "enlightened" teachers tell you to live in the here and now, they still have to step out of their *now* to plan for future marketing strategies, and how they are going to spend the money you pay them for lessons they don't live. My point is that we should strike a balance between internal exploration and external responsibilities.

The mindbody reflection method you'll learn here shows you how to detect when you are tuned out, why you are tuned out, and what makes it worthwhile for you to tune in. Rather than completely avoiding presenteeism, you can choose it wisely as refreshing breaks that can help you tune in again with stronger commitments to find deeper meaning and passion in your life.

Additionally, by spending more time in the embodied present, you can experience your body when it's working properly as well as detect early signs of when it's breaking down.

Tools to Inhabit the Embodied Present

Looking for Patterns

Determine when and where you tune out (presenteeism) most frequently:

Work: Days of the week? Assignments? Meetings? People?
Home: Mornings? Evenings? Weekends? Family members?
Other: Recreation? Worship? Politics?

Identify objects with emotional attachment (Wilson effect):

Cell phone? TV? Video games? Laptop? Internet? Other?

Identify most frequent reason for tuning out:

Lacking challenge? Insufficient meaning? Insufficient authority? Misunderstood? Not valued?

Identify the language you use most frequently to express yourself:

"I *feel* you should"? "I *think* you should"? "It *sounds* like"? "I *see* what you're saying"? "I *sense* what's happening"?

Dedicate Time to Practice MindBody Reflection

Commit to a time and place most likely for you to practice the method:

Mornings before work? At work? Evenings after work? Going for a walk? Sitting quietly?

Caveat: Do not try the mindbody reflection method while driving or listening to digital distractions.

The MindBody Reflection Method

I suggest that you first practice the MindBody Reflection Method (MBRM) as a valuable ritual during the times you chose until it becomes a familiar tool that you can use anytime. The MBRM trains you to detect when you're tuned out, how to tune in, and how to change what entices you to stay tuned out. One of the best ways to keep the commitment to practice the MBRM is to find a time that does not compete with your strongest digital companions. Find a situation with the weakest Wilson effect. Also, the two best settings to start the practice are sitting comfortably in a quiet place or going for a walk.

- Let's assume you decide to practice the MBRM sitting in a quiet place.

- Take a deep breath and slowly look around where you are. Notice something new (novelty)—it could be a detail on a window, a spot on the wall, and so on.

- After you identify the novelty (detail you never noticed before), pay attention to your body and notice what is happening: a twinge of connectiveness, slow breathing, tension in your shoulders, cold hands.

- Repeat the procedure several times: find novelty in your surroundings, then go back and identify what your body is doing. It does not have to be a body reaction to what you're discovering in your immediate surroundings. It's just a shifting from external novelty to body awareness. Spend as much time as you wish on each observation. Practice the shifting for a few minutes and go to the next step.

- Observe your surroundings (everything) for the duration of five slow breaths. Then, for the duration of the next five slow breaths, observe what your body is doing. Do the shifting after each five breaths for

155

three to four minutes. (The time period does not have to be precise.) Move on to the next exercise.

- Now notice what your eyes see, what your ears hear, what your body touches, what your nose smells, and what your mouth tastes. You're connecting *from your body* in the world with the world. Do this exercise for a few minutes before moving on.

- Notice your variety of body sensations: warm/cold areas, tense/relaxed areas, breathing from stomach or chest (fast or slow), emerging emotions (happy, safe, bored, excited, sad). You're connecting *from your body* with your body in the world. Shift back and forth from sensing the world from your body to sensing what your body is doing in the world. The two conditions do not have to be related. It's an exercise to increase awareness of embodiment that will help you identify when you're tuned out of your immediate present: a *disembodied* present.

Identifying Presenteeism

- Recall what you usually do to disconnect in the situation of presenteeism you choose: condition at work, home, friends. Elaborate on the memory of the presenteeism. Do you think about vacations, the Internet, people in your past, plans for the weekend? While you're reliving the presenteeism, embody the experience: What do you feel and sense? How does it manifest in your body?

- Shift from replaying the presenteeism memory to observing your mindbody reactions: What do you sense and feel after you replay the presenteeism? Do the shifting from the memory to your reaction of the memory for a few minutes, and move on to the next experience.

- Identify what takes you away from the embodied present when you're in presenteeism. In other words, what's lacking in the present that takes you to the past or future? Not enough challenge, authority, meaning, passion, interest? While you're identifying what's lacking in your chosen situation, embody the experience: What do you feel, sense? Stay in your embodied awareness for a few minutes before moving on.

- Identify what could entice you to embody the present in the presenteeism situation you chose. Perhaps opportunities to be more creative, have more choices, more authority, more acknowledgment from others? What do you feel and sense when you consider each possibility? For example, when you consider the options, does more authority have a different embodied expression than more acknowledgment? You're letting your mindbody reactions help you determine what you need to engage in the present. Stay in your body awareness for a few minutes before moving on.

- Whom would you have to confront to make the changes you want? Whom would you have to disappoint or upset? What would you have to give up? What do you feel and sense in your body when you consider what you need to face? Stay in your body awareness for a few minutes before moving on.

The Hidden Power

These seemingly simple exercises are intended to teach you mindbody awareness of when you embody *the world* in the world, and when you embody *yourself* in the world. In other words, knowing when you're embodying your internal and external experiences and when you're on automatic pilot. But just as important, experiencing the mindbody self when embodying the world with the senses, and embodying internal sensations while remaining within the world. You and the world remain interconnected, whether you were taught to separate each other or not. I strongly encourage you to understand that these deceptively simple differences in embodiment versus disembodiment have profound effects on how much empowerment you have in your life.

Let's move on to the next step toward inhabiting your present. First, a critical visit to your digital companions and other distractions:

- Identify which digital companion (cell phone, TV, Internet, video game, or other distraction) causes the most longing and frustration when you're not able to have access to it. Put simply, which distraction do you miss the most?

- Imagine a situation when the distracting condition you most want is not available for several days. What would you be missing? What could you do that's meaningful in its absence without going to another distraction?

- What do you sense and feel in your body when you imagine not having access to your chosen object or situation? Try to make the imagery as vivid as possible so you can experience the discomfort. Identify how and where you embody the discomfort. Look for patterns and unique mindbody reactions to the abstinence.

Now that you have embodied avoidance and its causes, let's evaluate the difference between *avoidance entertainment* and *approach entertainment*. Delaying responsibilities, disconnecting from significant people, discomfort when away from digital companions, and frustration when thinking you're missing out on what could be going on in your digital social circles are examples of avoidance entertainment. Although it may seem counterintuitive, including your digital companions as *part* of your responsibilities is the most important example of approach entertainment. Why? Because when you accept that you have as much right to personal entertainment as you do to connecting with your work, family, and friends, you will feel less resentment and more joy when you keep any of your commitments: meaningfully approaching all instead of resentfully avoiding some.

To add meaning and passion to what you do is not just about making things more interesting. Meaning is stifled when you do something because you *have* to do it. Creativity is depleted when you see responsibility and entertainment as different conditions. I am not trying to entice you with word gymnastics. I am asking you to stay with me so you can benefit from what I am proposing.

But first let's look at the usual objections: There are things you don't like that you *have* to do. There are people you don't like whom you *have* to include in your life. There are entertaining things that you do and boring things that you *have* to do.

Should you *try* to like what you would rather avoid? Should you *try* to make boring things more interesting? Should you *try* to like unpleasant people? The answer to these objections and questions is that as long as you believe that you *have* to do something, you will resent it, and most likely you will tune out. As long as you *try* to do something, you will not be fully committed. Thus, the two core factors in tuning in are *choice* and *commitment*.

Choice: We make pleasant choices because we *want* to and unpleasant choices because we *have* to. The wanted choice is an approach to pleasure; the unwanted choice is an avoidance of negative consequences.

Commitment: We make stronger commitments to tasks and people we like than to unpleasant tasks and people we would rather avoid.

So far, I have identified the basic operating factors in tuning in and tuning out. Now I have to give you solutions beyond the obvious.

The MBRM makes you aware of what, when, and where you're tuned in or on automatic pilot. This is necessary to know before you try to implement changes, but not sufficient because it does not tell you how to change what you find. Choice and commitment are strongly interrelated. Psychologically, degree of freedom is determined by the number of choices you have available. The more choices, the more freedom you experience. Commitment, wanted or not, reduces your sense of freedom because all other choices are rendered unavailable the moment you commit. For example, you want to commit to a good relationship, but as soon as you do, you feel entrapment rather than freedom—not necessarily because you made the wrong choice, but because you gave up all the other options available before you made the commitment. Thus, freedom increases with choices and decreases with commitments.

The more pleasurable the choice you make, the more willing you are to dismiss the other choices. But this does not mean your degree of freedom changes. Instead, you're more comfortable emotionally disconnecting from what is no longer available. Where am I going with all of this? Seeing the interrelationship of choice, commitment, and pleasure will make it easier to understand how to enter your embodied present and exit your disembodied presenteeism, anytime you choose. Let's use the example of choosing family versus Internet for one evening.

Choices: Internet, TV, taking a nap, having a drink, texting, going for a walk, and . . . family.

Commitment: to spend time with family.

Loss of freedom: no longer having the choices of Internet, TV, and so on.

Level of pleasure in your choice: low, because the conversations are predictable and with few areas of shared interest.

Freedom increases with number of choices, and choosing pleasurable options decreases the emotional attachment to options not chosen. Therefore, if you increase the pleasurable options you can have *within* the commitment you chose, it will be easier to disconnect from your emotional attachments to digital companions.

You can use the MBRM to practice this new way of making commitments:

- Commit to spending time with family one evening. Increase the freedom within this choice by finding new ways to interact: going for a walk rather than sitting at home; initiating conversations with topics of mutual interest; preparing a meal together that is new to all instead of engaging your laptop until dinner is ready.

- As you run these new options in your head, what are your body sensations and feelings?

- Allow your creativity to unfold and embody your reactions. Consider as many pleasurable options as you can conjure, within the commitment you made.

- Once you have a few a pleasurable options, share them with your family and have them contribute their own pleasurable options. But all options must be mutually satisfying. You want win-win, not compromises.

- Explore the chosen options with a sense of freedom.

- Commit to using this way of deciding in all areas of presenteeism.

To anticipate your question: How do you practice this method in a job where your employer is not interested in coauthoring freedom with you?

You increase the options of how to do what you're asked in ways that have more meaning and value to you. For example, you're given a boring project and you look for ways to do it differently and better than how co-workers do it. In other words, increase your choices of *how* to do what you're told. You see? Rather than trying to be more creative, you're increasing your degrees of freedom, which indirectly increase meaning and creativity. If after you try all your options the working conditions do not permit the internal freedom I am suggesting, you still have additional choices: You could start looking for another job, create your own job, take courses that make you more marketable. Is it easy? No. But it's better than letting your job make you a life member of the chronic-illness-learned-at-work club. And that's what too much presenteeism can do to you at work and in other settings.

Debriefing

If the concept of *from self to the world within the world* remains fuzzy or inconsequential, I implore you to trust that the evidence comes gradually as you experience the subtleties of embodiment. By practicing the different types of shifts, you will indirectly increase your awareness of when and why you tune out from the embodied present (all of you here and now). By shifting from automatic pilot to embodiment, you can decide to embrace the present or continue to live in the past or the future. Remember, embodiment does not have to be constant. It's an opportunity to change what keeps you "retired" from your present. Unfortunately, too many people go into retirement from the present at a very early age.

The causes of health are not triggered from past joy or future plans for joy. As you will learn in the "Cultural Brain" chapter, the immune system responds positively to meaningful pleasure in the embodied present and negatively when the pleasure is disembodied and void of meaning: *eudaimonic* versus *hedonic* pleasure. Big words, with bigger consequences than you could imagine. I'll explain in the "Cultural Brain" chapter.

chapter 8

The Cultural Brain

The brain is a coauthor of consciousness—a portal rather than the source. Culture is a collectively learned propensity to perceive the world. New brain-scanning instruments and computer-enhanced imaging such as functional magnetic resonance imaging (fMRI) consistently show the adaptability of the brain, which is called *neuroplasticity.* What were considered fixed functions based on a mechanical model of the brain are no longer supported by the latest research in neuroscience. And although the area of neuroplasticity research is well established, the cultural influence on brain function continues to be ignored. Fortunately, there's a relatively new interdisciplinary field called *cultural neuroscience* that is beginning to fill the gap.

HOW CULTURE SHAPES PERCEPTION

In this chapter, I'll discuss some fascinating results that show how cultures strongly influence the perception of our world, and just as important, how these changes affect the biochemistry, activity, and shape of the brain. Now we can convincingly argue that beliefs are more than abstractions without physical consequences. Your biology becomes the beliefs that you culturally learn to gain understanding of your world. But it's essential to clarify that I am not referring to the overused "mind over matter" adage. It's much more than one system controlling the other. Instead, it is a coauthoring of mind *and* body establishing meaning in cultural contexts. But before moving forward, I want to assure you that, more than listing a series of research studies that you can find in academic journals, I'll use the results to show you how the mindbody self learns to interpret its journey, and how to change what was considered impossible to achieve.

Relational Incompleteness

In previous works I proposed a model of how the brain makes interpretations based on what I call *relational incompleteness.* The brain is a *culturally adaptive system* designed to primarily seek contextual relevance. If the contextual conditions are unclear or unknown, the brain generates premises until it can find relevance. For example, if you go to a hospital and see a physician in a surfer's wetsuit, your immediate reaction is surprise because the situation is way out of context. In order to find contextual relevance, your brain begins to generate possible reasons for the mismatch: the doctor is crazy, the doctor was surfing when called to the emergency room, and so on, until you find an explanation that fits the context. In fact, if you're told that the doctor is dressed like a surfer because he is teaching a class in CPR for lifeguards, you might even smile when you think about the hospital's creative way of promoting the seminar.

Seeking contextual relevance to reach meaning is straightforward, but in order to perform this apparently simple task, the brain has to constantly redesign its working strategies to solve complex and unforeseen challenges. However, the brain is not like a computer: If we imagine the brain as hardware and thoughts as software, we can conclude that our brain is much more complex than the most advanced computer. There is no computer that can have its software modify its hardware—but that's exactly what the brain is capable of doing. Thoughts and emotions can change the structure and function of the brain. And the reason this marvelous task can be accomplished is that the brain has a design of *incompleteness* that can find meaning in the comparison with unanticipated conditions. Although my description may seem complicated, I'll explain how relational incompleteness works in the brain's culturally adaptive system. *Completeness* creates limits and the inability to handle anything outside its closed system. This is why computers periodically need new software and redesigned hardware to process their expanded capabilities. In contrast, our most recent ancestors, the Cro-Magnons, had the same cognitive abilities that we have. This means that our brain's design has not required an update for more than 40,000 years. Not even my beloved Apple computers can compete with that. And while we're on the subject of archaeology, the Neanderthals, who preceded the Cro-Magnons and had inferior intelligence and no developed language, are not our ancestors. Neanderthals first appeared around 100,000 years ago, and although they were mostly extinct around the time of the Cro-Magnon era, one group did not evolve from the other. There's recent evidence suggesting they coexisted but most likely did not interbreed. Because of the similarities they share with us, most anthropologists are now calling the Cro-Magnon "early modern humans."

You know that you are human because there are nonhuman species, tall because there are short people, female because there are males. In other words, meaning is reached by relating to opposites. This is the relational component of the brain. But let's suppose that you confront a creature from outer space—an unanticipated and unimagined entity. Although you may take for granted that you can make sense of the unforeseen, the reason you're able to do so is because of the relational incompleteness design of your brain. The creature from outer space was unanticipated and not part of your reality system, but since the brain's design is incomplete (culturally adaptive system), it allows for unfamiliar conditions to be incorporated and classified in relation with the familiar in your culture. For example, the creature from outer space could be human-like when related to the human head, but not to the human feet, luminous when related to the composition of human skin, without ears when related to our ears, and so on. The cultural brain is overdesigned to take us from the known present to the unknown distant future without losing meaning. The relational incompleteness model can help us understand how cultures sculpt the brain. The brain modifies its structure and function so it can adapt to the unique ways cultures choose to see and communicate their world.

The Eastern and Western Brain

As you have seen throughout this book, one of the most convincing ways to show how cultures affect the human brain is to compare how Eastern and Western perception differ. More than how your brain responds to your surroundings, the emphasis shifts to how your culture taught you to interpret information and make sense of what you perceive. You are the owner of a cultural brain. This is why I propose that cultural anthropology is the missing link of neuroscience.

Since Eastern cultures are more collectivist than Western cultures, they tend to focus on the relationships with the context they perceive. In contrast, Western cultures, being more individualist, pay more attention to isolated components than to their relationship with the context. When shown pictures of people and nature, and then asked to remember what they saw, Eastern participants remember the relationship between the figures in the picture (the tree is by lake, the man is standing under the tree), whereas Western participants remember the characteristics of individual figures (a tall man, an old tree, a shallow lake). Since the brain is taught these cultural preferences, fMRI images show that for Eastern participants, seeing one item in relation to another activates the same part of the brain; for Western participants, one item registers in one area and other items in another. Experiments also show this difference in perception when participants are asked to speak about themselves, and then about their mother or a close relative. Again, there's a difference in brain activity areas between Eastern and Western participants. The Eastern brain is activated in the same area for *self* as for *mother*, but the Western brain activates in one area for *self* and another for *mother*. Interestingly, the activated area of the brain is the same for Eastern and Western participants when relating to *self* (medial prefrontal lobe), but when *mother* is the subject, only the Western brain changes the area of activity.

Other studies on patterns of interest based on time spent watching objects show that eye movement for Westerners mostly fixes on the figure, while Eastern eye movement alternates between figure and background. These studies indicate that the Western analytical style of perceiving the world (focus on characteristics of a figure) and the Eastern holistic style of perceiving the world (focus on relationship between figure and context) are reflected in brain activity. Thus, to a great degree, culture sculpts the perceptual brain.

But what happens with these cultural differences as people age? If certain brain functions diminish as we age, Eastern and Western brains should show differences in the areas where they lose function. I promise good news at the end, but now let's follow this reasoning so we can learn what happens to the cultural brain with the passing of time. When you grow older, you have a combination of more time to practice what you do as well as more time to neglect what you don't do. Use it or lose it. When examining elderly East Asian participants, researchers discovered that they show better brain function in processing relationships between figure and context (what they learn to perceive) than older Western participants (what they learn to neglect). Investigators found the opposite effect when it comes to processing figures with their characteristics: Elderly Westerners did better than elderly East Asians. That is, older Westerners and older East Asians continued to show difference in styles of perception. Both maintained the capacity to perceive what their cultures taught them to identify, and lost function in what their cultures taught them to neglect.

The plot thickens . . . when older East Asians were compared with young East Asians in regard to processing figures with their characteristics, young East Asians did better. Does this mean there's a loss of function because of age? Not quite, but be patient. Investigators also found that when comparing older and young Westerners processing figures with their characteristics, there were no differences. But why, when compared with younger participants, did the older East Asians have diminished function and not the older Westerners? The reason can be explained culturally. Since Easterners are better at processing relationships with figures than processing individual characteristics of figures, they lost function of what is not their primary focus (culturally learned interest). But since Westerners do better with processing figures with their characteristics, they did not lose that function, and did as well as the young Westerners in the study. But here is the good news I promised: When the older East Asians were asked to focus on the characteristics of the figure rather than the relationship of figures, their function returned. The moral of the story is that what your brain learns to culturally perceive remains strong, while what it learns to culturally neglect loses function—but the function is dormant rather than lost forever.

How Language Sculpts the Cultural Brain

Language is one of the basic structures of cultures. If the brain were a closed system that did not allow variation in how we communicate, humans would have developed a universal language similar to animals. For example, the barking of dogs and the chirping of birds is the same everywhere. In contrast, there are approximately 6,500 languages in the world. The plasticity of our brain allows cultures to develop their unique languages. Some languages are more phonetic than others in that the sound of vowels does not change. For example, in Spanish the letter *a* is always pronounced *ah*. No exceptions. As we know, English is not a phonetic language; vowels change their sound based on the word. The letter *a* sounds different in the words *apple, able, author*. Scanning studies show different areas of the brain are affected when speaking a high phonetic language (Italian) versus a low phonetic language (English). Cultures with high phonetic languages activate areas of the brain related to identifying word sounds, whereas cultures with low phonetic languages activate areas of the brain identifying words. You may have noticed that, when in doubt, English speakers frequently ask others to spell a word, something that rarely happens with Spanish, Italian, and German languages because of the consistent sound of their vowels. The significant contribution of cultural neuroscience is that it shows us how cultures teach the brain to specialize in ways to perceive and communicate.

I'll share a personal experience to exemplify how cultures teach our brains to communicate based on cultural demands. My first language is Spanish; English is second. Since Spanish is phonetic, my brain learned to identify meaning more by sound than by letters. When I was in elementary school in the U.S., I did poorly in a spelling bee. Intuitively, I asked my teacher if I could write the word on a pad before spelling it. When I could see the word, I was able to phonetically decipher the spelling. After my little discovery, I won several spelling contests. What was happening is that my brain was taught to find meaning from the sound of words (phonemes), but since English does not have consistency in the sound of vowels, I got lost. I want to emphasize that the different areas of the brain that are activated by the cultural perception you learn become more specialized than those that are given secondary status. But just as the elderly East Asians were able to recuperate function of their neglected memory for individual characteristics, the brain's plasticity allows you to relearn almost anything your culture taught you to forget.

But when the brain is not working well, can we exclude cultural differences? Fortunately, culture is with us there as well. Dyslexia is a learning disorder that affects reading comprehension and writing. Very innovative studies show that Chinese children express their dyslexia in different parts of the brain than English children. One of the reasons for the difference is that the Chinese language requires processing a nonalphabetic writing system (characters), and Western languages like English process language alphabetically. Just to throw in a bit of neuropsychology for those interested in the affected areas of the brain, Chinese-speaking dyslexic children show a dysfunction of the middle frontal gyrus (the area related to processing language symbols). In contrast, English-speaking dyslexic children express their deficit in the left temporoparietal cortex and inferior frontal gyrus (areas related to alphabetical processing). But just as striking, there's reduced gray matter (outer areas of the brain that process signals from sensory organs) in the left parietal region for English-speaking dyslexics, and in the left middle frontal gyrus for Chinese-speaking dyslexics. Cultural learning is involved in the wellness and pathology of the brain. I argue that if cultures teach the brain where and how to focus perception, our shared beliefs certainly affect the causes of our health and the learning of our illnesses. In addition to language disorders, most *acquired illnesses* (not from birth) are strongly influenced by our cultural brain. There are certainly exceptions, but if we dig deep into the ecology of our mindbody, we find there are no cultural vacuums.

We can also generalize from cultural neuroscience research that cultures teach the brain how to process music (six-month-old babies pay more attention to music from their own culture than music from other cultures); where to solve mathematical problems (native English speakers activate language-related areas of the brain—left hemisphere—while native Chinese speakers activate areas of the brain related to movement—premotor cortex); how to estimate the size of geometric figures (East Asians and Westerners use different neural circuitries to estimate the size of a drawn line); and social preferences in people (Americans show activation of mid-prefrontal lobe area when shown silhouettes of bodies in dominant positions, whereas Japanese show activation in that same area of the brain when shown silhouettes of bodies in more subordinate positions).

Rather than supporting the reductionist neuroscience view that behavior is controlled by the neurochemistry of the brain, cultural neuroscience consistently shows that cultures teach the brain how to express the neurochemistry. Of course, these studies do not address differences within multicultural countries like the U.S. (African Americans, Native Americans, Hispanics, and so on). But what they do show is that culture is very active in determining how the brain processes its neuroplasticity: the culturally adaptive system.

For over a century, research has consistently shown that odors cannot be identified and abstracted with language as we do with colors. Developmental biologists explain the limitation with identifying odors as an evolutionary trade-off between greater need for vision than for olfaction. When subjects are asked to identify colors, they can group them by tints and hues, associate them with emotions, and use other ways to abstract with language what their visual sense is picking up. But subjects fail miserably when asked to do the same with a range of odors. Apparently our brains gradually lost some of the sense of smell that is no longer needed for survival. But as you know by now, this is not the end of the story. All the studies that pontificated their conclusions exclusively used Western subjects from highly developed nations and did not bother to consider how language coauthors perception in different cultures.

A recent study by neuroanthropologists Asifa Majid and Niclas Burenhult debunked the olfactory truism about the brain. They found that the Jahai people of the Malay Peninsula have a language that can abstract the perception of odors as well as other people can with colors. When the Jahai were compared with American participants, both groups did equally well identifying colors, but only the Jahai were able to accurately identify and abstract the odors presented in the study. This is another robust example of how culture weaves our perception and provides a language to describe what we perceive. Just as striking, we cannot continue to study the brain in a cultural vacuum.

Anthropologists Daniel Lende and Greg Downey introduced the term *neuroanthropology* in their book *The Encultured Brain: An Introduction to Neuroanthropology,* to propose an interdiscipline that studies the relationship between culture and brain. Neuroanthropology is very compatible with my model of cognition and biology coauthoring mind and body in cultural contexts.

Cultural Expression of Mental Illnesses

Generally, professionals diagnose mental illnesses as if they were immune to their own cultural biases. This is especially the case when the professional and the patient are from different ethnic groups. Schizophrenia is a mental illness that tends to be overdiagnosed in blacks by professionals from other racial or ethnic backgrounds. The symptoms of schizophrenia are complex and difficult to discern when the professional is not aware of what determines normality in the patient's culture. One of the reasons for this cultural bias is that most health-care professional schools exclude cultural anthropology from their curriculum.

As with most other mental illnesses, the symptoms of schizophrenia vary across cultures. The auditory hallucinations (hearing voices), delusions (thought disorder), disorganized speech, flat affect, antisocial behavior, and other symptoms of the illness are influenced by how patients learn to culturally perceive their world. Studies comparing the frequency and intensity of hallucinations in schizophrenics across cultures—using subjects from Austria, Georgia, Ghana, Lithuania, Nigeria, Pakistan, and Poland—found that the West African countries Ghana and Nigeria had the highest rates of auditory hallucinations and Austria had the lowest. While most countries also had high rates of visual hallucinations (seeing things that are not present), Pakistani and Georgian patients had significantly lower incidence.

Studies that looked at the effects of minority status and socio-economics of schizophrenics in the United States found results contrary to their expectations. Nonminority groups (whites) expressed more symptoms than the minority groups (blacks and Hispanics) studied. The results of these studies provide strong evidence against the theory that minority groups are more symptomatic because of their lower social status. Instead, the unexpected results are due to the identity and bonding factors of their cultures.

Other studies also looked at how the values of a culture (collectivist versus individualist) can affect symptoms of schizophrenia. Investigators included Korean American, African American, and Latino schizophrenics and found that Koreans had closer family ties (living with family, working in the family business) than the other groups. On the negative side, Koreans had the lowest self-esteem. How did social values affect the results? Of the three groups studied, the Koreans were the most collectivist. Their strong emphasis on family identity helps them with symptoms of isolation, whereas self-effacement and denial of individual worthiness for the good of the family works against them because the illness could tarnish the family image.

In addition to cultural values, language can also affect how professionals report and families view schizophrenia. Although the word *schizophrenia* comes from the Greek, meaning "splitting mental faculties," most English-speaking people are not familiar with its origin and view the word as simply describing a mental disorder. But countries like Japan and China that use characters (ideograms) to stand for symbols rather than single words, have three characters that together stand for schizophrenia: *mind, split, disease.* This powerful stigmatizing label for the illness has several cultural consequences. Kim and Berrios (2001) found that in Japan, only 16 percent of the schizophrenic patients knew their diagnosis, and only 33 percent of their family members knew it as such. Adding to reluctance to accept the cultural stigma, Japanese psychiatrists often refer to schizophrenia as "neurasthenia" or "autonomic nervous dysfunction" rather than using the real diagnosis: a coauthoring of doctor, family, and patient to reduce collectivist cultural shaming. These cross-cultural studies on schizophrenia also show differences in medication dosage, patient compliance, and forced medication. For example, in India it is more likely for families to force schizophrenic patients to take medication because of their collectivist sense of what is best for the group, whereas U.S. families are more reluctant because of their sense of individual rights.

Collectivism versus individualism is a major factor that continues to show significant difference in how genes express or suppress illnesses. Cultural neuroscience studies illustrate how cultures affect the expression of genes responsible for clinical depression and other mental disorders. But since reductionist researchers believe gene expression is the sole mechanism for most behavior, they frequently report finding the "depression gene," the "longevity gene," the "alcoholism gene," or any other isolated gene that could explain complex human behavior as if it were void of cultural influences. The results are quite convincing if you confuse correlation with cause. Just because a particular gene is frequently expressed in cases of depression, it does not follow that genetics is the cause.

But let's use evidence to debunk correlation as cause. First, let's look at the "evidence" presented in favor of the "depression gene." But also consider how the highly technical description can scare the general public and make them reluctant to question the findings. An individual gene can express different functions. The types of expression for genes are called alleles. Genes have short and long alleles. The short allele has low expression of a function (transcription), and the long allele has high expression. Serotonin is a neurotransmitter that affects mood, and when the levels are low, it is associated with clinical depression (low serotonin). The studies in question find that clinically depressed patients have more short alleles for serotonin expression than nondepressed people. This means that serotonin is lower in depressed individuals because of the short alleles that cannot express sufficient serotonin. Well, these impressive results can only lead to the conclusion that depression is all genetics. Who could argue with such highly technical results? I, and many of my colleagues, strongly argue against what I call myopic science.

Now let's look at what cultural neuroscience finds when collectivist and individualist cultures are studied. As you know by now, Asian cultures are more collectivist than Western cultures. They value group harmony more than individual achievement. The research that includes these two cultural perceptions as factors in depression finds that people from collectivist cultures have more short alleles for serotonin than individualist cultures. Therefore, based on the reductionist research, collectivist cultures should have higher incidence of depression than individualist cultures.

In other words, collectivist cultures have lower levels of serotonin, which should cause depression. Right? Wrong!

Although the collectivist cultures have lower expression of serotonin (short alleles), their cultural family bonding and cooperative behavior mitigate (minimize) the effect gene expression has on clinical depression. The point to remember is that the "depression gene" proponents do not bother to study how cultural differences can intervene with gene expression. When it comes to depression, family bonding trumps the effects of gene expression.

One of the most significant consequences of ignoring how cultures influence gene expression and stigma of illness is the effect it has on prognosis and patient response to treatment. As you will see in the next section, labels from *cultural editors* (doctors in hospitals, clergy members in places of worship, experts in their fields) can cause anything from inflammation to death.

CULTURAL PSYCHONEUROIMMUNOLOGY

I have proposed cultural psychoneuroimmunology (CPNI) as an interdisciplinary model to investigate how social and cultural contexts affect immune, nervous, and endocrine regulation. I want to transition conventional psychoneuroimmunology (PNI) rat research in labs to field studies with humans in their natural environments. I argue that academic labs are void of cultural contexts, and since rats are incapable of understanding the meaning of their actions and awareness of their mortality, results projected to humans lack major contributing factors that affect health and longevity.

In the mid-1960s my mentor, Dr. George F. Solomon, coined the term *psychoimmunology* after finding that psychological processes affect the immune system. Several years later, Dr. Robert Ader discovered that the nervous system is also involved, and renamed the interdisciplinary field *psychoneuroimmunology*. Additionally, other investigators found that the endocrine system also plays a part in the cognitive-biological connection, and expanded the already long name to *psychoneuroimmunoendocrinology*. In the U.S., however, the interdiscipline is commonly known as PNI. I will not go into greater detail because I have already written extensively in other works about the development of PNI. Instead, I'll focus on what I believe should be the next developmental stage of PNI research. Like most of the life sciences, PNI research has mostly ignored the cultural influence on mindbody processes. I introduced CPNI as the logical path to study cultural factors in the regulation of the nervous, immune, and endocrine systems.

Cultural neuroscience research consistently shows that shared beliefs sculpt perception. Now we can look at how the culturally adaptable brain affects other mindbody regulation. But I must tell you that most of the results are coming from cultural neuroscience and neuroanthropology (culture-brain interaction) because unfortunately PNI research continues to ignore culture. Let's look at the foundation for CPNI.

One of the most promising areas of cultural neuroscience research is based on a simple question: If an illness causes deficits in specific areas of the brain, what would happen if the brain could be taught to improve function in the affected area? This is different, however, from cases of brain damage from head injuries or strokes where patients are taught to compensate for the damaged area by learning to use a healthy part of the brain. The difference is that compensatory treatment is necessary when *significant* function is lost because of permanent brain tissue damage (as from a stroke). In contrast, the studies that I will share with you train patients to improve areas that have *reduced* function. Are you ready?

The HIV virus in children primarily affects two biological functions: the area of the brain for spatial memory (maze learning) and the CD8 and CD4 immune system cells responsible for suppressing and fighting the HIV virus. Ugandan children with HIV were trained to use a computerized instrument that improves spatial memory. Remarkably, when the children improved their skills in using mazes (spatial memory) their CD8 and CD4 immune cells increased their activity. Although not a cure, the intervention can diminish the progressive damage of the illness. These results are possible because of the neuroplasticity of the brain and its relationship with the immune system. Perhaps now you can see why I put you through the technical prepping.

Since these results were replicated with HIV-infected children in other cultures, one might conclude that the investigators were working with universal brain functions (the same results for all cultures, therefore no cultural influence). But, in addition to nutritional deficiencies, poor sanitation, intestinal parasites, and other environmental deprivations, children in these socioeconomically deprived areas in Africa live in cultures where they learn helplessness and hopelessness very early in life. Since these culturally learned behaviors are known to weaken immune function, they add a significant risk factor to the already aversive living conditions.

In my clinical practice I developed a treatment method based on two mindbody factors: the cultural adaptation of the brain (plasticity influenced by culture) and the brain's relationship with the immune system. The reasoning applied is similar to the HIV studies with children. That is, if we can teach a method that replicates the benefits a medication has on the immune system, we can enhance the effects of the medication and, in some cases, replace it with mindbody techniques. But before continuing, I want to be perfectly clear that *these interventions should always be done under the care of medical professionals.* The work I am going to describe was done with monitoring and approval of the patient's physician.

My patient had severe asthma requiring the use of inhalers several times a day. It was affecting his work and his marriage. Although he was a competent and responsible 31-year-old husband and father, he was allowing his controlling mother to determine his budget and monitor his checkbook. As you know by now, helplessness is one of the worst enemies of the immune system. I helped him set limits with his mother and to process that she was not going to like it. The symptoms improved as he regained control of his finances, but he was still affected by his mother's frequent attempts to make him feel incompetent. For example, although he was a very bright and well-respected computer programmer, his mother convinced him he was not smart enough to go to college.

The biocognitive technique I taught him was based on the following premises:

1. Asthma is an overresponse of the immune system causing bronchial constriction that impairs normal breathing.

2. Fast-acting inhalants (steroids) open bronchial pathways, suppress coughing, and relieve other constricting symptoms.

3. The brain can be taught to modify nervous, immune, and endocrine responses.

4. Mindbody techniques can replicate the effects of some medications—especially if the medication is fast acting (like steroids).

Under deep relaxation, the patient was taught to visualize the inhaler he used: to identify the color, shape, and details of the tube containing the medication. Anytime he had an actual asthma attack, he had to identify the first experience of relief after using the inhaler, close his eyes, bring the image of the inhaler to awareness, and embody the image in the area of the body he was feeling the relief. As the breathing improved, he would bring the image of the inhaler to his chest, and to his improved breathing. He practiced the procedure several times a day during asthma attacks as well as during periods without attacks. The objective was to teach him to embody an image in an area where he experienced relief. There was moderate improvement, but like anything in science, the best discoveries happen during unexpected conditions.

One weekend he and his wife visited his mother's lake house in the middle of spring (high pollen season). His mother, in her usual condescending manner, asked him if he was smart enough to bring his asthma medication. He instinctively told her he did. But later that evening he and his wife realized he had, indeed, forgotten to bring his inhaler. He felt stressed but was able to calm down during dinner. However, the nocebo (expected harm) from his mom was already predisposing him for an asthma attack. It happened in the middle of the night, and he panicked. His wife, who was also involved in the treatment, calmly told him: "The nearest pharmacy or hospital is 30 miles from the house. Your only choice is to do the technique that this crazy doctor taught you." He desperately agreed, sat very courageously, and began to bring the image of the inhaler to mind and remember the area of relief from the times he used the actual inhaler. The moment he was able to visualize the image of the inhaler and embody the memories of previous relief, his symptoms began to subside, and within 10 minutes his asthma attack was completely gone. In fact, he later told me that when he visualized the image of the inhaler, he could clearly see the expiration date! That's what the brain can do with practice.

Gradually he continued to apply the mindbody technique until he was able to reduce the use of his medication by 90 percent. Again, I remind you that this work was done under the supervision of his physician. The technique works best with fast-acting medication because it allows quick feedback to embody the image in the area of relief. I also use this method for patients with chronic pain who are on fast-acting medication (narcotics). Again, always done with consent from the patient's physician.

Now let's look at what studies can clarify for us about asthma. There's research evidence indicating that chronically angry mothers aggravate asthma in children younger than seven, and controlling mothers aggravate asthma in children seven and older. It's very tempting to speculate that these mothers are symbolically not letting their children breathe. But it's imperative to understand that if you have children with asthma, blaming yourself is the last thing I want you to do. Instead, if you feel you fit the profile, there's professional help available for parents of asthmatic children.

The good news from the research is that the best way to help children with asthma is for mothers to be more self-caring. Older children with the lowest incidence of asthma attacks have mothers who rate high on attending to their own wellness. See the advantage of self-care versus caretaker? Other research shows that sadness triggers cholinergic airway contraction, whereas happiness causes airway muscles to relax. In addition, family happiness suppresses cortisol, a stress hormone released in response to psychosocial conflict. I strongly believe *any* illness should be approached with a view of family as a microecology that affects all members: rather than pointing fingers, jointly discovering ways of changing cultural habits that are not conducive to wellness.

Addictions Are Not Disease

I want to approach the topic of addiction with the latest evidence for why some scientists are seriously considering alternatives to the medical model of addiction as disease. I argue that rather than disease, addictions are culturally learned strategies to avoid owning personal empowerment and maintain social isolation. The path to liberation requires choosing between cues of self-sabotage and invitations to worthiness. As you will see, it's not a question of willpower or avoiding professional help. It is quite the opposite. The arguments are highly controversial and emotionally laden. But let's look at why there's so much reluctance to let go of the medical model of addiction. Most of the research in favor of the disease hypothesis studies the biochemistry of how addiction affects the brain and behavior. Taken in isolation, the evidence appears indisputable. But if we include the sociocultural component of addiction, the biochemical "evidence" begins to crumble. Not because biochemistry is not involved, but rather because reductionist thinking assumes we behave solely based on our biochemistry. Before giving you evidence for my biocultural model of addiction, I propose an alternative to "a better world through chemistry": *Biochemistry does not control behavior; behavior coauthors biochemistry.*

Most of the studies supporting the disease model of addiction use rats kept in isolated cages or in enclosures with little opportunities for social bonding. Rats, like humans, are very sociable. When these socially deprived rats are put in another cage where they have a choice of drinking plain water or water with addictive drugs like heroine, they consistently choose the laced water until they die of overdose. Strong evidence? Not really.

When rats are placed in an environment where they can play, mate, and socialize, the picture changes drastically: They choose regular water instead of drugged water. But why did the investigators find this response to socialization? Pleasure-inducing drugs activate dopamine, a neurotransmitter (brain messenger) associated with rewards. When rats and humans create social bonds, they secrete oxytocin, a neuropeptide released during touching, breastfeeding, orgasm, and other bonding behavior. What effect does oxytocin have on dopamine? It decreases the secretion (down regulate) of dopamine. Social connections decrease the need for chemically induced pleasure! But let's never conclude that we are biochemical machines. Drugs can induce pleasure-seeking behavior, but social behavior can change biochemical reactions to pleasure without causing negative side effects.

Although the studies I mentioned used rats instead of humans because of obvious ethical reasons, there's plenty of evidence that the oxytocin hypothesis works just as well with humans. Some examples: During the Vietnam War, 40 percent of soldiers had tried heroin and close to 20 percent were addicted. When the soldiers left the hell of war and returned to loving families, only 5 percent became re-addicted to heroin.

Unfortunately, when confronted with the argument that addictions are not a disease, some therapists feel helpless and some addicts feel they don't want to give up their helplessness: a coauthoring that obstructs personal empowerment. Both feel anger masking the fear to avoid shifting paradigms. But what would happen if both groups helped each other overcome the fear of owning their strength and resilience? I propose that relapse would dramatically drop from the present 60 percent.

If the brain were insensitive to cultural influences, socialization would have no effect on drug addiction. Fortunately, this is not the case. The biggest contributor to the false premise that addictions are a disease, like diabetes and other legitimate illnesses, is that drugs alter gene expression. What this line of thinking consistently ignores is the research that shows how cultural beliefs and socialization also affect gene expression and its corresponding biochemistry. Most important, I am not suggesting that addiction should go untreated. Most emphatically, I propose the opposite: to change the cultural brain that learned to replace the pleasure of social bonding (eudaimonic) with drug-induced pleasure (hedonic). The cultural brain follows pro-social ethics.

Eudaimonic versus Hedonic Pleasure

I ended the "From Presenteeism to Embodied Present" chapter with two terms originating in classical Greek philosophy dating back more than 2,300 years. Aristippus (435–356 B.C.E.) proposed that the pursuit of pleasure should be the goal in life. Thus he is mostly associated with hedonist philosophy. In contrast, Aristotle (384–322 B.C.E.) viewed Aristippus's hedonism as crass and lacking meaning. The debate continues to this day, but cultural psychoneuroimmunology offers very credible evidence that, when related to healthy living, Aristotle won the argument. Let's go from ancient Greece to state-of-the-art mindbody science. There's a coordinated immune system reaction to stress called *conserved transcriptional response to adversity* (CTRA). When activated, it involves expression of genes that trigger inflammation as well as reduce antibody and antiviral strength, making you more vulnerable to disease. Studies show that people who lead a life based on the pursuit of hedonic pleasure (mostly seeking gratification of the senses) have higher levels of CTRA than people who engage in meaningful conduct that gives them pleasure (eudaimonic). In other words, finding pleasure in acts of generosity, civic mindedness, social bonding, and sharing knowledge is significantly better for your health than pleasure for its own sake.

In addition to owning a cultural brain, we function with an immune system that has morals—but not self-righteous intolerance that assumes exclusive ownership of ethics. In fact, rigid morality void of compassion is not good for your health.

THE PATHOLOGY OF DISEASE AND THE ANTHROPOLOGY OF ILLNESS

Physicians share technical beliefs to diagnose and treat *disease* based on tissue damage and biochemical abnormalities, whereas patients conceive their *illness* based on shared beliefs about maladies. The degree of agreement between the two perspectives varies across cultures. In most developed Western cultures, doctors and patients share the belief that infections are caused by pathogens. But if you go to some cultures in the Amazonian jungle, the Western symptoms of anemia become what their shamans call *limpu*: a terminal illness believed to be caused by the spirit of a stillborn who inhabits the body of the patient in order to remain on earth, eventually draining life out of the patient and moving on to another body. A Western physician with the technical belief that anemia is caused by vitamin B12 deficiency or hemorrhaging can only cure the disease in whites and mestizos (mixed race) who identify with whites, but not in natives who believe *limpu* is a terminal illness. I should clarify, however, that although a Western doctor's treatment is based on lab results that confirm the anemia diagnosis, it is not sufficient to save a patient who believes the anthropology of the illness (*limpu*) rather than the pathology of the disease (anemia). However, the distinction between disease and illness I am describing is not common practice in most medical establishments.

Western medicine treats hot flashes of menopause based on evidence of hormonal imbalances. Although there are alternative treatments within Western cultures, there's little disagreement that hormonal changes are involved. But when we examine how other cultures diagnose and treat menopause we find very intriguing differences. In Bolivia and other South American countries, hot flashes are called *bochorno*: the Spanish word for shame. And although their doctors understand the hormonal origin of the condition, some also use the word *bochorno* to describe their patients' hot flashes. This is an interesting example of both doctors and patients using the cultural label of the condition. Of course, menopause is a normal female development, not a disease or illness.

But, labels have mindbody consequences. PNI studies show that the experience of shame increases *tumor necrosis factor* immune-system molecules that signal inflammation. However, in Japan, menopause is called *konenki*, meaning "turn or change in life." In Chinese medicine, the character for *next* and the character for *spring* are used jointly to represent menopause as *second spring*: an opportunity to recognize and honor women for reaching a stage of accumulated wisdom and maturity.

One culture responds to hot flashes with shame and another with opportunities to share wisdom and accept respect in the community. Consequently, South American women who subscribe to the *bochorno* label have lower self-esteem, more hormonal imbalance symptoms, and inflammation than their Japanese counterparts who gain social status when they reach menopause.

The studies that found shame causes inflammation also report other valuable information. Although shame causes inflammation, it does not affect cortisol—a hormone widely studied in stressful conditions. One of the shortcomings of PNI is that it has almost exclusively focused on cortisol and other stress hormones released during fight-or-flight conditions. The shame studies are a refreshing exception showing that more complex negative emotions that go beyond basic fears can cause inflammation present in cancer, cardiovascular disorders, and autoimmune diseases. Additionally, recent research is strongly indicating that inflammation could be one of the major causes of depression, and that antidepressant medication may not be the most effective treatment. In fact, if the shame studies had only measured cortisol, which was not affected, the results would have failed to show that shame is bad for your health.

The *Diagnostic and Statistical Manual of Mental Disorders* (DSM) published by the American Psychiatric Association determines the criteria to classify mental disorders. Wisely, the latest edition (DSM-5) has retained and expanded the glossary for culture-dependent syndromes. The DSM-5 expansion of cultural variables in diagnostics recognizes the effects of personalizing illness when confronted with disease. Dr. Eric Cassell very eloquently defines illness as what the patient feels going to the doctor and disease as what the patient has on the way home from the doctor's office. I would add that both perceptions embody what the patient's culture expects will happen *after* the diagnosis: helplessness or hope.

To outline the numerous ways that cultures conceive illness to understand disease is beyond the scope of this section, but a few examples will give you a sense of how cultural biases shape the perception of maladies. You'll see how stigmas about equating psychological problems with "being crazy," feeling intense fear as a sign of weakness, and reluctance to take medication for problems of the mind shape the cultural interpretation of mindbody dysfunctions.

Ataque de nervios: A Spanish-language term meaning "attack of nerves," used by Caribbean Hispanics to describe a set of symptoms including screams, uncontrollable crying, tremors, and verbal and physical aggression when experiencing loss of control. *Ataques de nervios* are culturally learned reactions to family tragedy (death, serious accidents) or dissolutions of relationships (divorce, estrangement with relatives). This configuration of intense response to family adversity is culturally acceptable and serves to avoid abnormal behavior labels such as hysteria and other dissociative disorders.

Amok: A sudden episode of dissociation (detachment from reality) followed by depression, transitioning later to violent behavior toward persons or objects. Amok syndrome was originally associated with Malaysian cultures, but similar patterns are also seen in the Philippines, Polynesia, and Papua New Guinea. The episode is more prevalent in men, and appears to be triggered by insults perceived as disrespectful or false accusations. The same syndrome is reported in Puerto Rico as *mal de pelea* (Spanish for "fighting sickness"). *Amok* serves as a cultural rationalization to defend a man's honor without the psychiatric diagnosis of brief psychotic disorder. The word *amok* was introduced to the English language in the 17th century to describe "murderous frenzy" traditionally regarded as occurring exclusively in Malaysia. In a more general sense, the word *amok* refers to people or conditions wildly out of control or causing frenzy.

Mal de ojo: A Spanish phrase meaning "evil eye." From Mediterranean cultures to many other parts of the world, *mal de ojo* refers to a syndrome of screaming without apparent cause, insomnia, vomiting, diarrhea, and fever, mostly affecting infants and older children and, less frequently, women as well. Believers attribute the cause of *mal de ojo* to a malicious or intensely jealous person with power to cast spells by looking at or wishing harm on vulnerable individuals. The concept of *mal de ojo* goes as far back as the Old Testament and other Western and Eastern sacred texts. Affected cultures use talismans and other symbolic means to protect against the curse of *mal de ojo*.

Taijin-kyofu-sho (TKS): In Japanese culture, an intense fear of offending others because of personal looks, body odor, facial expressions, or body movements is known as TKS; TKS syndrome is defined as a mental disorder in the Japanese official diagnostics manual. These mental health professionals recognize that culturally defined illnesses need to be treated differently than pathologically determined diseases. Although TKS meets criteria for a diagnosis of social anxiety disorder (SAD) in most countries, the specific effort in Japanese culture to avoid offending one's group or culture should be considered when designing treatment. More specifically, clinical research shows a difference between TKS and SAD. Whereas SAD diagnosis is based on individuals intensely fearing being embarrassed, TKS individuals fear embarrassing others.

Although most health professionals are willing to consider that cultural beliefs affect biological processes, their reductionist training and financial consequences for shifting paradigms continue to obstruct their acceptance of a cultural brain. To bring neuroanthropology and cultural neuroscience to mainstream health care would challenge the Cartesian split that views patients as either physically or mentally sick. I am very encouraged, however, by the increased research in how exalted emotions (compassion, empathy, love) and elevated cognitions (admiration, dignity, modesty) affect our nervous, immune, and endocrine system. But as important, how our cultural beliefs influence the biology of our experiences.

Tools to Repattern the Brain

As you've learned from the research I presented in this chapter, cultural beliefs can sculpt most of your perception because of your brain's plasticity. But it's not only pliability that coauthors the cultural brain. Just as mind and body cannot be separated to understand the vastness of their oneness, culture is interwoven with the world we perceive. Culture is the fabric that brings meaning to who we are and horizons to what we perceive. But since the mind-body-culture interconnection is the result of over 150,000 years of subtle refinements, we're not aware of the power we have to redesign perceptual patterns that bring anguish to our lives. Let's approach the practical applications as if you had just discovered new tools that were always with you.

Reweaving Your Perception

Principle: The cultural fabric can be rewoven because the brain perceives a solid world with fluid interpretations.

When we perceive the physical world of living beings and objects, our interpretation and memory of their *tangibility* registers as fluid units of mind-body-culture. Although our perception cannot change the physical composition of what we perceive, we can reinterpret (recontextualize) the meaning of our perception. For example, although a chair is solid, the interpretation of the chair that the brain archives is fluid.

When we perceive the world of ideas, concepts, and symbols, our interpretation and memory of their *intangibility* also registers as fluid units of mind-body-culture.

Our perception cannot change the nonphysical composition of what we perceive, but we can reinterpret (recontextualize) the meaning of our perception. For example, although a table is a solid object, and the concept of happiness is not, the interpretations that the brain archives are fluid. Thus, the brain has plasticity and culture has fluidity. Nothing is carved in stone.

- Go to your favorite place and allow your mindbody to slow down and reduce the noise. Take a deep, long breath and consider that your perception of the world is woven by your culture.

- Entertain this concept of cultural weaving for a few minutes and observe your mindbody reaction, without interfering.

- Recall a period in your life when you were overwhelmed by a challenge (illness, bad marriage, financial crisis). Recall how you handled the situation and the greatest concern at the time. Embody what you sense and feel while you're remembering the challenge.

- What was your greatest fear? Perhaps it was not being able to change or accept the outcome. What and where do you feel in your mindbody? Allow it to surface and move on without attaching to the memory.

- Bring back the same memory of the challenge, but this time look at the *cultural weaving* you gave to your perception at the time. For example, how does your culture weave the perception of illness, divorce, or financial crisis? What are the stigmas? What is the emotional price to pay?

- Separate the cultural weave from the challenge, and experience the difference. For example, financial loss is the challenge, and the cultural weave is the shame that some cultures bring to failure.

- Identify what you did to overcome the challenge and the stigma from the cultural weaving of the challenge. For example, the challenge of losing a job requires finding other employment, whereas the cultural stigma woven in the challenge requires dealing with the shame and loss of social status. Embody what you feel on both conditions. Most likely, you dealt with both conditions without knowing they were woven as one.

- Of the two conditions, which remains unsolved? For example, a financial situation was remedied, but not the shame (cultural weave).

- Begin to look at challenges as culturally woven perceptions. When you do, you'll be able to recognize the cultural spins given to our struggles. Then, based on what you learned from your culture, decide if the weaving requires laundering.

Debriefing

The considerations in these exercises may seem obvious, but at the time of crisis we don't recognize the difference between how we respond to the disruption of order, and how our cultures weave the implications of the disorder. For example, individualist cultures may conceptualize (culturally weave) bankruptcy as lessons on the way to success, whereas collectivist cultures weave it as permanent shame to the family or group. Governments and institutions reflect cultural weaving in their laws and business consequences. For example, shameful conduct is the cultural weaving of business failure in Japan; in some cases it's considered a crime, and in the extreme, it leads to suicide. In Saudi Arabia, there's no minimum age for marriage. Men can divorce their wives without legal justification, and the dissolution is granted immediately. The Philippines remains the only country in the world where divorce is not legal. The next set of exercises provides tools to unweave cultural stigmas and biases.

Focus only on the cultural weaving component of your challenge. Identify which archetypal wound was woven to the challenge. For example, shame for financial loss, abandonment for divorce, or betrayal for illness. Although the shame and abandonment wounds are reasonably associated with the circumstances, the connection of betrayal with illness may need clarification. Illness is often (not consciously) associated with betrayal of the body.

Refresher

The archetypal wounds that most cultures weave are: shame, abandonment, and betrayal. Their respective healing fields are honor, commitment, and loyalty to the mindbody self: Cultures can disempower you with archetypal wounds, and you can regain personal power with self-caring healing fields. Thus, cultures weave wounds as well as healing fields to our perception of the world. Self and environment are woven in a coauthorship of external conditions and cultural preconceptions. Review the "Causes of Health" chapter's section on forgiveness.

Here are the steps to healing archetypal wounds:

- After you determine the archetypal wound woven by you or others to your challenge, embody the emotions and sensations. Determine if the wound remains unresolved. If it is, bring the corresponding healing field to awareness. If the wound has been *truly* healed, find one that remains open.

- Bring to awareness how you're going to resolve the archetypal wound with the corresponding healing field. For example, if the archetypal wound is shame, imagine what you can do to honor you. It does not need to be related to the wounding circumstances. Embody what you feel and sense as you imagine honorable conduct.

- If the archetypal wound is shame, engage in honorable self-caring deeds for the next few days, and pay attention to the thoughts, sensations, and emotions that surface. If abandonment is the archetypal wound, engage in self-caring commitments; and if it's betrayal, engage in self-caring loyalty. The self-caring deeds can be as simple as committing to enjoy your work, honoring your conduct in special relationships, and loyalty to what you consider worthy in your personal activities.

- When confronted with new challenges, determine what you need to do to correct the disruption, and what you need to do to avoid or heal the archetypal wound your culture weaves to the challenge.

These exercises encompass different degrees of the topics covered in this chapter. As you learn to reweave dysfunctional perceptions, your mindbody responses will be activated accordingly. In other words, as you reweave a perception of helplessness with a perception of empowerment, you trigger gene expressions related to the causes of health, resolve cultural stigma associated with life challenges, and embody new language that recontextualizes (shifts cultural meaning) how your cultural brain was taught to read your identity and relationship with your culture. But remember, the recontextualizing requires experiencing (embodying) the shift of felt meaning from one interpretation to the other—living the transition from helplessness to empowerment.

chapter 9

Growing Older versus Cultural Aging

This chapter is based on my theory that growing older and aging are different processes. The principles you will learn come from the best teachers I could find: hundreds of centenarians from different cultures who showed me why genetics is not the key to healthy longevity.

THE GERONTOLOGY OF MACHINES

Growing older is mostly determined by the passing of time, but aging is how we experience time based on our cultural beliefs. Until recently, there was little medical interest in viewing the passing of time as nothing more than genes expressing their inevitable deterioration. I propose that, although gerontology studies the aging process, it mainly focuses on the pathology of aging while ignoring the causes of health in the process of growing older. Additionally, the branch of medicine that specializes in the health care of the elderly (geriatrics) shows profound ignorance of how cultural contexts affect our biology. Fortunately, the assumption that sentient beings can be studied and treated with mechanical models is changing rapidly. The life sciences are finally welcoming the contributions of cultural neuroscience, neuroanthropology, and other disciplines that bring natural contexts and cultural factors to the forefront. What could this mean for you? That you no longer have to live with the belief that aging is an inevitable genetic sentence. Clocks measure objective time, but subjective time is measured by the hypothalamus. The hypothalamus is located above the brain stem, and one of its primary functions is to communicate with the nervous and endocrine systems through the pituitary gland. Most remarkable, however, is that in addition to regulating circadian rhythms (24-hour physiological cycles), this internal clock also responds to how cultures perceive time passing. Aging is the time that your biology learns to travel through cultural space.

There are several reasons why a majority of the health sciences are reluctant to shift their mechanical paradigm in the face of credible empirical evidence that we cannot be reduced to our parts. Most of the medical research is done in laboratories using rats as their subjects, and making conclusions from statistical averages. For the sake of economic and clinical efficiency, this model makes sense. But it ignores that we are not rats, we do not live in antiseptic labs, individuals are not averages, and we are cultural beings with beliefs that affect our health and longevity. In fairness, some of the research in pharmacology and other branches of medicine is done with rats and other animals because the procedures would be highly unethical and illegal if performed on human beings. But I leave the cruelty-to-animals issues to the organizations that can argue those concerns better than I.

My point is that when humans are studied in their natural settings, the cultural perception of their environments is considered, and their individuality is assessed, we find a world beyond how rats respond when exposed to medieval torture in the name of science. But we can't ignore that there would be no prevention for polio without Jonas Salk experimenting with monkeys before courageously trying the vaccine on himself and his family. By the way, Salk's vaccine uses an inactivated virus that is very safe, but it has to be injected. Several years later, Albert Sabin developed the oral vaccine. Although cheaper to manufacture, the oral version uses a weakened *activated* virus that can cause polio in three out of one million dosages, still making it extremely safe when considering the risk-benefit factor. I remember taking the oral vaccine when I was in elementary school. Thankfully, Salk and Sabin are responsible for eradicating polio from most of the world.

The mechanistic model is also applied to aging research using animals to learn how certain chemicals affect genes related to longevity—again, assuming gene expression happens in a cultural vacuum. In the "Cultural Brain" chapter I discussed research that shows how cultural contexts can affect the expression or suppression of genes related to health and longevity. For example, the so-called longevity genes are found in only 35 percent of centenarians. The centenarians I have studied also show approximately 25 percent correlation between their advanced age and their parents' longevity. The unaccountable percentage is what I propose cultural factors can answer for us. But keep in mind that cultures influence what we eat, our level of activity based on age, where we live, how much risk we take in our lives, life expectancy, and the rituals that enhance or diminish our immune system's defense against foreign bodies. It's all about culture, but as you will see, cultures can be beneficial or detrimental to your health and longevity.

THEORIES OF AGING

Modern theories of aging in social sciences were developed in industrialized Western countries to determine retirement age and how to care for the elderly. Shortly after World War II, the *disengagement theory* was the first of three major psychosocial theories to explain the aging process. The disengagement theory wins the prize for the most depressing of the three. It proposes that aging is an inevitable and mutual withdrawal or disengagement that decreases connections between the aging person and their social systems. In other words, you disconnect from society because you're aging. Next, the *activity theory* proposes that if the elderly stay active and maintain their social connections, the aging process is delayed and quality of life improves. The third is the *continuity theory*: It states that older adults will usually maintain the same activities, behavior, and relationships as they did when they were younger. But as you might suspect from a biocognitive perspective, all three theories used elderly American subjects, and did not consider individual differences or cultural factors. In other words, aging is the same all over the world.

Subsequently, anthropologist Margaret Clark came to the rescue. She was able to show that anthropology and gerontology could mutually benefit from working together in the areas of human development and aging. Clark proposes that aging is a series of adaptations to the social systems embedded in cultures. In other words, aging is strongly affected by how we adjust (adapt) to the constraints of our cultures. Some of the constraints include retirement age, age limits for hiring, gender restrictions, family authority, medical biases, rites of passage to elderly status, and many other challenges imposed by social systems rather than by our biology.

But although anthropology is much more sensitive to the power of culture in the aging process, Clark and her former student Sharon Kaufman (now a pioneer in her own right) also noted that early anthropologists documented cultural patterning of the life cycles, but they rarely studied these patterns beyond childhood. This was mostly due to the influence psychoanalytic theory had on cultural anthropology. In general, psychoanalytic theories do not go beyond early childhood psychosocial development. Recent research in anthropology confirms Clark's adaptation theory in Western societies as well as how other cultures with core values compatible with healthy aging are less stressful. Cultures that view growing older as opportunities to gain wisdom and social status have healthier and longer-living elderly populations. This finding makes sense when you view aging as adaptations to cultural constraints. Fewer anti-aging constraints result in healthier adaptation to the passing of time.

Jay Sokolovsky remembers when he was studying anthropology in the early 1970s that there was little interest in researching elderly Americans. In his book *The Cultural Context of Aging*, he noted that anthropology was mostly studying small tribal populations in Africa, Amazon, and other areas where people were still hunters and foragers. But American social pressure to look "forever young" has disillusioning effects that create major adaptation difficulties for its aging population. Sokolovsky is encouraged to see that some of the marketing for the elderly is moving from focusing on *retirement* communities to promoting *active-living* centers. Although these are salesmanship strategies, there's a recognition that the perception of aging is changing in the right direction. Most important, however, is that shifts in perception can change the cultural constraints that Clark and other anthropologists see contributing to unhealthy aging.

PORTALS OF ADVERSITY

While bringing gerontology and anthropology together to study the aging process is necessary, I believe it's not sufficient to explain how cultural constraints affect longevity. How does difficulty in adapting to cultural constraints affect our biology? Why is it that some people who experience major cultural constraints (sexism, racial prejudice, extreme poverty, physical abuse) live long, healthy lives? These are some of the questions that led me to study the outliers that defy their cultural norms. Who are these extraordinary people? When looking for the causes of healthy aging, there's no better sample than those who reach considerable longevity relatively free of illness: healthy centenarians. Interestingly, many of the centenarians I studied experienced major traumas in their lives (rape, concentration camps, and other infamies). In fact, easy lives were exceptions rather than the expected profile of healthy longevity. So what's going on? Before we look for answers, I will clarify that these centenarians come from different cultures, races, socioeconomics, gender, environments, and educational backgrounds—individualist and collectivist cultures from five different continents. So it's reasonable to conclude that there are common factors across all cultures that contribute to healthy longevity. In other words, we can identify the best fit between individual characteristics and cultural demands. I can tell you that in all the research I've done and all the theories I've encountered, I was never able to reach a satisfactory either/or con-clusion. It was always the best of both worlds. And my work with healthy centenarians is no exception.

Language is a tool to frame what we want to communicate. New concepts can venture so far from the known that they can cause turbulence: entering the unknown without shifting to new navigational tools. Consequently, I'll introduce new words to replace old concepts. For example, if I use new terms to revise the concept of *adjusting to cultural constraints*, I can explore ways to expand the boundaries of its meaning. Let's consider that *resilience* is different from *adjustment*. The more resilience (ability to recover and grow), the better we can respond to cultural constraints. Also, constraints cause adversity. For example, if your options to find a job are constrained by your age, it will cause adversity: unemploy-ment → no income → no food.

As we explore the new terms, I ask for your patience so I can show you that I am not indulging in semantic games. Words are tools of perception, but they have to be embodied before they can generate new meaning: experiencing a semantic shift. For exam-ple, the statement, "You're so cool, I would kill to be like you," is interpreted as a high compliment *if* you understand English and are familiar with American slang. But if you come from a remote culture, the literal interpretation of your intended compliment would be: *This person is willing to commit murder to be like me when my temperature drops.*

Of course, the "foreigner" in my example would have to be liv-ing in a cave to be so linguistically disconnected. But if that were the case, the literal interpretation of the intended compliment would cause a discharge of cortisol and other stress hormones from believing that someone is willing to commit murder. But if our caveperson learns the intended meaning of the words *cool* and *kill*, oxytocin, a hormone associated with social bonding, would be the biological response to feeling admired. My point is that cultures transform words into biosymbols (language that affects our biology).

The biocognitive terms I am introducing modify Clark's concept of adjusting to cultural constraints. The word *constraint* implies restriction with rigid boundaries—a journey with roadblocks requiring adaptations that affect aging. In other words, although the way you adjust (adapt) to constraints imposed by your culture influences how you age, it does not explain how the process works and how individuals respond differently.

The Cultural Portal Theory of Aging

Based on my research with healthy centenarians worldwide, I developed a theory of cultural aging: culturally defined segments (portals) of expected beliefs and conduct. The portals include newborn, infancy, childhood, adolescence, young adult, middle age, and old age. Each portal has implicit rules that attribute cause to what you do in that culturally defined stage. If you are an outlier who defies the cultural expectations of a portal, you will be admonished until you comply or choose to be an outcast. But what happens if you become a worthy outlier? I suggest you enter centenarian consciousness: an opportunity to live the causes of healthy longevity. I'll use the old-age portal to illustrate some of the cultural entrapments.

Retirement is one of the cultural expectations in the old-age portal. Is it biologically defined? No. Retirement age ranges from 45 in Turkey to 70 in Australia. Some of the consequences for defying cultural aging include:

- Compulsory age retirement regardless of competence and passion for the work you do.

- Difficulty finding employment beyond retirement age.

- Health insurance costs based on group averages rather than on individual health.

- Admonishments if you don't act, dress, and look your age.

- Admonishments if you fall in love with someone younger.

- Admonishments if you are healthy and medication-free.

Here are some sample dialogues of admonishments for defying the old-age portal:

- "Doctor, my right shoulder hurts.": "What do expect at your age?"

- "Doctor, how was my blood workup?": "I am having a hard time believing that at your age there's nothing wrong with your health."

- "I fell in love with a person 10 years younger than I am.": "Be careful, you're wanted for your money."

- "I want to go back to college.": "At your age? Enjoy your retirement."

The importance of understanding the underlying restrictions of portals is that your biology is strongly influenced by the cultural attributions (causes) you give to your actions. If you believe that you're "too old" for something, your biology will comply.

Fortunately, I found *outlier consciousness* in almost all the healthy centenarians I investigated. I'll share a couple of examples from my field notes of how they refuse to be controlled by cultural portals:

- I asked a 101-year-old man to define middle age: "That's a dumb question. You find out when you die."

- I asked a 102-year-old carpenter when he was planning to retire: "Why should I retire from something I enjoy so much?"

- I asked a 100-year-old woman how she would respond if people tell her that she's too old to do something she loves: "I'd tell them to fuck off."

Now ask yourself, what portal have you been duped to believe you should be in? In the tools section, I'll show you ways to break from cultural portals, and how to avoid their negative aging consequences.

A Language for the Theory of Cultural Portals

The cultural belief that intellectual and physical function diminish with the passing of time strongly determines how we age while growing older. In other words, cultures tell us how we should deteriorate across time. This is a bold statement that I strongly defend and invite you to consider. I am not denying that as we grow older there's some natural wear and tear. Instead, I am arguing that genetics is not as crucial in the aging process as mechanistic science claims.

The theory of cultural constraints proposes aging is caused by adjustments we are required to make without alternative paths to growing older—inevitable adjustments to the cultural hurdles we encounter on our personal journey. This is certainly the case if you give in (adjust) to the constraints. But I learned from the outliers I studied that you don't have to surrender if you are willing to step out of the collective reality you are taught to believe. When you become a rebel with a worthy cause, you can question the imposed portals that cultures determine are the only way to transition through life. I suggest *resilience to adversity in cultural portals* describes more accurately what determines unhealthy aging as well as healthy growing older.

Let's look at how the terms I introduce can help us understand the difference between aging and growing older. In American psychology, resilience is defined as *the ability to properly react to stress and adversity.* The research in this area studies how people overcome physical and emotional trauma. In other words, how they suffer trauma and are able to bounce back without permanent damage. But some French social scientists also study people who, in addition to overcoming trauma, grow from the experience. From my fieldwork with centenarians, I find that they tend to experience the resilience with growth that French researchers find in their work with trauma. And this type of resilience is what I believe is one of the major causes of health in the process of growing older. The good news is that this mode of response to adversity can be learned at any age. It's not in your genes; it's in your expectations for a brighter future.

The most intriguing finding in the resilience-with-growth research is that people who thrive in the face of adversity expect a better future during and after the trauma. Despite the initial physical and emotional pain of trauma, they maintain a sense of humor and hope for recovery. More important, their positive expectations enable them to learn from the negative experience. But I caution that this strategy is not a matter of thinking happy thoughts to deny the suffering. Pollyannaish wishful thinking is far from what takes place in resilience with growth. It can be a gift and a lesson. Remember, this book is about changing cultural perception rather than modifying behavior. (The proper tools to shift paradigms will be available at the end of this chapter.)

One of the ways cultures inadvertently teach us *victimhood consciousness* is by underestimating our human resilience. For example, research in post-traumatic stress disorder (PTSD) misses the mark because it assumes that most people who experience trauma are going to be seriously damaged. This happens because the populations studied are those who seek help due to their difficulty adjusting to the trauma they've suffered. Similarly, gerontology studies the diminishing function in aging with people who seek help for their pathology across time. Both areas of research know little about people who experience trauma with healthy resilience, and elderly people who grow older with minimum wear and tear. Fortunately, recent studies in healthy longevity and resilience with growth are finding that these *outliers of wellness* are not as uncommon as expected. But as Abraham Maslow (one of the founders of humanist psychology) warned us, *when all you have is a hammer, everything looks like a nail.* I tend to stay away from health-care professionals who carry hammers.

NAVIGATING ADVERSITY

Research in positive psychology is challenging the science of gloom and doom to look beyond the damage caused by adversity. Mishaps, misfortunes, and afflictions can be fertile ground for enhancing quality of life. But the process is different from the proverbial "When life gives you lemons, make lemonade." This well-intended advice is more positive thinking than positive psychology. What is the difference? We find the answers in the underlying lessons of resilience with growth. Staying in the proverbial mode, resilience experiences the bitterness of the lemon and changes the approach to life rather than the taste of the lemon.

Lawrence Calhoun and Richard Tedeschi pioneered the concept of Posttraumatic Growth (PTG) to investigate positive growth within highly challenging and traumatic contexts. People who fit the PTG profile show change in three areas of their lives:

1. **Personal change:** increased self-confidence from evidence of surviving and overcoming a significant challenge.

2. **Interpersonal change:** increased appreciation of family and friends who showed support during the crisis.

3. **Change in philosophy of life:** greater ability to appreciate what was taken for granted before the traumatic event.

By no coincidence, these shifts in meaning are also evident in centenarians who live in relatively good health. But the most fascinating finding in my investigations is that centenarians who have not experienced major adversities have the same characteristics found in the PTG studies. In other words, they don't have to be rattled by trauma to experience meaningful lives.

Rather than waiting for adversity to scare you into a more appreciative and confident person, you can learn these characteristics anytime you choose. But what do you think would happen if you began to live a consciousness that nourishes appreciation and self-confidence without having to wait for adversity to knock? Not only will you indirectly learn the causes of healthy longevity, but you will also thrive in the face of adversity without succumbing to victimhood. Is it easy? Not with the wrong tools, but very possible when you create evidence that you're worthy of a good life. Just as you can learn to trigger genes that express illness, you can find the meaning in life that expresses your inherited causes of health.

Embracing Uncertainty

Considering that uncertainty is defined as something doubtful or unknown, how can you prepare for what you can't predict? You cannot. The best you can do is to prepare for the worst and hope for the best. But if instead of preparing for what *could happen*, you focus on how to engage the change required by what *actually happens*, you can embrace uncertainty. But why am I leading you into another potential quicksand? No, it's not because I am testing your patience. It's because I am going deep into what makes centenarians thrive where others age prematurely and die.

Drawing from what we know from research in PTG, shifts in meaning after a traumatic experience are what drive resilience with growth. So we can assume that people who are able to embrace uncertainty are good at making meaningful changes; they seem to have an internal compass that guides them in the direction of what needs to change during traumatic storms. And again, whatever comes naturally to healthy centenarians, you can learn and succeed as they do. Fair enough? As we continue to explore this vital subject, I want to assure you that I am introducing you to the science of human potential that remains fairly inaccessible to the general public. It's research that explores our propensities for health rather than our limitations from illness.

Let's look at the conditions that support and encourage the changes centenarians are able to accomplish during adversity.

PTG research shows that *self-confidence* and *appreciation* are the individual characteristics involved in changing *personal, interpersonal*, and *philosophy of life* meaning. So, two characteristics are needed to make changes in three areas. What my fieldwork with centenarians can add to this formula is the ingredients necessary for self-confidence and appreciation. Once you learn them, you can incorporate them in your centenarian consciousness.

- **Self-confidence:** a trust in your abilities, qualities, and judgment.

- **Appreciation:** the recognition and enjoyment of the good qualities of someone or something.

Self-confidence and appreciation stem from the capacity to recognize value in self and others. Envy is the biggest enemy of both characteristics because it has to devalue self to covet what is given value in others. The devaluing also prevents appreciation for others because value is placed on what the person possesses rather than who the person is. Thus, envy hinders development of the characteristics needed to navigate adversity and embrace uncertainty. Not surprisingly, envy is rarely found in the lives of centenarians. Before preparing a fertile terrain for the agents of meaningful change, I had to identify its main detractor (envy) to emphasize how it can sabotage attempts to value self and others.

If we can identify how valuing self and others is learned, it will indirectly show us how to build self-confidence and appreciation. Keep in mind that most biocognitive learning methods are designed to be indirect. Why? Because shifting the meaning that maintains behavior requires more than reasoning what needs to change. For example, try to convince an addict to quiet the habit because it can be lethal. Reasoning is not sufficient because chemical dependence is a mindbody experience supported by an underlying meaning of insensitivity to personal health. And yes, I know how the addiction model makes this proposal difficult to accept. Nevertheless, if after treating an addiction the underlying mindbody meaning does not change, relapse remains highly likely.

Tools to Shift MindBody Meaning

One of the most effective ways to recontextualize (transform) mindbody meaning is to experience conditions that are radically incompatible with what you want to change. In the "Permanence, Control, and Other Illusions" chapter, I discuss the essential needs hidden in lamentations. We're going to recruit admiration (one of the essential needs) to neutralize envy (detractor) as well as to nourish self-confidence and appreciation (characteristics for resilience with growth). Experiencing the mindbody meaning of admiration creates a terrain that's friendly to health enhancers and incompatible with detractors of resilience with growth. First, create a semantic space (concept), then embody (experience) the meaning of the concept.

1. Conceptualizing the shift of mindbody meaning.

- A move from self-doubt to self-confidence requires valuing self.

- A move from ungratefulness to appreciation requires valuing others.

- Admiration is the mediator of the transition.

- Envy is the detractor of the transition.

2. Experiencing the shift of mindbody meaning.

- To initiate the experience of self-valuation, recall and embody past evidence (memories) of your worthy actions.

- To fortify the experience of self-valuation, initiate and embody new worthy actions.

- To initiate the experience of eradicating envy, recall and embody past evidence (memories) of admiring worthy people.

- To fortify the experience of eradicating envy, initiate and embody admiring new worthy people.

As you can see, the biocognitive process of shifting embodied meaning is straightforward:

1. Identify a concept that defines the meaning of what you want to accomplish.

2. Determine the enhancers and detractors of your desired outcome.

3. Recall and embody memories of times when you experienced the desired outcome.

4. Initiate and embody new experiences that fortify your desired outcome and weaken its detractors.

5. Associate with people who are willing to coauthor liberation from self-entrapment.

But I want to be very clear that experiencing the shifts in meaning (embodiment) is one of the key differentiating factors between biocognitive methods and cognitive therapies, which assume that simply replacing one behavior for another is sufficient to accomplish lasting change.

Debriefing

Now you can understand how cultures teach us to behave and attribute causes to what we experience, based on predetermined periods (portals) across time. These portals are mostly responsible for how you age and how you confront adversity. Most important, however, once you recognize how portals limit your growth, you can choose to rebel as outlier and create liberating rituals in new subcultures that support the causes of health and the lessons of longevity. Everything I illustrate about centenarian consciousness can be learned at any age. And yes, I repeat this centenarian wisdom throughout the book to counteract the constant bombardment of helplessness by the marketers of disease. But it's important to remember that not all of your coauthors are going to agree with your paradigm shift, because some are not willing to confront their own portal constraints or are more comfortable in known misery than unknown joy. Rather than masochists, they are blind to their own human potential.

Growing older brings some natural wear and tear, and some misfortunes and traumas are inevitable on our journeys. But if instead of trying to predict the future we learn to confront change, we will unleash our inherent resilience with growth rather than succumb when adversity comes our way.

chapter 10

Navigating Adversity with Uncertainty as Your Guide

Ith minor variations, Western dictionaries define adversity as *a state or instance of serious or continued difficulty or misfortune*. I propose that since most challenging conditions in life are culturally interpreted, their solutions must be sought within cultural contexts.

THE CULTURAL FACES OF ADVERSITY

Including obvious life-threatening circumstances such as fires, earthquakes, physical assaults, and so on, cultures teach us how to avoid or confront adversity. For example, the Chinese character for adversity also means opportunity. One of the difficulties in responding to adversity is that we tend to stick with the rules that worked in the past rather than explore new ways to deal with misfortunes in the present. Most adversity conditions require shifts of operating rules. For example, you expect to stay at your job until retirement, but suddenly you're told that you're no longer needed. The abrupt disruption of *expectations*, *routines*, and *attachments* forces you to reevaluate a future that appeared stable until the unwanted change derailed your plans. Although the future is not predictable, we make assumptions as if we could control the unforeseeable. So far, these descriptions are familiar to most without new revelations. But I deliberately start with basic concepts to gradually increase their complexity before introducing tools to navigate the uniqueness of uncertainty.

The Nature of Adversity

When you ask people in situations of intense adversity to describe their experience, they usually focus on their mindbody reactions: "incredible," "overwhelming," "frightening," "unexpected." These responses describe how they experience adversity without considering its disruptive nature. After researching worldwide how people react to adversity, it became clear to me that cultures teach us how to respond to what adversity disrupts: expectations, routines, and attachments. I remember in watching the news during the Gulf War how American and British soldiers described a desert windstorm. The American soldier: "Wow, this is an incredible wind, it's blowing everything away." The British soldier: "It's a bit windy." Same storm, two different culturally learned responses to adversity: One expresses disruptions with excitement, the other with restraint.

Adversity triggers uncertainty in three areas of life: expectations, routines, and attachments. In the example of losing your job, all three areas are affected. You have to change your expectations of retiring from the job, end the routines related to the job, and relinquish the emotional, financial, and status attachments to the job. Not an easy task.

But if in addition to considering the mindbody responses to adversity (overwhelming, frightening, etc.), we focus on the three areas affected by the uncertainty (expectations, routines, and attachments), we regain control faster and reduce the damage of traumatic conditions.

Expectations

The first awareness of uncertainty comes to mind during adversity when you realize that your present condition and future plans are no longer viable—uncertainty of what lies ahead. It's the sobering realization that what you considered a reliable transition from your present to your future is not going to happen.

Routines

A major part of our mindbody stability is grounded in what we do habitually in our daily lives. Those daily behaviors and activities that we take for granted give us the necessary predictability to experience certainty—an invisible safety net that comes to mind only when abruptly removed. Returning to the job example: Before going to bed, you know why you're going to get up in the morning, have your coffee, watch the news, drive to work, and so on. Suddenly these activities are taken away, leaving you in a *routine vacuum*. The mundane becomes relevant because of its absence, and the old adage "You don't know what you have until you lose it" comes to life.

Attachments

To understand the attachment component of adversity, let's bring back the term you learned in the "From Presenteeism to Embodied Present" chapter, the Wilson effect: how we tend to extend our emotional self to objects or conditions that provide us with safety, companionship, and reliability. Think of attachments as emotional ropes that tie you to the known and predictable experiences in your life. Interestingly, attachments also include negative conditions and people. But why would you attach to situations that cause you discomfort? Because being able to predict good or bad circumstance increases the psychological certainty we need to maintain mindbody stability. At the end of the chapter, I'll show you ways to deal with the three areas of uncertainty triggered by adversity, but now let's continue to explore the nature of uncertainty.

One of the reasons I propose that uncertainty is the best guide to navigate adversity is because understanding how your life is disrupted allows you to focus on what needs to change, and on finding the right tools. For example, knowing how to sail a sudden shift in direction and strength of the wind is necessary to navigate a storm at sea. But we can see that whether a storm at sea or the loss of employment on land, adversity causes uncertainty in the same three areas: expectations, routines, and attachments.

Research shows that if you encounter uncertainty during unpleasant conditions, the intensity of negative emotions increases; if the conditions are pleasant, positive emotions intensify. So it seems that the psychological effects of uncertainty may have more to do with what you feel than with the unknown aspect of uncertainty. More important, however, is that although adversity is associated with negative experiences, uncertainty is also present in positive circumstances that are difficult to predict. This recognition adds clarity to the navigational tools in that when confronted with adversity, it's important to focus on the unknown component as well as what you're feeling at the time the uncertainty unfolds.

But let's see what happens if you jump into adversity without considering what you're feeling at the time. If you're having a good day, adversity "ruins" the positive emotions. If you're having a bad day, adversity "increases" the negative emotions. When you're aware that the emotions you have when adversity lands affect the intensity of how you respond, you are able to improve how you navigate the unknown. If you are having a good day when adversity visits, recognize you have a foundation of positive emotions to confront the unknown with empowerment. In contrast, when you're having a bad day, recognize you have a foundation of negative emotions to confront the unknown with helplessness. The former feeds your strength, and the latter fuels the fire. This does not mean, however, that you should suppress your emotional reaction to adversity. Instead, feel the uncertainty (good or bad), and move from a position that enhances resilience.

Research also shows that uncertainty increases awareness and curiosity of the moment. This mechanism makes us pay more attention to out-of-order conditions of adversity. Although we know that adversity is defined as a situation of *continued difficulty and misfortune*, uncertainty brought by good fortune can also disrupt the same three areas affected by negative destabilizing. For example, let's flip the misfortune of losing your job to the good fortune of getting a substantial promotion in another city. See where I am going with this? The *expectations* of remaining in the city where you work, the *routines* related to where you work, and the *attachments* to the home and friends where you live will change as drastically with the good fortune condition as if you were fired. Although one is negative and the other positive, both trigger uncertainty caused by having to shift from the predictable to the unknown. But there's more to uncertainty . . .

Research shows that uncertainty can lead to procrastination. If you're involved in a task and you don't know what to do next, there's a tendency to procrastinate (postpone the task) to relieve anxiety caused by the uncertainty of not knowing how to proceed. In cases of procrastination, one of the most common self-defeating strategies is to wait until the last minute to have a built-in excuse in case of failure. When it comes to avoiding discomfort, our brains excel at creating immediate relief with little attention to the cost of delaying commitments.

As you can see, we're adding pieces to the uncertainty puzzle to increase your navigational skills during adversity. It's like building a compass that can guide you when predictability is swept out from under you. Another interesting research finding is that adversity increases cooperation. Have you noticed how helpful people become with strangers during situations of shared danger? Being on a rough plane ride, stranded on a bus, responding to a natural catastrophe: The humanity in each of us comes out during adversity. Of course, there are those who take advantage of human tragedy for personal gains. On the positive side, in attempting to decipher the complicated rules of initial romantic attraction, researchers find that keeping a new date guessing how much they are liked will pique their interest. In other words, not knowing where you stand (uncertainty) increases interest more than if you are certain of how well you are perceived. Interestingly, this area of research is referred to as "the pleasures of uncertainty."

Uncertainty Avoidance

Looking at uncertainty avoidance is one of the ways to study differences in how cultures experience adversity. Based on their history of adversity, cultures learn how to deal with the fact that the future is unpredictable. For example, due to the constant threat of natural disasters (volcano eruptions, earthquakes, and tsunamis), Japan is one of the highest uncertainty avoidance countries in the world. In addition to natural catastrophes, it did not help the Japanese fear of uncertainty to have two of their cities (Hiroshima and Nagasaki) devastated by atomic bombs, leading to their surrender in World War II. Latin America and Germany are also considered to have the highest level of uncertainty avoidance, whereas the U.S., U.K., and Denmark have the lowest. Of course, since the U.S. and U.K. are multicultural, they have more within-country difference than Denmark. As with most topics presented in this book, the mindbody self learns to love and fear from the tribe.

Beyond the Cultural Constraints of Adversity

If we interpret our world and assign cause to what we perceive based on cultural contexts, we can certainly recontextualize (redefine felt meaning) the function and response to adversity. Borrowing from the Chinese concept of adversity as the flip side of opportunity, let's change the connotation of adversity and create navigational tools from what we know about uncertainty. But before going further, let's look at how the Western meaning of adversity got its foreboding label. The process went from the Old French *avers* (contrary, opposing) to Modern French *adverse* (antagonistic, unfriendly) to finally Middle English *adversity* (calamity, misfortune). The encouraging news is that the root word for these transitions comes from the Latin *advertere*, which means, simply, "to turn toward." This Latin root is closer to the Chinese interpretation than the Old French spin of the word. The Latin makes adversity a turning point and the Chinese an opportunity. By lacking a value judgment, they can include the negative as well as the positive conditions. And this is precisely how we're going to approach adversity. But it should be noted that to recontextualize adversity does not imply that misfortunes are less painful.

Instead, their outcome includes an opportunity to turn toward positive growth.

The New Face of Adversity

I define adversity as *a derailing of stability requiring constructive change.* It's an opportunity to grow toward a desired outcome that's not available until a shift of expectations takes place. Like any other concept of the mindbody self, the new meaning of adversity should be embodied as a living philosophy and applied science. In other words, more than a disruption of good or bad fortune, biocognitive adversity is simply a derailing of stable conditions requiring a change of objectives.

Changing the felt meaning (how you experience symbol, word, concept) of adversity is not an intellectual replacement of interpretations. Depending on your culture, you are taught to experience adversity as misfortune or opportunity. But the face of adversity that I am introducing is much more than either. Rather than seeing misfortune (negative value) or opportunity (positive value), the new meaning makes adversity a turning point, without denying the corresponding emotions. In other words, experience the joy of good fortune and the anguish of misfortune knowing that both conditions require changing expectations, routines, and attachments—moving from business as usual toward new business.

Armed with a more empowering definition of adversity, let's see how uncertainty fits into our new approach. I've discussed uncertainty from the perspective of *what* it disrupts. But what about looking at *why* it disrupts? We know uncertainty causes instability in the areas of expectations, routines, and attachments, and that it can intensify positive or negative emotions, trigger procrastination, and increase awareness. But why does it have so much power in so many areas of our lives? There are many mathematical, philosophical, experiential, and metaphysical definitions of uncertainty, but for our purpose, let's focus on its elegance and simplicity.

From its most basic characteristic, we know that uncertainty disrupts stability. But so does falling disrupt balance, running disrupt walking, nightmares disrupt sleep, and so on. Thus, disruption of stability alone is not sufficient to define uncertainty. When we add loss of predictability to disrupting stability, we get closer to unraveling the uniqueness of uncertainty. For example, if you fall and disrupt your walk but are able to resume your walking, uncertainty does not enter your world. If, on the other hand, when you fall you sprain an ankle, your predictability to resume your walk is disrupted. In this case you have disruption of stability and predictability. But there is more . . .

There are two types of uncertainty: expected and unexpected. For example, you know you're scheduled for gallbladder surgery in two weeks. Some of the uncertainty in this case is expected in that you know when it starts, but not how it ends. But if you have a sudden gallbladder attack that requires immediate surgery, the uncertainty is unexpected. Both scenarios have unexpected outcomes, but you can plan for the former, and not for the latter. The expected and unexpected aspects of uncertainty help us identify another ingredient of uncertainty: control, or better yet, uncontrollability. Therefore, the inability to control uncertainty is another factor to consider. Thus, uncertainty is disruptive, unpredictable, and uncontrollable.

Uncertainty and Cognitive Control

There's extensive research in how we make decisions during conditions of uncertainty, but recent studies are exploring the connection between uncertainty and cognitive control. We know adversity creates uncertainty, we know the areas that affect us, and we know the types of uncertainty we experience. Now let's look at *cognitive control*, an area of neuroscience that studies how our thought processes shift to adjust to external conditions. What takes place when you're driving a vehicle is one of the best ways to explain the dynamics of cognitive control. You drive to work every day without noticing that some of your behavior related to the task happens automatically: shifting gears, making turns, braking, and so on. But you can recall that when you were learning to drive, everything you did was quite conscious and deliberate. After you gain competence in driving, your brain allows you to inhibit the routine tasks until an unexpected situation breaks the pattern and activates your driving awareness so you can attend to the change. This inhibiting and activating mechanism (cognitive control) is present in most of what you do. Have you noticed when you're immersed in a task and suddenly realize you finished it without noticing how you did it? This is one of the best examples of inhibited cognitive control. Interestingly, contrary to expectations, research shows that high multitaskers are more distractible and process information less efficiently than low multitaskers. So if you think that multitasking is productive, the evidence goes against common sense.

Let's look at how this research in cognitive control relates to uncertainty and how we can use the information to create practical tools to navigate adversity.

There are several factors we can consider to understand how uncertainty unfolds and how our cultures teach us to respond. We know that uncertainty avoidance is one of the factors that differ across cultures—from low tolerance of uncertainty (Japan) to high tolerance of uncertainty (U.S.). We also know that cultures teach us how to interpret adversity. Most Eastern cultures interpret adversity as opportunity, while more Western cultures frame adversity as misfortune. These two culturally interpreted factors of uncertainty have profound implications on how people respond to adversity. Additionally, we can examine how cognitive control works in shifts from stability to instability.

In general, anytime we encounter out-of-order and unpredictable conditions, all the habitual behaviors that were functioning automatically and out of awareness (inhibited) are dropped and cognitive control takes over to monitor the new condition and find ways of coping. For example, you're driving along relying on habit (brake, gas, turn) and suddenly a car on the opposite side of the road jumps lanes and is coming toward you head-on. Instantly, your automatic behavior stops and your brain shifts to monitor the situation so it can give you information on how to proceed. There are only two options: take action or postpone action. As the uncertainty increases, so does the postponement. This is an important factor to remember because the postponement comes from lacking sufficient information to help you decide on the best action. Recall what I discussed about procrastination? The puzzle continues to make more sense.

One of the tools we can extract from knowing that uncertainty postpones action is to practice strategies to detect relevant information from new conditions. You practice looking for relevant information during low levels of uncertainty and then apply your new skills to conditions of higher levels of uncertainty. For example, while driving, stop your automatic (inhibited) behavior and practice anticipating what drivers will do around you. This is a form of mindfulness that's reached quickly by detecting novelty in your surroundings. In the tools section, I'll show you other techniques to navigate adversity with your new friend, uncertainty, as your guide.

Bringing together adversity, the uncertainty it causes, and the process of cognitive control gives us new understanding of how we respond to unpredictability in general, and how cultures teach us to interpret the context in particular. But independent of your cultural understanding of adversity, you can learn new ways to interpret and confront adversity in your life. Given that adversity triggers fight-or-flight stress hormones, knowing how to respond can make a positive difference in your health and longevity. The greatest lesson I learned from the healthy centenarians I studied is that they instinctively respond to adversity with remarkable flexibility because they simply view uncertainty as a natural part of life.

Tools to Navigate Adversity
with Uncertainty as Your Guide

Now that you know how the private self is culturally taught to behave in unknown territory, you can learn healthy ways to confront the unpredictable. To give you quick access to the material, I'll outline the properties of the three main players in this chapter: adversity, uncertainty, and cognitive control.

Adversity

Three main areas of life affected by adversity:

- Expectations
- Routines
- Attachments

Uncertainty

Three characteristics of uncertainty:

- Disruptive
- Unpredictable
- Uncontrollable

Cognitive Control

Two main functions of cognitive control:

- Inhibit habitual behavior during stable conditions
- Activate immediate attention to monitor unstable conditions and make decisions

Recontextualizing Adversity and Uncertainty

- Adversity as a shift of direction
- The same rules for positive or negative conditions that affect stability
- Uncertainty as the unruly guide for unknown territory

Changing the Felt Meaning of Adversity

This exercise is designed to change the old felt meaning of adversity to the new. It does not imply, however, that you have to suppress or ignore the negative or positive emotions associated with the mindbody meaning you learned from your culture. Instead, you move from your usual response toward finding a new direction. Although the procedure is deceptively simple, it goes to the core mindbody meaning of symbols and recontextualizes rather than replaces one label with another. Put more simply, the new meaning will be felt differently because it incorporates a new mindbody signature.

- Go to your chosen quiet place and slow down your mindbody activity. Breathe deeply and slowly without effort.
- Let your mind wander, and follow it as a passive observer—like watching clouds pass by your visual field. You're creating a working experiential scenario to change felt meaning.
- Bring forth a memory of a situation of adversity that had relevance in your life. Make the experience as vivid as you can and pay attention to your mindbody reactions.

- When you can experience the felt meaning of the adverse condition, you have identified your present embodied adversity (before shifting to the new meaning).

- Now replay the same memory superimposing the new meaning of adversity. In other words, rather than associating adversity with misfortune (Western) or opportunity (Eastern), the meaning becomes *change of direction*.

- Using the change of direction perspective, focus on the options to change direction that come to mind. Before, the attention went to misfortune consciousness; now it goes to changing direction consciousness. You will be surprised how this simple shift of operative consciousness opens paths that went unnoticed before.

- Practice this exercise several times with the same memory or with other instances of adversity until you can experience the new felt meaning. As you experience the new meaning and apply it to actual situations of adversity, you create and deepen neuromaps (brain-cell connections) that reflect a new perception you choose to interact with your world.

Applying the New Felt Meaning of Adversity

In this next exercise, you use the new felt meaning that moves you from interpreting adversity as misfortune or opportunity to a signal for changing direction. You can use the new meaning to confront the three areas affected by adversity: expectations, routines, and attachments. Instead of focusing on misfortunes or good fortunes, explore options for moving toward changing expectations, routines, and attachments. You can go to this next exercise now or take a break and return to it later.

- To create the contemplative quietude in your favorite place, take a few deep and slow breaths before starting this exercise.

- Bring back to your mindbody awareness a memory of adversity, or imagine one that could happen in the future. Noting that the new meaning of adversity leads toward a change of direction, imagine what expectation, routine, and attachment need to change. First, experience the effect of the adversity, and then shift to the change mode. In other words, identify what expectation needs immediate change, then identify the felt meaning: How does the imagined change of expectation manifest in your mindbody? Observe without intervening as if you were watching a metamorphosis from caterpillar to butterfly.

- Follow the same shift to the change mode for the routines and attachments affected by adversity. Identify what routines need to change, and what attachments need to be released. Then observe the *biocognitive metamorphosis* (the mindbody transition of felt meaning) as you did with the expectations. It's a transformation of meaning, not a replacement of behavior. See the Glossary for more details on *biocognitive metamorphosis*.

- Practice this exercise as much as needed to experience the change in felt meaning when you find a new direction. Just as the previous exercise that focused on changing the felt meaning of adversity, now focus on the felt meaning of changing the direction of expectations, routines, and attachments. For example, what do you experience (mindbody) when you find a new direction for expectations, routines, and attachments after adversity hits?

Embracing Uncertainty

In this exercise you're going to recontextualize uncertainty as a guide, rather than an agent of chaos. You know that adversity is the cause of uncertainty in the three areas of life that you just explored, but now you can focus on how uncertainty causes instability. Using another analogy, look at adversity as the storm with strong wind and rain, uncertainty as the rough waves created by the storm, and you as the captain of a boat navigating the unknown conditions. The storm (adversity) requires a change of expectations, routines, and attachments of your journey because the rough waves and rain (uncertainty) *disrupted* your course and made it *unpredictable* and *uncontrollable*. Now that you know the makeup of uncertainty, you can confront it with the right tools to assess and bring order to the disruption, unpredictability, and uncontrollability in each of the areas affected: expectations, routines, and attachments. As you know by now, I use narratives and analogies as biocognitive shortcuts to explain complicated interconnecting conditions. In fact, anytime you want to explore strategies to deal with complicated situations in your life, create a story of how you can confront what you most dread using the tools you're learning in this chapter and other areas of interest in the book. When you're ready to start the next exercise, go to your favorite place of solitude and bring your mindbody to a tranquil place.

- Create a scenario for an upcoming difficult condition as if you were a director of a play. This time you're going to learn how to effectively navigate the ingredients of uncertainty (disruption, unpredictability, and uncontrollability). Notice I used the word *navigate* rather than *solve*. The reason for this difference is that uncertainty is a process (the rough waves) to be navigated rather than fixed.

- Identify what is disrupted in your scenario and embody the experience. For example, your plans to take a vacation must change (expectations).

- Identify what is unpredictable and embody the experience. For example, you no longer know when you can take the planned vacation.

- Identify what is uncontrollable and embody the experience. For example, you no longer have control of when and where you can go on your vacation.

- Notice which of the three ingredients of uncertainty affected you most. Was it the disruption, unpredictability, or uncontrollable part of the experience?

- Focus on the chosen condition and embody it once again to identify its mindbody signature (how you experience it). Allow it to unfold without interpretation.

- Bring back from memory other factors of uncertainty that also affected the chosen condition. For example, if you chose uncontrollability, look for other circumstances in your life that were affected by loss of control.

- Look for areas in your life where you presently feel disruption, unpredictability, or loss of control. Here you're identifying existing underlying uncertainty in your life. In other words, you might have unresolved uncertainty ingredients in your life that are causing unnoticed damage.

- Use the tools you learned to confront adversity and its uncertainty consequences to address any unresolved or hidden uncertainty in your life. These exercises allow you to confront past and future uncertainty as well as help you identify unresolved conditions that are ignored or avoided in your life.

Always start with the least threatening and move on to the more difficult as you gain navigational experience.

- With any of the exercises in this chapter, you can also apply the concept of cognitive control to help you clarify what is inhibited (automatic pilot) and what needs to be activated (what requires purposeful attention). For example, as with all overlearned behavior (driving skills), misery can be so prevalent in your life that it could be inhibited without awareness of the damage it causes.

Debriefing

The exercises you practiced give you a new perspective to address adversity and uncertainty. Rather than trying to control them, you can approach their effects as transitional conditions that must be navigated. This strategy removes the anxiety of trying to avoid shifts in expectations, routines, and attachments caused by the disruption, unpredictability, and uncontrollability of uncertainty. Instead, each of the conditions affected by adversity is confronted as a temporary condition of instability that needs to be navigated rather than resolved. You navigate with the proper tools until you reach the shores of stability—then you can decide what to keep and what to discard on your journey of the mindbody self. The most effective method to learning these strategies is to start with the most relevant section, master it, and move on to another. Avoid trying to absorb all the exercises in one sitting. This book is a resource to visit anytime you need a guiding compass, rather than a map to memorize and discard.

chapter 11

Biocognitive Tools for Life

n this final chapter I'll show you additional ways to deepen and consolidate what you've learned about your mindbody self. I'll introduce new topics with tools to apply them. The format is different in that the lessons are a compilation of mindbody principles and indirect teaching methods I've been refining for the past 25 years. As with all mindbody lessons, embody and incorporate them as well as create evidence to support and strengthen what you learn. As you've done throughout the book, I strongly recommend that you refer to the book's glossary anytime you find a new term or concept that remains unclear. I also encourage you to practice and revisit the applications you learn here and in previous chapters when challenges unfold.

LONGEVITY

The Cultural Portals of Aging

As you learned in previous chapters, growing older is the passing of time, whereas aging is what you do with time based on your cultural beliefs. But how does it really work? Culturally defined segments (portals) of expected beliefs and conduct strongly influence how our biology responds to time. The portals of newborn, infancy, childhood, adolescence, young adult, middle age, and old age are woven by your culture and perceived as biological barriers rather than imposed cultural expectations based on the passing of time. Each portal has implicit rules that attribute cause to what you do in that culturally defined stage. The most important implication is that your biology will respond to stress depending on the causes you learn to assign at each cultural portal. For example, a cultural attribution of "I am too old for this" can compel you to give up activities you love simply because your culture, as opposed to your biology, determines the boundaries of your joy. Additionally, if you try to reinstate an activity from an earlier portal (young adult) to a portal that restricts the activity (older adult), the most likely cause you might give to any difficulty you encounter will be based on the present portal. For example, if you used to jog regularly when you were in your 20s and start jogging again at 70, your muscle aches and other discomforts would be attributed to your age rather than being out of shape. But if you have a medical checkup and find that you're healthy, you can retrain your cardiovascular system and muscles to respond as well as they did in your young-adult portal. The power of reinstating healthy rituals to later portals is that when you retrain your mindbody, it gives you irrefutable evidence that cultural portals are determining most of your limitations.

The Tarahumara natives of Copper Canyon, Mexico, known for their running endurance, play an ancient game called *carrera de bola* (Spanish for "race of the ball") that consists of kicking and chasing a ball for as long as 200 kilometers. They run barefooted and have been tested for their endurance by Harvard investigators. The older Tarahumara consistently outrun the younger, demonstrate better running style, and have superior cardiovascular conditioning—more evidence that aging is what you do with the passing of time determined by your cultural beliefs. But the cultural beliefs have to be turned into action.

On the other side of the scale of cultural biases, organizations in collectivist cultures tend to promote their workers based on gerontocracy (preference to the elder) as opposed to meritocracy (preference to achievements). This system is biased against the young because it assumes that abilities automatically increase with age. As much as we should champion honoring growing older, it does not follow that the passing of time makes us more competent and deserving of recognition. The issue to consider here: Some people grow lazier and more opportunistic as they age. Interestingly, organizations that promote their employees solely on creativity, commitment, and competence outperform competitors that continue to practice gerontocracy. I hope you can see why I prefer to celebrate what we do meritoriously with the passing of time rather than the accumulation of time.

The MindBody Self model is an invitation to join a revolution. But as paradigm shifts go, there are different degrees of acceptance. It's not a question of in or out. It's rather how much you're willing to accept joyfully. The issue with age is so powerful and relentless because from day one we are classified by time duration. And when space mindfulness is introduced, it's like telling the fish that there's something beyond their water. So, to break the "fishbowl effect," turbulence is required. Our choices are to live in accumulation of time consciousness or to inhabit space consciousness: One takes pride in the passing of time; the other celebrates the wisdom of what is accomplished in space across time.

Stepping Out of Portals

Although each portal has unique rules to keep you constrained, before you can step out you first have to recognize that there's life beyond the cultural fishbowl. The recognition of the limitations and the decision to rebel apply to all portals. But each portal also has expectations of what you are entitled to do. Let's identify the constraints and entitlements of each portal and learn ways to modify them. Look at all the portals so you can identify with yours and notice how those you love identify with their portals. It's a cultural wake-up call.

Old-Age Portal

This portal defines what you can no longer do in the present and future that was allowed in past portals. For example, strenuous physical activity, falling in love again, good health, physical strength, good memory, and expectations for a bright future are redefined based on the premise that aging is a process of diminishing returns. On the entitlement side of the old-age portal, you are taught to expect senior discounts, special parking spaces (some cultures consider old age a handicap), help with carrying groceries, and social services offering a cane at a certain age whether it's needed or not. These entitlements are based on the premise that the passing of time should be rewarded because you are weaker and less able to take care of yourself. Of course, people with physical disabilities and legitimate needs should be aided and protected at any age, rather than solely based on their age.

- Identify the restrictions and entitlements of the old-age portal that are affecting you.

- In consultation with your health-care provider, identify what you no longer do physically and mentally that you can begin to gradually reinstate in your life: physical activity, taking courses, learning a new language, romance, and so on.

- As you begin to step out of the old-age fishbowl, be mindful that the admonitions from family and friends will surface "for your own good." You may encounter statements like "Relax and enjoy your retirement," "You're not as young as you think," and many other creative ways to keep you in the portal. Please understand that these coauthors are responding from their own fishbowls and are unable to see beyond their culturally imposed limitations.

- Look for coauthors your age or older who live as outliers and rebels. Pay attention to how they thrive outside the fishbowl. If you don't know any, find heroes you can imitate. For example, Dr. Shigeaki Hinohara is a Japanese physician who at age 104 continues to practice medicine and gives 150 lectures a year.

- If you can afford it, without depriving yourself, refuse senior discounts and other entitlements for being old. If you cannot reject the entitlements because of financial or physical limitations, accept them gracefully as recognition of what you have done for others. Always bring to mind and embody a memory of your kind conduct when you receive senior benefits. If you cannot recall any at the time, do something as soon as you can to serve others.

- If you're physically able, give up your seat to someone younger in public places. You will be amazed at the energizing power of this offering.

- Move from entitlement consciousness to a resource of wisdom that you can share with others.

Middle-Age Portal

Although all portals exist only in your cultural brain, the middle-age portal is a major marker: your first confrontation with the need to shift from young to older. As you know from other chapters, middle age varies by cultures. Studies show that those who look younger than their age believe middle age starts 10 to 15 years later than those who look older than their age. Why? Because the portals are cultural markers that affect how your biology unfolds.

- Identify the restrictions and entitlements of the middle-age portal that are affecting you.

- What are you giving up, and expecting in the future, based on middle-age consciousness? Participating in sports you enjoy? Youthful clothing and hairstyles? Plans for further education? Correcting or ending unhealthy relationships? Examples of the entitlement side of middle age include permission for less attention to weight and looks, excuses to give up dreams or delay them until retirement, more tolerance for job dissatisfaction, and plans for retirement guided by fear-based financial advice.

- Identify the restrictions and entitlements you want to modify. Bring enjoyment to the gradual changes and patience for those who disagree with your decisions to rebel.

- As you begin to step out of the middle-age fishbowl, be mindful that the admonitions from family and friends will surface "for your own good." You may encounter statements like, "You need to start planning for your retirement," "It's time to settle down and give up your unrealistic expectations," and many other creative ways to keep you in the portal. But please understand that these coauthors are responding from their own fishbowls and are unable to see beyond their culturally imposed limitations. If you change, then they know they have an option to change: This scares those whose cultural weaving is dyed in the wool.

- Look for coauthors your age or older who live as outliers and rebels. Pay attention to how they thrive outside the fishbowl. If you don't know any, find heroes you can imitate. For example, people who are starting new careers, new families, and living their dreams rather than accepting their age as index of having spent half of their longevity.

- Transition from a middle-age consciousness that determines when you reach the second half of your time on earth to a consciousness that's devoted to reinventing your expectations and awakening your dreams. Julia Child wrote her first cookbook at age 50, and Taikichiro Mori was an economics professor who left academia at age 55 to become a real estate investor and the richest man in the world (*Forbes* magazine's 1993 ranking). They are two of a growing number of outliers who have refused to be limited by the illusion of middle age.

Young-Adulthood Portal

This portal is more generous than others because it allows you to feel invincible with a long life ahead of you. Growing older is the least of your concerns and you can afford to waste time with what will later be deemed foolish mistakes. But like all portals, these young-adult considerations are culturally derived. In some cultures the pressure to be married and start a family begins early. A college education is a given in some cultures and an impossibility in others. Having many children is expected in some low socioeconomic cultures, whereas in some higher socioeconomic cultures the expectation may be to have only as many children as you can afford to put through college. Some cultures dictate that marriages be arranged by the families of groom and bride, some forbid marriage outside of the culture's religion, while others encourage marriage with family members. Again, culture rules the game.

- If you identify with the young-adult portal, look for restraints and entitlements you may be living without awareness: working for a gerontocracy organization, being pressured to marry and start a family, making poor decisions because you have all the time in the world to learn, procrastinating academically or professionally.

- Commit to a strategy that breaks the fishbowl effect. Be patient but firm with others who want to keep you within the cultural expectations of the portal.

- Bring old wisdom to your young mindbody to operate at your best. Learn from outliers and rebels your age who progress at their speed without allowing cultural editors to restrain them.

Adolescence Portal

In this portal you're neither child nor adult: You're in a cultural limbo where your adult identity is suspended until you perform rites of passage that can range from killing your first wild beast to legally purchasing your first beer or cigarettes. Some of the restraints include being too young for certain cultural privileges or too old to have childhood dreams. The entitlements include excuses to be irresponsible, lazy, and insensitive. Portal entitlements are implicit expectations from yourself and your culture, such as adolescents believing that the world is out there to serve them, and parents expecting such behavior from adolescents.

- Find an honorable ritual in your culture and make it your rite of passage. For example, while peers are destroying their bodies with drugs, travel to a venerable place and return with mature convictions to explore your talents and share your honorable experiences with others less fortunate than you.

- Learn strategies to deal with the mind-set of replacing family bonding with digital distractions— less texting and more live social bonding with family and mature friends.

- Find heroes close to your age who are on paths to positive growth, and allow yourself to feel enough admiration to learn from them.

- Surround yourself with people who can teach you qualities that you want to improve.

- Do not allow cultural editors to determine your limitations. Instead, explore your potential to achieve what you did not believe was possible.

- When you feel invincible, use the experience to embrace your excellence rather than abuse your body.

- Learn to eat healthful food and create workout rituals to enter adulthood with wellness consciousness. View your adolescence as a gift to be enjoyed and protected.

Childhood Portal

Although it is unlikely that children will read this section of my book, I'll describe some of the cultural universals, unique restraints, and entitlements of the child portal. With few exceptions, most cultures view childhood as a period when innocence must be protected. Sadly, some of the exceptions include parents selling their children to human traffickers who hook the children on highly addictive drugs (heroine) and sell them as sex slaves. There are approximately 20 million to 30 million slaves (sex or forced labor) in the world. The average cost of a slave is $90.

On the brighter side, the childhood portal for most cultures includes physical and emotional security, nourishment, education, and love. Some of the restraints include limited potential for education and success in extreme poverty cultures, as well as compulsory early marriages (in some cultures, 12 is the average age for girls to marry). The less dramatic side of entitlements includes allowing children to be obnoxious, excusing inappropriate behavior, and permitting them to use illness as a way to avoid responsibilities.

Some of these restrictions and entitlements happen, however, without parents' awareness that they are coauthoring them. In some cases, the allowances are based on guilt from parents who had very restrictive childhoods and go to extreme permissiveness to compensate. The recommendations that follow are intended for parents and teachers.

- The best way to teach children, and especially to correct them, is to ask questions. The Socratic method (teaching by asking questions) works best for several reasons: 1. It offers a model of correcting behavior by self-discovery, and cooperation rather than shaming and controlling. 2. Children tend to equate bad behavior with being a bad person—a generalization made because of developmental reasons (early-childhood inability to abstract from the particular to the general). 3. Fear teaches avoidance with little assimilation of pro-social alternatives.

- Suppose a four-year-old spills a glass of orange juice. You might say with an angry face, "See what happened? I told you not to play with your glass." The child already knows what happened and only focuses on your angry face.

- A Socratic alternative: You ask with a curious face, "What happened?" The child looks at you with a fearful face. If you don't receive an answer, you ask: "Did you spill your glass? What can you do to fix it?" No answer. "Do you want me to show you what *we* can do to fix it?" "Okay," the child answers (we hope), but if not, the next statement works either way. "Let's get a paper towel and wipe the table." After the job is done with your help, you give your child a hug and say, "See how you fixed the problem? I am very proud of you."

I am aware that these very simple examples are not earthshaking lessons. But the reason I use them is to give you the underlying psychology of the lesson and the neuropsychological reasons for the approach.

Because of the power that cultural editors (parents at home, teachers in the classroom) have on children, their first reaction after a misdeed is to look at the facial expression of the adult. When young children fall, the first thing they do is look at the facial expression of the adult to decide if the pain is worthy of crying. Of course, when the pain is strong they cry without your permission. When they make a mistake or misbehave, the best facial expression is curiosity.

When you ask what happened, you invite discovery rather than fear. When you ask what can be done, you facilitate solutions rather than helpless shame. And when you hug after the job is done, you reward a job well done rather than dependence.

In early childhood, the brain has the most plasticity to absorb as much information as possible, but the plasticity is open to establish neuromaps of helplessness or empowerment. These early neural associations are strengthened by repetition that gradually influences the formation of cultural selfhood: I am bright, I am awkward, I am loved, I am helpless, and so on. But just as important, facilitating self-discovery minimizes early learning of archetypal wounds as cultural controls.

I want to be clear that I am oversimplifying the developmental process because children are resilient, even in dysfunctional families. Having said that, there is strong neuropsychological data that shows abused children have a higher level of baseline cortisol (stress hormone) that carries on to adulthood. The good news, as always, is that the pliability of the brain can reverse most of what the nervous, immune, and endocrine system learned in order to cope with childhood adversity.

- You can use the information from the childhood portal to identify the teaching method you experienced in your childhood and how you may be applying it to yourself or your family. If it was love and understanding, congratulations. But if not, identify what you want to change that continues to affect you and those you choose to love.

- Commit to using the Socratic method when you fail to meet your expectations and when others do not live up to yours. If you're consistent and patient, your neuromaps will change, and your cultural self will be nourished.

The Anti-Aging Photo Experiment

Your brain archives what you accomplish, not how long it takes you to accomplish it. My colleague Dr. Ellen Langer, a professor of psychology at Harvard University, has conducted a series of experiments that consistently show how context (external conditions) can reverse the effects of aging. In just one week of living *as if* they were 20 years younger in a retreat that replicated the earlier era,

80-year-old men reversed frailties considered to be part of "normal aging." The men improved their strength of grip, gait, appetite, sleep, vision, mood, memory, and other biological markers of age. Some of the participants who came to the study using canes left a week later without them, and carrying their own suitcases. A control group was instructed to *reminisce* about younger days without living *as if* they were younger. Both groups stayed at the same retreat, but the experimental group lived in an area where everything (furniture, music, TV programs) simulated life as it was 20 years earlier. The control-group participants reminiscing about the past and living in an area of the retreat that maintained the looks of the present showed little or no improvement. The control group *talked about* the "good old days," while the experimental group *relived* the experience. Here you can see the difference between recalling memories and embodying them.

Based on the Langer studies and my own clinical work, I developed a technique I call the *anti-aging photo experiment.* My colleague and dear friend Dr. Christiane Northrup (a world-class expert on women's health) and I have independently taught the anti-aging technique to hundreds of women who report noticeable facial changes in the selfies they take on day one and day seven of the experiment. The improvements include reduced facial stress, livelier eyes, and tighter skin. I emphatically state that these experiments are not scientifically designed, nor do they represent research evidence. Nevertheless, the "before" and "after" head shots of most of the participants show undeniable improvement in facial features. I am now extending the experiment to measure other aging markers such as level of energy, sleep, and vitality. By the way, men can also try the experiment.

So keeping in mind that the technique is nothing more than a way to explore the benefits of self-caring, I will outline the procedure:

- Find a head-shot photo of yourself from at least 10 years ago, when you had more energy, looked younger, and were in a happy period of your life.

Upload the photo to your cell phone so you can view it as needed.

- Take a selfie head shot and have it available on your cell phone. This will serve as the before photo. At the end of the seventh day, take another selfie that will serve as the after photo.

- Rate yourself before and after the experiment. In the scale below, a score of 1 is lowest, 5 middle, and 9 highest. Circle the number that best describes how you feel in each category before and after the seven-day experiment. For example, a rating of 2 in energy is very low and a rating of 8 is very high. To make the measurements more accurate, after you rate yourself at the start of the experiment, do not look at your pre-experiment scores or your day one selfie until you finish your post-experiment rating.

Pre-experiment Rating

General Energy Level:	1 2 3 4 5 6 7 8 9
Sense of Wellness:	1 2 3 4 5 6 7 8 9
Self-Caring:	1 2 3 4 5 6 7 8 9
Youthfulness:	1 2 3 4 5 6 7 8 9
Sleep:	1 2 3 4 5 6 7 8 9

Post-experiment Rating

General Energy Level:	1 2 3 4 5 6 7 8 9
Sense of Wellness:	1 2 3 4 5 6 7 8 9
Self-Caring:	1 2 3 4 5 6 7 8 9
Youthfulness:	1 2 3 4 5 6 7 8 9
Sleep:	1 2 3 4 5 6 7 8 9

- After completing the experiment, also rate your subjective measure of overall satisfaction with facial changes comparing day seven to day one selfies. A score of 1 is lowest, 5 middle, and 9 highest.

Post-experiment Satisfaction with Photo Changes
Overall Photo Change: 1   2   3   4   5   6   7   8   9

Instructions for the Seven-Day Experiment

- Three times a day, look at the photo from the past. Take a deep breath and bring back memories of how you felt and the things you were doing that you enjoyed in those days.

- Embody the feelings and sensations, and allow them to grow. If you remember your enthusiasm from those earlier days, observe how you experience it in your body now and allow the feeling to expand. *Always look at the younger photo as you embody the positive memories.*

- Whatever good feelings you had, bring them to your present and experience them for the rest of the day *as if* you were that same person. For example, if your recall your high energy from those earlier days, embody the experience and function at that level of energy for the rest of the day.

- Do things that you enjoyed in the earlier days and imagine you're as young as you were at the time of the photo. Look at the photo so you see your youth.

- Look at the photo before you go to bed and take the good feelings and memories to your sleep.

- Follow this procedure for seven days. It's better not to share the information with anyone to avoid biases that could interfere with the experiment.

- Rate the *after* part of each category, and the scale for your level of satisfaction with the day seven photo when compared to the day one photo. Look for details and general looks.

- After completing the experiment, make gradual changes in your life to bring you closer to the joy and vitality that slipped away from earlier days. A commitment to give up "normal aging" and incorporate youthful growing older is necessary to maintain the gains from the photo experiment. In other words, the experiment is a wake-up call to enter wellness. To maintain gains, in addition to implementing youthful consciousness, repeat the experiment every few months until no longer necessary.

- Find coauthors of youth consciousness and nourish the relationship. If you are satisfied with the results of the experiment, teach it to others who can appreciate your offer.

Drs. Langer, Northrup, and I have seen how positive gains from our experiments are lost within weeks if people allow cultural editors to drag them back to their designated portals. For example, if you come out of the old-age portal and start doing things for yourself and others, coauthors of the old-age portal may try to bring you back with statements like, "Grandma, don't get up to make our coffee, let me do it." Well-meaning, rather than promoting wellness.

I remember when I went to Cuba to investigate some of the centenarians there, a 102-year-old man invited me for a walk so he could tell me about his healthy longevity. When we started to cross the street, he grabbed my arm and told me he was going to help *me* cross. I asked why he did that, and he responded, "To show you how shitty it feels when people assume you're too old to take care of yourself." He laughed heartily and took a puff of his cigar.

The Initial Context of Illness and Its Critical Mass

In my biocognitive theory I propose that most acquired illnesses (not from birth) start when conditions lose their initial preservation function. What was initially needed to protect us continues to operate beyond its intended purpose. For example, a child learns to sleep lightly when she is afraid that her alcoholic parents are going to kill each other during hostile arguments in the middle of the night. The initial vigilance has a function: Waking up allows the child to confirm that the parents survive another night of hostility. But in light sleep the nervous, immune, and endocrine processes are deregulated. As long as light sleep registers as a protection function, mindbody damage is minimized. A few years later, although the parents are divorced and the child is living with her recovering alcoholic mother in a safe environment, the light sleep continues beyond its protective function. Since it no longer registers as preservation, the sleep deprivation takes its toll and expresses illness. The dysfunctional condition reaches a critical mass.

Keeping my promise from the "Coauthoring the MindBody Self" chapter, I'll explain how *evidence-based medicine* (EBM) leaves essential *evidence* out of its limited approach to disease by undervaluing the narrative of the patient's illness.

I'll use the example of sleep deprivation to illustrate my argument. The majority of fibromyalgia cases I've treated show an initial trauma that started with functional light sleep. One case, a six-year-old girl, slept lightly because her uncle, who lived at home, would come into her room in the middle of the night and fondle her genitals. This went on for over a year until her uncle moved out. Although the danger was gone, she continued to have problems with her sleep. In her early 20s she was eventually diagnosed with fibromyalgia: an illness that includes chronic pain in specific areas of the body, depression, low energy, inflammation, and sleep disturbance. The first doctor she consulted found no lab *evidence* (false negative) to match her complaints and referred her to a psychiatrist. If there's no physical evidence, then it must be imagined. The psychiatrist belonged to the camp that believes fibromyalgia does not exist, and treated her for depression. Again, the patient's narrative was irrelevant. She did not improve with the antidepressant protocol, and was referred to a rheumatologist who believes that fibromyalgia exists. Notice the struggle to have some EBM practitioners validate the patient's anguish? Finally, the rheumatologist and I worked with the patient, and within two months the fibromyalgia symptoms were gone. We addressed the learning of the illness, and taught her how to retrain her cultural brain to change the signals of distress she was sending to her nervous, immune, and endocrine systems.

I propose that if EBM includes the patient's narrative in the evidence, it will cease to operate as a one-sided diagnostic and treatment medical model. As it stands, EBM would be more accurately described as body evidence to treat the mindbody of a cultural brain. But again, in fairness, I am generalizing to bring to your attention how professional arrogance can diminish the patients' contributions to their healing. Fortunately, functional and narrative medicines are leading the way to an inevitable paradigm shift in health care.

- If you have an ailment, without blaming yourself, see if you can find an initial protective function it provided, and how it became the pathology of disease (clinical evidence) and the anthropology of illness (your cultural experience of the evidence). In other words, there are two processes going on that you can address with your health-care professional.

- The physical evidence is your disease (abnormal blood values, organs and systems dysfunctions), and the felt meaning is your illness (fear, guilt, blame, stress, social disconnection, decreased control over your body, pain). While your health-care professionals know best how physiology works, you know more than anyone how your physiology feels. Choose health-care professionals who understand

243

the healing power of incorporating your narrative with the evidence they provide to treat and diagnose your ailment.

- Let your health-care professional work on the physical dysfunction while you explore ways to change how you're responding to the discomfort. Rather than a mind and body split, you want a mindbody coauthoring of two sources of wisdom: Your health-care professional treats the causes of the pathology and you embrace the causes of health.

- The causes of health can enhance any health-care treatment: setting emotional limits, social bonding, service to others, self-caring, forgiveness, breaking bread with family and friends, taking a break from the news, meditation, laughter, disengaging from blaming, resolving resentments, hope, hugs, stepping out of cultural portals, creating laudable rituals, admiration for worthy heroes, and most important, knowing that you are the recipient of over 150,000 years of mindbody refinements to support your wellness.

- When you commit to a wellness journey, whether to end an illness that has a cure or to reduce the anguish of a disease that awaits the discovery of a cure, be patient with your mindbody. Rather than expecting radical change, pay attention to your mindbody's subtle ways of moving toward health.

- All diseases will eventually be cured. But this does not mean that you wait helplessly until the discovery comes. Stephen Hawking, considered the Einstein of our times, was diagnosed with ALS (Lou Gehrig's disease) when he was 21 and was not expected to live more than four years. At 75 he continues to write best-selling books on physics while functioning as director of the Centre for Theoretical

Cosmology at Cambridge University. He does all this activity confined to a wheelchair and using a voice synthesizer to communicate. There's no question Hawking is an extraordinary human being, but at some level, so are you.

BIOCOGNITIVE KOANS FOR WESTERN MINDS

A koan is a riddle used in Zen Buddhist meditation to abandon ultimate dependence on reason and gain sudden intuitive enlightenment. Koans purposely have no logical solutions. Some examples of koans include: What is the color of the wind? What is the sound of one hand clapping? What is Zen? The interaction between teacher and student is elaborate and complex. The student's response to a koan gives the teacher a sense of how much progress the student is making toward enlightenment.

In my version of koans for Western minds the objective is more modest than reaching enlightenment. It is, rather, taking the Eastern concept of roundabout (incidental) learning and giving it a Western spin. Without having to seek enlightenment, it opens pathways to insights that are not available using *unconditional meaning*. For example, the unconditional meaning for the word *eyeglasses* is defined as "an instrument to correct or assist defective vision"—nothing else. *Conditional meaning* is determined by context. In the desert, eyeglasses can be used to start a fire using the lens to intensify sunlight and direct it to paper or twigs. If you don't have utensils, eyeglasses can be used to stir your coffee, and so on.

While Zen koans are used to disconnect from linguistic meaning to find enlightenment, our Western version of koans provides transitions from unconditional to conditional semantics in order to shift felt meaning. Returning to the above example: Your brain assimilates a conditional meaning that expands the unconditional function of eyeglasses. By the way, biocognitive koans for Western minds are also useful for Eastern minds that want to learn from

the West. The best way to understand the koan version I am introducing is to try it.

*Biocognitive koan: Cultures are powerful contributing architects
to your reality, but you are the coauthor of their influence.*

- Sit in a quiet place and read the statement above
  slowly while breathing gently and deeply.

- Let reactions surface and observe how they manifest
  in your mindbody. Pay attention to subtle shifts
  in sensations, thoughts, and emotions. Do not
  interpret—observe.

- Repeat, several times in your mind, the first part
  of the koan above: *Cultures are powerful contributing
  architects to your reality.* Let reactions surface and
  observe how they manifest in your mindbody. Pay
  attention to subtle shifts in sensations, thoughts,
  emotions, and meaning. Do not interpret—observe.

- Repeat the second part of the koan above several
  times: . . . *but you are the coauthor of their influence.*

- Let reactions surface and observe how they manifest
  in your mindbody. Pay attention to subtle shifts in
  sensations, thoughts, emotions, and meaning. Do not
  interpret—observe.

- Repeat the full koan several times with one
  exception: Replace the word *but* with the word *and.*
  Now it becomes: *Cultures are powerful contributing
  architects to your reality,* and *you are the coauthor of
  their influence.* Let conditional meanings surface and
  observe how they manifest in your mindbody. Pay
  attention to subtle shifts in sensations, thoughts, and
  emotions. Do not interpret—observe.

- Now repeat this new meaning: *But* consciousness presents challenges. *And* consciousness opens converging pathways to resolutions.

- Conceptualize the felt meaning of language as your mindbody experiential landscape. When you shift from unconditional to conditional felt meaning, you expand the possibilities of your experiential landscape.

You can use the biocognitive koan method with any felt meaning you want to shift or expand. For example, if you want to expand the meaning of setting limits, you can start with an unconditional interpretation of *caretaker* and transition to conditional:

- Take care of others

- Take care of others to be liked

- Take care of others when I can

- Take care of others in emergencies

- Take care of others who take care of me

- Take care of me

- Not take care of others, and give them permission to not like my new limits

- Taking care of others is a choice, not an obligation

You can see that the objective is to move from rigid unconditional meaning to flexible conditional *felt* meaning. But I caution that the transitioning requires more than reasoning the changes: This would only accomplish disembodied change in meaning (in your mind rather than your mindbody). Instead, the biocognitive koan method requires embodying each of the steps that lead to a final transition. In other words, what do you experience (sense, feel) when you express each stage of the koan? When you repeat and embody *take care of others to be liked*, you gain insights to the purpose. When you repeat *not take care of others and give them permission to not like my new limits*, you may feel more anxiety, but doing so expands the conditional meaning of the koan because it allows you to see how you obstruct your personal development.

Now I am going to use a famous Zen koan with another Western twist to the Eastern method. Rather than finding answers or enlightenment, you contemplate a proposed solution until you find a practical application to navigate adversity in your life. But before you start, be aware that I am not an enlightened teacher:

Biocognitive koan: *What is the color of the wind?*

Koan solution to contemplate: *Passage is the color of the wind.*

- Sit in a quiet place, breathing gently and deeply.

- Repeat the koan several times in your mind: *What is the color of the wind?*

- Let reactions surface and observe how they manifest in your mindbody. Pay attention to subtle shifts in sensations, thoughts, and emotions. Observe, without interpreting.

- Repeat the proposed solution several times in your mind: *Passage is the color of the wind.*

- Let reactions surface and observe how they manifest in your mindbody. Pay attention to subtle shifts in sensations, thoughts, and emotions. Observe without interpreting.

- After you practice the method as many times as you wish, ask yourself: *What color do I give the turbulent winds of my life, and how do I interfere with their passage?*

- Let reactions surface and observe how they manifest in your mindbody. Pay attention to subtle shifts in sensations, thoughts, and emotions. This time: *observe, interpret,* and *embody.*

With this method, you learn to embody disembodied cognitions to find tangible insight. You can create your own koans and propose solutions that are intuitive rather than rational: whatever comes to mind without concern for the connection. For now, there's no need for enlightenment.

Throughout the book, I propose embodiment as the essential factor in experiential change of behavior. Embodiment reaches the foundation of beliefs that maintain behavior. Trying to make a change without embodying felt meaning is like telling a thief that stealing is morally wrong and expecting a shift in moral conduct.

It has been a delightful experience writing this book for you in anticipation that it will provide tools for lasting change. But as you can surmise, a paradigm shift such as what I offer requires a new language, patience to learn it, and trust that it will work when you transition from the impossible to the reachable.

I strongly recommend that you refer to the Glossary when needed, and apply the mindbody tools when turbulence comes around. If at times the language and concepts were difficult to navigate, I want to assure you that, rather than "dumbing down" the material like a quick-fix formula, I trusted your intelligence and relied on your capacity to see that expanding your cultural self requires perseverance, despite what others might think when you become a rebel with a worthy cause.

Glossary

adversity. With minor variations, Western dictionaries define adversity as a state or instance of serious or continued difficulty or misfortune. See **biocognitive adversity**.

aging. A dysfunctional assimilation of cultural beliefs and their portals that define how our biology *should* respond to the passing of time. See **growing older**.

aliquid nihil. A Latin term meaning "giving something for nothing back," *aliquid nihil* is what I call my method to navigate adversity in meaningful relationships. When you go into a period of giving without expecting anything back, you enter a consciousness of generosity that comes from self-sufficiency. This does not mean self-deprivation. It's an opportunity to nourish yourself while offering nourishment to your partner. See **quid pro quo**.

alterity. In anthropology, the term means "otherness" as it relates to how we perceive other cultures and individuals in relation to our own sense of self.

amok. A sudden episode of dissociation (detachment from reality) followed by a depression, transitioning later to violent behavior toward persons or objects. Amok syndrome was originally associated with Malaysian cultures, but similar patterns are also seen in the Philippines, Polynesia, and Papua New Guinea.

anchors of misery. People who obstruct your mindbody progress and keep you connected with negativity and helplessness; those committed to misery and to bringing everyone else down into their despair.

archetypal wounds. Mindbody wounds resulting from the turbulence of abandonment, shame, and betrayal. In biocognitive theory, these wounds are viewed as archetypal because they are found in all cultures with different degrees of interpretation.

ataque de nervios. A Spanish-language phrase meaning "attack of nerves," used by Caribbean Hispanics to describe a set of culturally influenced symptoms including screams, uncontrollable crying, tremors, and verbal and physical aggression when experiencing loss of control.

belief horizons. The limits or edge of our knowing. Within the limits, information is perceived as familiar, and outside the limits it is interpreted as foreign.

beyond the pale. Historically, early tribal cultures enclosed their members' dwellings within fences or walls (pale) to protect against wild animals and enemies. If you remained within the enclosure, you were protected, accepted, and required to work for the collective benefit of the tribe. But if you went "beyond the pale," you were no longer considered a contributor to the best interest of the tribe: To venture out for your own benefit did not serve tribal needs. See **within the pale.**

biocognitive. Term coined by Dr. Mario Mártinez in 1998 to define his theory of mind-body-culture. In his biocognitive theory, Martinez proposes that cognition and biology *co-emerge* within a cultural history to find maximum contextual relevance. Biocognition challenges the limitations of the conventional sciences that reduce life to its biological components and dismiss mind as a neurochemical expression. Rather than an epiphenomenon of biology, cognition co-emerges with biology in an inseparable coauthorship of phenomenology and physicality within cultural horizons.

biocognitive adversity. A derailing of stability requiring constructive change; an opportunity to grow toward a desired goal not available until a shift of expectations takes place. See **adversity.**

biocognitive metamorphosis. A biocognitive analogy to describe how transitioning of felt meanings is not the same as replacing one condition for another. Instead, a transformation takes place in which a new foundation co-emerges, analogous to the metamorphosis of caterpillar to butterfly. Biocognitive theory argues against behavioral theories that define change as replacement of one behavior for another without considering the root meaning of the symbol that maintains the behavior.

bioinformation. The exchange of information by living beings, including the language, emotions, symbols, and biological responses expressed during communication.

bioinformational field. Mindbody information interpreted in culturally determined contexts.

biosymbol. A symbol (word, sign, concept) assimilated by the biology of the recipient. Biosymbols are learned early and are mostly taught by cultural editors. For example, if you are taught that going out in the rain can make you sick, the symbol "rain" gains a stressful quality that can trigger stress hormones.

centenarian consciousness. The consistent beliefs and rituals of healthy centenarians (100 years or older) across cultures. Although affected by their cultures, their healthy longevity is strongly related to how they rebel from restrictive collective beliefs.

coauthorship. A mutual contribution and participation with an event or a person. Communication is always a coauthored engagement, and it is never a one-way process void of coupling.

complexity compass. A variability guide to navigate the complexity of our turbulence. It disconnects our reruns by shifting from confirming the known to discovering novelty. Rather than pointing to fixed locations, it guides based on the instability that emerges from the turbulence: finding novelty in the complexity.

collective unconscious. The term coined by Swiss psychiatrist Carl Jung, referring to structures of the unconscious mind shared among beings of the same species.

contextual co-emergence. Attributes simultaneous cause to the biocultural histories that are exchanged between communicators (at all levels) in a shared bioinformational field that seeks maximum contextual relevance. *Co-emergence* is a biocognitive term that offers a new causality in biology. Rather than the conventional assumption that life processes emerge one from another, in bio-cognition, causality co-emerges simultaneously and is perceived sequentially. Although the emergent upward and downward causality of academic biology may be necessary, they are not sufficient to explain the complexities of life.

cortisol. A steroid hormone produced in humans in the adrenal gland. Cortisol is released in response to stress and low glucose concentration in the blood.

cultural anthropology. The comparative study of human societies and cultures and their development. How different cultures construct their shared beliefs.

cultural brain. A model of the brain proposed by Dr. Mario Martinez that views culture as one of the main sculptors of neuroplasticity. Martinez argues that cultures teach the brain how to perceive and communicate with our world. See culturally adaptive system.

cultural editors. Authority figures in cultural contexts who mold our identity through lessons, admonitions, and examples. Cultural editors influence our conception of self-worthiness and self-attributes.

cultural logistics. Established mores based on cultural meaning rather than academic logic or reasonable agendas. Some cultural logistics can be logical in the academic sense, while others counter what may appear unreasonable or illogical to other cultures.

cultural neuroscience. The study of how cultural values, practices, and beliefs shape and are shaped by the mind, brain, and genes across different measures. Cultural neuroscience bridges theory and methods from psychology, anthropology, psychoneuroimmunology, neuroscience, and genetics.

cultural paradigm. A conceptual working model with inherent cultural assumptions, rules of engagement, and attributions.

cultural portals. Culturally defined life periods of how to behave and what to expect depending on age (infancy, childhood, adolescence, young adulthood, middle age, and old age). The portals convey powerful forewarnings to maintain collective identity and tribal control with admonitions such as "You are too old for that" or "What do you expect at your age?"

cultural psychoneuroimmunology. An interdisciplinary model proposed by Dr. Mario Martinez to investigate how social and cultural contexts affect immune, nervous, and endocrine regulation. It moves psychoneuroimmunology rat research in conventional labs to field studies with humans in their natural environments. Martinez argues that academic labs are void of cultural contexts, and since rats are incapable of understanding the meaning of their actions and awareness of their mortality, results projected to humans lack major contributing factors that affect health and longevity.

cultural weave. The interpretations cultures coauthor to perceive the world. According to biocognitive theory, we perceive the fabric that cultures weave of self and environment. The plasticity of the brain and fluidity of the cultural weave make it possible to change mindbody perceptions we learn to interpret the world.

culturally adaptive system. A self-regulating system that can change its structure and its function to adapt to cultural demands. Dr. Mario Martinez coined this term to explain how the brain learns to perceive based on cultural conditions. See **cultural brain**.

default mode. A neuroscience term to describe a default state during decreases in neural activity.

drift. A biocognitive term to identify the synchronistic co-emergence of interconnectedness. The drift is nonlinear and unpredictable; it unfolds without apparent sequence. Although the drift cannot be sought linearly, shifting from confirming expectations to a discovering mode increases the probability of entering its portals.

elated quietude. A deep stage of contemplation in which the joy of entering periods free of thoughts and distractions is noted without derailing the experience. In the beginning stages of contemplative practice, the joy of quieting the mind is so exciting that it takes one out of the experience.

embodiment. To identify how and where cognition is experienced in the body and the role the body plays in shaping the mind within a cultural context. Rather than an object in relation to culture, mindbody must be considered as the subject of culture. See Thomas Csordas's article "Embodiment as a Paradigm for Anthropology" in the bibliography section of the "From Presenteeism to Embodied Present" chapter.

eudaimonic pleasure. Proposed by Greek philosopher Aristotle to counter Aristippus's concept of hedonic pleasure (pleasure for its own sake), eudaimonic pleasure is the pursuit of personal fulfillment and realizing human potential. Research in psychoneuroimmunology shows Aristotle's concept is a strong contributor to wellness, while the Aristippus hedonic pleasure has the opposite effect. See the "Cultural Brain" chapter for a discussion on how the immune system responds to hedonic versus eudaimonic mindbody processes. See **hedonic pleasure**.

evidence-based medicine (EBM). An approach to medical practice intended to optimize decision making by emphasizing the use of evidence from well-designed and well-conducted research. One of the limitations of EBM is that it does not consider the patient's narrative as contributory evidence.

explorer horizon. Seeks novelty to expand the extent of the domain. Paradigm shifts generate conflict between the explorer and regulator horizons because new information challenges established principles of the domain. Sets the rules for risk taking. See **internal horizon** and **regulator horizon**.

feedforward. An out-of-order event in the present with unfolding meaning or relevance in the future; a component of interconnectedness and its synchronistic portals.

felt meaning. The mindbody experience triggered by words, memories, images, and symbols; what one feels physically and emotionally. See **biocognitive metamorphosis**.

fishbowl effect. Term borrowed from French philosopher Michel Foucault, who used it as a metaphor to illustrate how we can remain trapped with ideas and behavior unable to see we can step out with new ways to perceive. Dr. Mario Martinez proposes that the boundaries of the fishbowl are determined by our cultures. Thus, we are not aware we are constrained in a cultural fishbowl.

fMRI (functional magnetic resonance imaging). Scanning device that shows brain activity in real time based on blood flow. Looks at how the brain responds to specific conditions such as thoughts, emotions, memories, and beliefs.

forgiveness. The mindbody forgiveness process has two sequential stages: The first reinstates one's empowerment and the second one's worthiness. When we recall and embody the felt meaning of the healing field corresponding to our wound, we experience the *alpha event*: recognition of our goodness, so we may recover our sense of empowerment that has been depleted by the misdeed. Whereas in the alpha event we recognize our deeds of honor, commitment, and loyalty, in the *omega event* we feel grateful for recognizing them. Recognition of our goodness reinstates our empowerment, and gratitude recovers our worthiness. The alpha event begins our liberation and the omega event completes it.

growing older. A natural process of time passing that we all experience. Although there are some physiological changes, they do not necessarily have to be pathological. See **aging.**

guardians of the heart. An experiential biocognitive model that views relationships as opportunities to heal the archetypal wounds of abandonment, shame, and betrayal that we rerun when love comes our way. By offering our hearts for reciprocal safekeeping, a guardianship is established to coauthor healing fields of commitment, honor, and loyalty within a covenant of safety.

healing fields. MindBody Code resolution of archetypal wounds that go beyond intellectually reasoning the solutions. The healing field for abandonment is commitment mindfulness; honor mindfulness for shame; and loyalty mindfulness for betrayal.

hedonic pleasure. Proposed by Greek philosopher Aristippus; to pursue pleasure and avoid pain as life goals to find happiness. See **eudaimonic pleasure.**

indeterminate locality. A biocognitive term to conceptualize how nonlinear communication is archived through multiple complexity localities that are not accessible until they co-emerge into linear processes. Indeterminate locality provides an alternative to the improper use of quantum nonlocality when defining nonlinearity. Quantum nonlocality has no *travel origin* and it applies to subatomic particles, whereas indeterminate locality has complex multiplicity of *travel origins* and takes place above atomic levels. While indeterminate locality is based on complexity theory, nonlocality is a quantum physics event. It is an error of category to use these two terms interchangeably.

individuation. A term coined by Swiss psychiatrist Carl Jung to describe the process of becoming aware of one's selfhood, one's makeup, and the path to discover one's true inner self. In biocognitive theory, individuation is expanded to identify the mindbody self we coauthor with our tribe, to recognize the difference between who we are and what we are expected to be, and to become our most worthy self. Our true nature is living our excellence.

infinite nesting. Repetitive patterns of disordered order in fractals containing all the information from the total pattern. This complexity theory concept is extrapolated in biocognition to explain the default modes of operative consciousness.

internal horizon. Defines the extent of the domain's established principles: What is beauty in the domain of aesthetics? What is morality in the domain of ethics? What is deity in the domain of religion? And so on. The internal horizon governs the cultural identity of the domain. See **regulator horizon** and **explorer horizon**.

interpretation cluster. A cluster of thoughts, emotions, sensations, memories, and context interpreted to make sense of an experience. Rather than passively storing our thoughts and emotions, we assign meaning to each of the factors associated with our experiences. For example, assertiveness may mean disrespect in some cultures, and a given right in others. Each condition has a cluster of thoughts, emotions, associations, and interpretations of what it means to be assertive.

konenki. Japanese word that describes menopause as "a turn" or "change in life." It reflects how Japanese culture views changes related to menopause as an opportunity to recognize and revere a woman's place of wisdom and maturity. See **second spring**.

koan. A Zen Buddhist riddle given to meditation students to break the habit of intellectualizing insights. The riddle has no logical solution; it's intended to exhaust the reasoning process of linear thinking, to arrive at experiential knowing, void of explanations. Some examples are: *What is Zen? What is the color of the wind? What is the sound of one hand clapping?*

lived theory. Living a theory entails embodying its principles in the form of actions. To live a theory, its principles must become rituals.

meeting of horizons. The communication exchanged between two fields of bioinformation. The horizons are the permeable boundaries of fields that assimilate or reject new bioinformation.

middle way. From Buddhist psychology, the optimal position between opposites.

mindbody. The mind and the body viewed as one. The coauthoring of cognition and biology shaped within cultural contexts.

mindbodycultural oneness. The inseparable learning process that takes place within cultural contexts. Perception is viewed as a unified field of cognition and biology finding meaning in culturally determined contexts. Change requires involvement of all parts as one.

narrative medicine. A patient-centered approach to diagnostics and treatment in medicine that includes the patient's experience of their symptoms and conceptualization of their illness.

neuroanthropology. The study of the coauthoring relationship between culture and brain; how culture influences the development, structure, and function of the brain.

neurophenomenology. The study of experience, mind, and consciousness as embodied conditions of the human mind.

novelty. The new. Whatever emerges for the first time is novel. In complexity theory, stability is defined as a range of repetition, from minimum variability in quantum flux to long and complex patterns of repetition in periodic and chaotic processes that can only be detected with recurrent methods. While periodic and chaotic series show greater recurrence than randomness, creative processes (biological, economic, etc.) are less recurrent than randomness. Thus, novelty is a unique condition of recurrence between chaos and randomness that can be measured by quantifying the scarcity of recurrences. In biocognition, the reductionist model of biology is replaced with principles of complexity theory interacting with cultural variables.

operative consciousness. The mind-body perceptual field determined by cultural presuppositions and beliefs. We perceive within the cultural horizons of our beliefs.

paradigm. A conceptual model or theory offering new assumptions, rules of engagement, and attributions based on evidence that no longer supports what it's replacing.

paradoxical intention. A term coined by Dr. Viktor Frankl, founder of logotherapy, to describe a self-contradictory or counterintuitive way of facing a condition or circumstance that results in the opposite of what was intended. The process is mostly subconscious or not well planned.

perceptual investment value. The implicit worth given to an intention, person, event, or action.

portal. Gates that express the total mindbody condition rather than its reducible physical locations. For example, the brain is a portal rather than the physical locality of thoughts. Portals are doors expressing the total bioinformational field.

pseudo-humility. Minimizing, rationalizing, or denying compliments and achievements for fear of immodesty. Most cultures teach against appearing boastful or conceited at the expense of acknowledging self-worthiness.

psychoneuroimmunology. An interdisciplinary field that investigates the connection between behavior and nervous, immune, and endocrine regulation.

quid pro quo. A Latin phrase that literally means "something for something." It represents the implicit expectation that one should always get something back for what they give. "You scratch my back, I scratch yours." When relationships are mostly based on quid pro quo, they become ledgers to keep score, void of generosity and gratitude. See *aliquid nihil.*

recontextualize. Rather than merely redefining the cognitive meaning of a context (semantic shifting), it is a process that re-visions the *felt meaning* of a context; the embodiment of biosymbols that define new contexts.

regulator horizon. Activates when there's a challenge or violation of the established identity of the domain. It determines what to accept or reject and how to admonish transgressions. The regulator horizon determines and governs the enforcement rules of the domain. See **internal horizon** and **explorer horizon**.

relational incompleteness. The brain is an incomplete interpreter that reaches meaning based on contextual relevance. Self is a relational entity that finds meaning with coauthors of identity within a culturally constructed context. Self-identification is a potentiality that co-emerges at the horizons of the relationship it coauthors. The interpreting brain interacts with the world to complete its interpretation, and the relational self finds identity in the relationship.

ritual. A behavior or event that gives inclusive meaning to the individual, family, or culture. For example: breaking bread, celebrating birthdays and holidays with family and friends, etc. A ritual identifies our relational self with our cultural belongingness.

ritualizing. Elevating the value of a behavior or event to a venerable place in one's life. Taking the mundane to a condition of honorable identity.

routine. A behavior or event that reflects what we do with some regularity. A routine identifies what we must do to maintain status quo. For example: going to work, taking a shower, shopping, etc. See **ritual**.

routine vacuum. When adversity disrupts routines that are part of daily life. For example, sudden unemployment requires giving up all the routines associated with going to work, such as chatting with colleagues, coming home at the end of the day, and so on.

segments of nothingness. The experience in between thoughts and observations during contemplative practices; gaps without contexts.

Samatha. A Buddhist meditation practice used to quiet the mind by focusing on the breathing or other one-pointed attention to mantras, mandalas, mudras, and so on.

self-referent fallacy. An interpretation of the actions or circumstances of others based on our own experience.

second spring. A term used in Chinese medicine to describe menopause. The Chinese characters for *next* and *spring* are used to define menopause as a woman's second spring. See *konenki*.

***taijin-kyofu-sho* (TKS).** In Japanese culture, an intense fear of offending others because of personal looks, body odor, facial expressions, or body movements. TKS syndrome is defined as a mental disorder in the Japanese official diagnostics manual.

tumor necrosis factor (TNF). A molecule that signals inflammation usually triggered by infection and other immunological damage. PNI research shows that TNF can be activated by the experience of shame.

uncertainty. A condition of reduced predictability. In biocognitive theory, by identifying the areas affected, uncertainty can be used as a compass to identify the out-of-order factors caused by adversity; adversity is the cause and uncertainty is the effect. See the "Navigating Adversity with Uncertainty as Your Guide" chapter.

unselfing. A biocognitive term to express the process of detaching from the social and cultural labels of self. Unselfing occurs during deep levels of meditation or contemplation. It is a groundless awareness that rids self of all its masks and labels. Without proper guidance, unselfing can be a frightening experience. In pathological processes, it manifests as dissociative and depersonalization states during extreme anxiety reactions. Contemplative adepts can enter unselfing states at will without deleterious effects.

variability guide. A searching mode that orients based on the novelty that emerges from the instability of turbulence. Sudden shifts from known to unknown time/space conditions require a navigational guide that replaces confirmation with discovery: entering unpredictable conditions without imposing linear order. See **complexity compass**.

victimhood consciousness. The mind-set (operative consciousness) that views the world as overwhelming with little hope of overcoming life challenges. One of the ways cultures inadvertently teach us victimhood consciousness is by underestimating our human resilience.

Vipassana. Also called insight meditation, it concentrates on the present moment. It consists of observing, with bare attention, the body (*rupa*) and the mind (*nama*) as well as the insights that emerge from the observations.

Wilson effect. Dr. Mario Martinez coined the term "Wilson effect" to describe how we tend to extend our emotional self to conditions that provide us with safety, companionship, and reliability. The name Wilson was inspired by the Tom Hanks film *Cast Away*. Isolated on an island after an airplane crash, Hanks's character finds a Wilson volleyball amid the wreckage, names it Wilson, and gives it human qualities—all to deal with his profound isolation.

within the pale. A phrase from the 17th century meaning to stay within the limits of established law or decency. The word *pale* is defined as an enclosure or boundary. Although civilization began during the Ice Age, when outliers went beyond their physical boundaries to explore harsh environments, the phrase "beyond the pale" has taken the connotation of exceeding appropriate limits. In biocognitive theory, going beyond the pale means breaking from established cultural beliefs that constrain your personal development. See **beyond the pale**.

Bibliography

Chapter 1: Coauthoring the MindBody Self

Birth, Kevin K. *Objects of Time: How Things Shape Temporality*. New York: Palgrave Macmillan, 2012.

Clifford, James. *Returns: Becoming Indigenous in the Twenty-First Century*. Cambridge, MA: Harvard University Press, 2013.

————. *Routes: Travel and Translation in the Late Twentieth Century*. Cambridge, MA: Harvard University Press, 1997.

Csordas, Thomas J. "Somatic Modes of Attention." *Cultural Anthropology* 8, no. 2 (1993): 135–56.

Fenker, Daniela B. et al. "Novel Scenes Improve Recollection and Recall of Words." *Journal of Cognitive Neuroscience* 20, no. 7 (2008): 1250–65.

Geertz, Clifford. *The Interpretation of Cultures*. New York: Basic Books, 1977.

Marguerat, Yves. "The Exploitation of Apprentices in Togo." In *The Exploited Child*, edited by Bernard Schlemmer, 239–247. London: Zed Books, 2000.

Marques, José M. et al. "The 'Black Sheep Effect': Extremity of Judgments Towards Ingroup Members as a Function of Group Identification." *European Journal of Social Psychology*, 18, no. 1 (2006): 1–16.

Moore, Carmella C. and Holly F. Mathews. *The Psychology of Cultural Experience*. Cambridge, UK: Cambridge University Press, 2001.

Turner, Victor. *The Ritual Process: Structure and Anti-Structure*. London: Aldine Transaction, 1966.

Chapter 2: Life beyond the Pale

Frankl, Viktor E. *Man's Search for Meaning*. New York: Pocket Books, 1997.

Garber, Judy and Steven D. Hollon. "Universal Versus Personal Helplessness in Depression: Belief in Uncontrollability or Incompetence?" *Journal of Abnormal Psychology* 89, no.1 (February 1980): 56–66.

Gleick, James. *Chaos: Making a New Science*. London: Penguin Books, 2008.

Grant, Adam. *Originals: How Non-Conformists Move the Word*. New York: Viking, 2016.

Jung, Carl G. *Man and His Symbols*. New York: Dell, 1968.

Leinaweaver, Jessaca B. "Improving Oneself: Young People Getting Ahead in the Peruvian Andes." *Latin American Perspectives* 35, no. 4 (July 2008): 60–78.

Martinez, Mario E. "The Biocognition of Personal Ethics: Does the Immune System Have Morals?" 9th International Conference on Ethics Across Curriculum. Milltown Institute, National University of Ireland, Dublin, November 2007.

Payer, Lynn. *Medicine and Culture*. New York: Henry Holt and Company, 1996.

Triandis, Harry C. "Collectivism and Individualism as Cultural Syndromes." *Cross-Cultural Research* 27, no. 3–4 (August 1993): 155–80.

Rabow, Jerome, Sherry L. Berkman, and Ronald Kessler. "The Culture of Poverty and Learned Helplessness: A Social Psychological Perspective." *Sociological Inquiry* 53, no. 4 (October 1983): 419–34.

Chapter 3: Entering the Biosymbolic World

Chung, Ruth H. Gim. "Gender, Ethnicity, and Acculturation in Intergenerational Conflict of Asian American College Students." *Cultural Diversity and Ethnic Minority Psychology* 7, no. 4 (November 2001): 376–86.

Haidt, Jonathan. *The Righteous Mind: Why Good People Are Divided by Politics and Religion*. New York: Vintage Books, 2012.

Hwang, Wei-Chin. "Acculturative Family Distancing: Theory, Research, and Clinical Practice." *Psychotherapy: Theory, Research, Practice, Training* 43, no 4 (2006): 397–409.

Kastanakis, Minas N. and Benjamin G. Voyer. "The Effect of Culture on Perception and Cognition: A Conceptual Framework." *Journal of Business Research* 67, no. 4 (2014): 425–33.

Lancy, David F. "'First You Must Master Pain': The Nature and Purpose of Apprenticeship." *Anthropology of Work Review* 33, no. 2 (December 2012): 113–26.

Lears, T. J. Jackson. "The Concept of Cultural Hegemony: Problems and Possibilities." *American Historical Review* 90, no. 3 (June 1985): 567–93.

Martinez, Mario E. "Effectiveness of Operationalized Gestalt Therapy Role-Playing in the Treatment of Phobic Behaviors." *Gestalt Review* 6, no. 2 (2002): 148–66.

Portis-Winner, Irene. *Semiotics of Culture and Beyond*. New York: Peter Lang, 2013.

Sandstrom, Kent L. et al., *Symbols, Selves, and Social Reality: A Symbolic Interactionist Approach to Social Psychology and Sociology*. New York: Oxford University Press, 2013.

Winkelman, Michael and John R. Baker. *Supernatural as Natural: A Biocultural Approach to Religion*. Upper Saddle River, NJ: Pearson/Prentice Hall, 2008.

Chapter 4: Permanence, Control, and Other Illusions

Burger, Jerry M. "Desire for Control and the Illusion of Control: The Effects of Familiarity and Sequence of Outcome." *Journal of Research in Personality* 20, no. 1 (March 1986): 66–76.

Gino, Francesca, Zachariah Sharek, and Don A. Moore. "Keeping the Illusion of Control Under Control: Ceilings, Floors, and Imperfect Calibration." *Organizational Behavior and Human Decision Processes* 114, no. 2 (March 2011): 104–14.

Ji, Li-Jun, Kaiping Peng, and Richard E. Nisbett. "Culture, Control, and Perception of Relationships in the Environment." *Journal of Personality and Social Psychology* 78, no. 5 (2000): 943–55.

Ju, Se Jin and Woo Kyeong Lee. "Mindfulness, Non-attachment, and Emotional Well-Being in Korean Adults." *Advanced Science and Technology Letters* 87 (2015): 68–72.

Kierkegaard, Søren. *The Concept of Anxiety: A Simple Psychologically Orienting Deliberation on the Dogmatic Issue of Hereditary Sin*. Princeton, NJ: Princeton University Press, 1980.

Langer, Ellen J. "The Illusion of Control." *Journal of Personality and Social Psychology* 32, no. 2 (August 1975): 311–28.

Martinez, Mario. *The Man from Autumn: A Psychological Novel*. Montevideo, Uruguay: Delamancha, 2012.

Martinez, Mario E. "Embodying the Four Immeasurables: A Biocognitive Approach to Tibetan Buddhist Contemplative Practices." Luminous Mind Center, Nashville, TN, October 2009.

Martinez, Mario E. "The Process of Knowing: A Biocognitive Epistemology." *Journal of Mind and Behavior* 22, no. 4 (Autumn 2001): 407–26.

Rinpoche, Sogyal. *The Tibetan Book of Living and Dying*. San Francisco: Harper, 2012.

Sahdra, Baljinder, Phillip Shaver, and Kirk Brown. "A Scale to Measure Nonattach-ment: A Buddhist Complement to Western Research on Attachment and Adaptive Functioning." *Journal of Personality Assessment* 92, no. 2 (2010): 116–27.

Solomon, Sheldon, Jeff Greenberg, and Tom Pyszczynski. "A Terror Management Theory of Social Behavior: The Psychological Functions of Self-Esteem and Cul-tural Worldviews." *Advances in Experimental Social Psychology* 24 (1991): 93–159.

Chapter 5: An Anthropology of Self-Esteem

Becker, Maja et al. "Cultural Bases for Self-Evaluation: Seeing Oneself Positively in Different Cultural Contexts." *Personality and Social Psychology Bulletin* 40, no. 5 (2014): 657–75.

Cai, Huajian et al. "Self-Esteem and Culture: Differences in Cognitive Self-Evaluations or Affective Self-Regard?" *Asian Journal of Social Psychology* 10 (2007): 162–70.

Deci, Edward L. and Richard M. Ryan. "The Importance of Universal Psycho-logical Needs for Understanding Motivation in the Workplace." In *The Oxford Handbook of Work Engagement, Motivation, and Self-Determination Theory,* edited by Marylène Gagné, 13–32. New York: Oxford University Press, 2014.

Geertz, Clifford. "On the Nature of Anthropological Understanding: Not Extraor-dinary Empathy . . ." *American Scientist* 63, no. 1 (1975): 47–53.

Markus, Hazel R. and Shinobu Kitayama. "Culture and the Self: Implications for Cognition, Emotion, and Motivation." *Psychological Review* 98, no. 2 (April 1991): 224–53.

Triandis, Harry C. and Michele J. Gelfand. "Converging Measurement of Horizon-tal and Vertical Individualism and Collectivism." *Journal of Personality and Social Psychology* 74, no. 1 (1998): 118–28.

Chapter 6: The Causes of Health

Ahn, Andrew C., Muneesh Tewari, Chi-Sang Poon, and Russell S. Phillips. "The Limits of Reductionism in Medicine: Could Systems Biology Offer an Alterna-tive?" *PLOS Medicine* 3, no. 6 (2006): e208.

Bell, Adrian V., Peter J. Richerson, and Richard McElreath. "Culture Rather than Genes Provides Greater Scope for the Evolution of Large-Scale Human Prosociality." *Proceedings of the National Academy of Sciences* 106, no. 42 (2009): 17671–74.

Eisenberger, Naomi I. "The Pain of Social Disconnection: Examining the Shared Neural Underpinnings of Physical and Social Pain." *Nature Reviews Neuroscience* 13, no. 6 (2012): 421–34.

——— et al. "The Neural Sociometer: Brain Mechanisms Underlying State Self-Esteem." *Journal of Cognitive Neuroscience* 23, no. 11 (2011): 3448–55.

Gimlin, Debra. "The Absent Body Project: Cosmetic Surgery as a Response to Bodily Dys-appearance." *Sociology* 40, no. 4 (August 2006): 699–716.

Hahn, Robert A. *Sickness and Healing: An Anthropological Perspective.* New Haven, CT: Yale University Press, 1995.

Kashdan, Todd. *Curious? Discover the Missing Ingredient to a Fulfilling Life.* New York: William Morrow, 2009.

Martinez, Mario. *The MindBody Code: How to Change the Beliefs that Limit Your Health, Longevity, and Success.* Louisville, CO: Sounds True, 2014.

———. "The Process of Knowing: A Biocognitive Epistemology." *Journal of Mind and Behavior* 22, no. 4 (2001): 407–26.

Morelli, Sylvia A., Jared B. Torre, and Naomi I. Eisenberger. "The Neural Bases of Feeling Understood and Not Understood." *Social Cognitive and Affective Neuroscience* 9, no. 12 (2014): 1890–96.

Rankin, Lissa. *Mind Over Medicine: Scientific Proof That You Can Heal Yourself.* Carlsbad, CA: Hay House, 2013.

Talhelm, Thomas et al. "Liberals Think More Analytically (More 'WEIRD') Than Conservatives." *Personality and Social Psychology Bulletin* 41, no. 2 (2015): 250–67.

Temoshok, Lydia R. "Connecting the Dots, Linking Mind, Behavior, and Disease: The Biological Concomitants of Coping Patterns; Commentary on Attachment and Cancer; A Conceptual Integration." *Integrative Cancer Therapies* 1, no. 4 (December 2002): 387–91.

Turner, Victor. *The Ritual Process: Structure and Anti-Structure.* London: Aldine Transaction, 1966.

Chapter 7: From Presenteeism to Embodied Present

Abdolzahra, Naami, Neda Smaeeli Far, and Arezu Pourmahdi. "Prediction of Students' Happiness Based on the Components of Their Socioeconomic Status." *International Journal of Psychology and Behavioral Research* 3, no.1 (2014): 67–74.

Bloom, D. E. et al. *The Global Economic Burden of Noncommunicable Diseases.* Geneva: World Economic Forum, 2011.

Clayton, Russell B., Glenn Leshner, and Anthony Almond. "The Extended iSelf: The Impact of iPhone Separation on Cognition, Emotion, and Physiology." *Journal of Computer-Mediated Communication* 20, no. 2 (March 2015): 119–35.

Csordas, Thomas J., ed. *Embodiment and Experience: The Existential Ground of Culture and Self.* Cambridge: Cambridge University Press, 2003.

———. "Embodiment as a Paradigm for Anthropology." *Ethos* 18, no. 1 (March 1990): 5–47.

Easterlin, Richard A. et al. "The Happiness-Income Paradox Revisited." *Proceedings of the National Academy of Sciences* 107, no. 52 (2010): 22463–68.

Gimlin, Debra. "The Absent Body Project: Cosmetic Surgery as a Response to Bodily Dys-appearance." *Sociology* 40, no. 4 (August 2006): 699–716.

Gosselin, Eric, Louise Lemyre, and Wayne Corneil. *Présentéisme et absentéisme: Compréhension différenciée de phénomènes apparentés.* Gatineau, QC: Université du Québec en Outaouais, Département de relations industrielles, 2011.

Greer, Steven and Marianne Brady. "Natural Killer Cells: One Possible Link Between Cancer and the Mind." *Stress & Health* 4, no. 2 (April/June 1988): 105–11.

International Labour Organization. *Occupational Safety and Health: Synergies Between Security and Productivity.* Geneva: International Labour Office, 2006.

Hesketh, Ian and Cary L. Cooper. "Leaveism at Work." *Occupational Medicine* 64, no. 3 (April 2014): 146–7.

Johns, Gary. "Presenteeism in the Workplace: A Review and Research Agenda." *Journal of Organizational Behavior* 31, no. 4 (May 2010): 519–42.

Moore, Jon T. and Mark M. Leach. "Dogmatism and Mental Health: A Comparison of the Religious and Secular." *Psychology of Religion and Spirituality* 8, no. 1 (February 2016): 54–64.

Przybylski, Andrew K. et al. "Motivational, Emotional, and Behavioral Correlates of Fear of Missing Out." *Computers in Human Behavior* 29, no. 4 (July 2013): 1841–48.

Chapter 8: The Cultural Brain

Adler, Shelley R. *Sleep Paralysis: Night-Mares, Nocebos, and the Mind-Body Connection.* New Brunswick, NJ: Rutgers University Press, 2011.

American Psychiatric Association. *Diagnostic and Statistical Manual of Mental Disorders: DSM-5,* 5th ed. Arlington, VA: American Psychiatric Association, 2013.

Austin, James H. *Zen-Brain Reflections.* Cambridge, MA: The MIT Press, 2006.

Azar, Beth. "Your Brain on Culture." *Monitor on Psychology* 41, no. 10 (November 2010): 44.

Bibliography

Banerjee, Anwesha. "Cross-Cultural Variance of Schizophrenia in Symptoms, Diagnosis and Treatment." *Georgetown University Journal of Health Sciences* 6, no. 2 (2012): 18–24.

Baracz, Sarah J. and Jennifer L. Cornish. "Oxytocin Modulates Dopamine-Mediated Reward in the Rat Subthalamic Nucleus." *Hormones and Behavior* 63, no. 2 (2013): 370–5.

Brent, Lauren J. N. et al. "Ecological Knowledge, Leadership, and the Evolution of Menopause in Killer Whales." *Current Biology* 25, no. 6 (March 2015): 746–50.

Cassell, Eric J. *The Healer's Art: A New Approach to the Doctor-Patient Relationship.* Harmondsworth: Penguin Books, 1978.

Chiao, Joan Y., ed. *Cultural Neuroscience: Cultural Influences on Brain Function.* New York: Elsevier, 2009.

——— et al., eds. *The Oxford Handbook of Cultural Neuroscience.* Oxford, UK: Oxford University Press, 2016.

Chiao, Joan Y. and Katherine D. Blizinsky. "Culture-Gene Coevolution of Individualism-Collectivism and the Serotonin Transporter Gene." *Proceedings of the Royal Society B: Biological Sciences* 277, no. 1681 (February 2010): 529–37.

Cohen, Irun R. *Tending Adam's Garden: Evolving the Cognitive Immune Self.* San Diego: Academic Press, 2000.

Doidge, Norman. *The Brain's Way of Healing: Remarkable Discoveries and Recoveries from the Frontiers of Neuroplasticity.* New York: Viking, 2015.

Dickerson, Sally S. et al. "Immunological Effects of Induced Shame and Guilt." *Psychosomatic Medicine* 66, no. 1 (2004): 124–31.

Fagan, Brian. *Cro-Magnon: How the Ice Age Gave Birth to the First Modern Humans.* New York: Bloomsbury Press, 2010.

Fredrickson, Barbara L. et al. "A Functional Genomic Perspective on Human Well-Being." *Proceedings of the National Academy of Sciences* 110, no. 33 (2013): 13684–89.

Glaser, Ronald and Janice K. Kiecolt-Glaser, eds. *Handbook of Human Stress and Immunity.* San Diego: Academic Press, 1994.

Hofstede, Geert. "Culture's Recent Consequences: Using Dimension Scores in Theory and Research." *International Journal of Cross Cultural Management* 1, no. 1 (April 2001): 11–17.

Ji, Li-Jun, Kaiping Peng, and Richard E. Nisbett. "Culture, Control, and Perception of Relationships in the Environment." *Journal of Personality and Social Psychology* 78, no. 5 (May 2000): 943–55.

Kusnecov, Alexander W. and Hymie Anisman, eds. *The Wiley-Blackwell Handbook of Psychoneuroimmunology.* Hoboken, NJ: Wiley-Blackwell, 2013.

Lende, Daniel H. and Greg Downey, eds. *The Encultured Brain: An Introduction to Neuroanthropology.* Cambridge, MA: The MIT Press, 2015.

Lim, Leslie. "Taijin-Kyofu-Sho: A Subtype of Social Anxiety." *Open Journal of Psychiatry* 3 (2013): 393–398.

Lynch, Elizabeth and Douglas Medin. "Explanatory Models of Illness: A Study of Within-Culture Variation." *Cognitive Psychology* 53, no. 4 (December 2006): 285–309.

Lyubomirsky, Sonja, Laura King, and Ed Diener. "The Benefits of Frequent Positive Affect: Does Happiness Lead to Success?" *Psychological Bulletin* 131., no. 6 (2005): 803–55.

Majid, Asifa and Niclas Burenhult. "Odors Are Expressible in Language, as Long as You Speak the Right Language." *Cognition* 130, no. 2 (2014): 266–70.

Márquez, Samuel et al. "The Nasal Complex of Neanderthals: An Entry Portal to their Place in Human Ancestry." *Anatomical Record* 297 (2014): 2121–37.

Martinez, Mario E. "The Biocognitive Space of Autoimmune Disorders: Autogenic Communication with Psychoneuroimmunological Profiles." Poster presented at the 11th annual meeting of the PsychoNeuroImmunology Research Society, Titisee, Germany, May 2004.

Miller, Andrew H. and Charles L. Raison. "The Role of Inflammation in Depression: From Evolutionary Imperative to Modern Treatment Target." *Nature Reviews Immunology* 16 (2016): 22–34.

Nagano, Jun et al. "The Parenting Attitudes and the Stress of Mothers Predict the Asthmatic Severity of their Children: A Prospective Study." *BioPsychoSocial Medicine* 4, no. 1 (2010): 4–12.

Pariante, Carmine M. et al. "Do Antidepressants Regulate How Cortisol Affects the Brain?" *Psychoneuroendocrinology* 29, no. 4 (May 2004): 423–47.

Robins, Lee N. et al. "Vietnam Veterans Three Years after Vietnam: How Our Study Changed Our View of Heroin." *American Journal on Additions* 19, no. 3 (May–June 2010): 203–11.

Ryan, Richard M., Veronika Huta, and Edward L. Deci. "Living Well: A Self-Determination Theory Perspective on Eudaimonia." *Journal of Happiness Studies* 9, no. 1 (2008): 139–70.

Solinas, Marcello et al. "Environmental Enrichment During Early Stages of Life Reduces the Behavioral, Neurochemical, and Molecular Effects of Cocaine." *Neuropsychopharmacology* 34, no. 5 (April 2009): 1102–11.

Solomon, George F. and Rudolf H. Moos. "Emotions, Immunity, and Disease: A Speculative Theoretical Integration." *Archives of General Psychiatry* 11, no. 6 (December 1964): 657–74.

Tezuka, Hiroyuki. "Success as the Source of Failure? Competition and Cooperation in Japanese Economy." *Sloan Management Review* 38, no. 2 (January 1997): 83–89.

Weng, Helen Y. et al. "Compassion Training Alters Altruism and Neural Responses to Suffering." *Psychological Science* 24, no. 7 (2013): 1171–1180.

Zaki, Jamil and Jason P. Mitchell. "Equitable Decision Making Is Associated with Neural Markers of Intrinsic Value." *Proceedings of the National Academy of Sciences* 108, no. 49 (2011): 19761–66.

Chapter 9: Growing Older versus Cultural Aging

Becker, Bettina. "Challenging 'Ordinary Pain': Narrative of Older People Who Live with Pain." In *Narrative Gerontology: Theory, Research, and Practice,* edited by Gary Kenyon, Phillip Clark, and Brian de Vries, 91–112. New York: Springer Publishing Company, 2001.

Buettner, Dan. *Blue Zones: Lessons for Living Longer from the People Who've Lived the Longest.* Washington, DC: National Geographic, 2008.

Calhoun, Lawrence G. and Richard G. Tedeschi. "Early Post-traumatic Interventions: Facilitating Possibilities for Growth." In *Posttraumatic Stress Intervention: Challenges, Issues and Perspectives,* edited by John M. Violanti, Douglas Paton, and Christine Dunning, 135–152. Springfield, IL: C.C. Thomas, 2000.

Clark, Margaret. "The Anthropology of Aging: A New Area for Culture and Personality Studies." In: *Middle Age and Aging: A Reader in Social Psychology,* edited by Bernice L. Neugarten. Chicago: University of Chicago Press, 1968.

Kaufman, Sharon R. *The Ageless Self: Sources of Meaning in Late Life.* Madison, WI: University of Wisconsin Press, 1986.

Lock, Margaret. *Encounters with Aging: Mythologies of Menopause in Japan and North America.* Berkeley: University of California Press, 1993.

Luborsky, Mark R. and Ian M. Leblanc. "Cross-Cultural Perspectives on the Concept of Retirement: An Analytic Redefinition." *Journal of Cross Cultural Gerontology* 18, no. 4 (December 2003): 251–71.

Manciaux, Michel, comp. *La resiliencia: Resistir y rehacerse.* Madrid: Gedisa, 2003.

Milam, Joel E., Anamara Ritt-Olson, and Jennifer B. Unger. "Posttraumatic Growth among Adolescents." *Journal of Adolescent Research* 19, no. 2 (March 2004): 192–204.

Neugarten, Bernice. "Personality and Aging." In *Handbook of the Psychology of Aging,* edited by James E. Birren and K. Warner Shaie, 626–649. New York: Van Nostrand Reinhold, 1977.

Poseck, Beatriz Vera, Begoña Carbelo Baquero, and María Luisa Vecina Jiménez. "La experiencia traumática desde la psicología positiva: Resiliencia y crecimiento postraumático." *Papeles del Psicólogo* 27, no. 1 (2006): 40–49.

Sokolovsky, Jay, ed. *The Cultural Context of Aging: Worldwide Perspectives,* 3rd ed. Westport, CT: Praeger Publishing, 2009.

Willcox, D. Craig et al. "Genetic Determinants of Exceptional Human Longevity: Insights from the Okinawa Centenarian Study." *Age* 28, no. 4 (2006): 313–32.

Chapter 10: Navigating Adversity with Uncertainty as Your Guide

Austin, James H. *Zen-Brain Reflections.* Cambridge, MA: The MIT Press, 2006.

Bar-Anan, Yoav, Timothy D. Wilson, and Daniel T. Gilbert. "The Feeling of Uncertainty Intensifies Affective Reactions." *Emotion* 9, no. 1 (2009): 123–27.

Mushtaq, Faisal, Amy R. Bland, and Alexandre Schaefer. "Uncertainty and Cognitive Control." *Frontiers in Psychology* 2 (September 2011): 249.

Ophir, Eyal, Clifford Nass, and Anthony D. Wagner. "Cognitive Control in Media Multitaskers." *Proceedings of the National Academy of Sciences* 106, no. 37 (2009): 15583-87.

Sirois, Fuschia M. and Timothy A. Pychyl, eds. *Procrastination, Health, and Well-Being.* London: Academic Press, 2016.

Whitchurch, Erin R., Timothy D. Wilson, and Daniel T. Gilbert. "'He Loves Me, He Loves Me Not . . .' Uncertainty Can Increase Romantic Attraction." *Psychological Science* 22, no. 2 (2011): 172–75.

Chapter 11: Biocognitive Tools for Life

Carey, Nessa. *The Epigenetics Revolution: How Modern Biology Is Rewriting Our Understanding of Genetics, Disease, and Inheritance.* New York: Columbia University Press, 2013.

Foucault, Michel. *The Order of Things: An Archaeology of the Human Sciences.* New York: Vintage, 1994.

Hawking, Stephen. *A Briefer History of Time.* With Leonard Mlodinow. New York: Bantam, 2005.

Jablonka, Eva. "Behavioral Epigenetics in Ecological Context." *Behavioral Ecology* 24, no. 2 (2013): 325–26.

Kahneman, Daniel. *Thinking, Fast and Slow.* New York: Farrar, Straus and Giroux, 2013.

Langer, Ellen J. *Counterclockwise: Mindful Health and the Power of Possibility.* New York: Ballantine Books, 2009.

Lieberman, Daniel E. "Strike Type Variation among Tarahumara Indians in Minimal Sandals Versus Conventional Running Shoes." *Journal of Sport and Health Science* 3, no. 2 (June 2014): 86–94.

Northrup, C. *Goddesses Never Age: The Secret Prescription to Radiance, Vitality, and Well-Being.* Carlsbad, CA: Hay House, 2015.

Pinto Bustamante, Boris Julián. *Imaginación, bioética, y medicina basada en narrativas: Relación médico-paciente, contingencia e imaginación.* Saarbrücken, Germany: Editorial Académica Española, 2012.

Sekida, Katsuki. *Zen Training: Methods and Philosophy.* New York: Weatherhill, 2005.

Straus, Sharon E. et al. *Evidence-Based Medicine: How to Practice and Teach It*, 4th ed. London: Churchill Livingstone, 2010.

Index

A

Abyss of uncertainty, 96–98
Academic logic, 30–31, 254
Acceptance
    of cultural brain, 186
    gaining, 27
    new paradigms and, 125
    reluctance to accept greatness,
        113–114
    safety and, 32
Acculturation, 65–66
Acquired illness, 170, 242
Activity theory, 195
Addictions
    disease and, 180–182
    as dysfunctional distraction, 59
    fear triad and, 96
    model, 205
    rituals compared to, 132
    as self-destructive patterns, 76
    smoking, 14
Ader, Robert, 175
Adjusting to cultural constraints,
        198–199
Admiration, 98–100, 187, 206, 234,
        244
Adolescence portal, 234
Adversity
    applying new felt meaning,
        221–222
    changing felt meaning, 220–221
    conserved transcriptional response
        to adversity (CTRA),
        182–183
    beyond cultural constraints of,
        214–215
    cultural faces of, 209
    debriefing, 225

defined, 251
as derailing of stability requiring
        constructive change,
        215–216
in Eastern and Western philoso-
        phies, 217
embracing, 223–225
illness as embodiment of, 151–152
intense, 210
nature of, 210–213
navigating in aging, 203–204
new face of, 215–216
portals of, 197–199
recontextualizing, 220
self-valuation in times of, 108–110
as state or instance of serious or
        continued difficulty or
        misfortune, 209
tools for navigating, 219–225
uncertainty and cognitive control
        in, 216–218
uncertainty avoidance and,
        213–214
as uncertainty in attachments,
        211–213
as uncertainty in expectations, 210
as uncertainty in routines, 211
Western meaning of, 214
Aesthetics, 1, 62–63, 71, 258
Affiliation self-esteem, 107, 118
Aging
    anti-aging photo experiment,
        237–241
    cultural portal theory, 199–201,
        227–229
    debriefing, 207–208
    embracing uncertainty, 204–206
    gerontology of machines and,
        193–195

method for cleaning out, 99–100
Langer, Ellen, 82, 237–238, 241
Language
    acquiring, 57
    biocognitive, 75
    cultural, 27
    cultural brain sculpted by, 168–171
    of cultural self, 41–42
    of love, 128
    mindbody, 15
    mind-body, 40
    for new concepts, 198
    oral, 8
    for theory of cultural portals,
        201–202
    written, 8
Law of attraction
    belief in, 89–90
    disproving, 89–90
    as New Age concept, 87
    New Thought Movement and, 88
    overview, 86–87
    questioning, 101
Leader archetype, 46
Leder, Drew, 153
Lende, Daniel, 171
Life beyond the pale
    anchors of misery in, 28–30
    challenging cultural beliefs, 36
    from collectivist to individualist
        perception, 38–39
    complexity compass for, 33–36
    cultural beliefs in, 25
    cultural editors and archetypes in,
        43–46
    cultural logistics *versus* academic
        logic, 30–31
    cultural portals in, 39–40
    debriefing, 53
    defined, 252
    discovering architects of limita-
        tions, 36–38
    discovering novelty and setting
        benign boundaries, 49–51
    horizons of cultural editors and
        archetypes, 46–48
    language of cultural self in, 41–42
    mindbody self and, 2
    overview, 25–26
    price of, 31–32
    resolving panic, 51–52
    structure of change in, 26–28

tolls for navigating, 48–53
    uncharted pathways in, 32–33
Life within the pale
    cultural rules and, 2–4
    mindbody self and, 2
    strategies for, 31
Limits, setting benign, 129, 136
Lived body, 152
Lived theory, 259
Longevity. *See also* Aging; Growing
        older
    biocognitive tools for, 227–245
    development, 62
    gene, 174, 195
    health and, 13, 47–48, 118, 175,
        207, 218
    as learned, 33, 37
    novelty in, 22
    perception, 4
    secret to, 132
Loss of control, 51–52, 185, 224
Love
    accepting, 79
    answering who loves you, 107–108,
        110
    choosing, 237
    compassion and, 78
    exalted emotion, 80–81
    fear of, 29
    healing power of, 87
    language of, 128
    pathways, 13
    rescuing from dread, 98
    self-, 134, 138
Love-based emotions, 11
Lover archetype, 46
Loyalty, 98, 191

M

Majid, Asifa, 171
Mal de ojo, 186
Mal de pelea, 185
Maslow, Abraham, 202
Matriarchal lineage, 3
Matter over mind, 55
Meaning. *See also* Felt meaning
    brain determining, 46
    conditional and unconditional, 245
    explicate, 59
    implicate, 59

Acknowledgments

True to my biocognitive concept of coauthorship, we never create in a vacuum. Being a product of our shared history, comprehensive acknowledgments would be longer than any book. Here, I limit my gratitude to those most associated with this book. My dear friend and colleague Dr. Christiane Northrup, who introduced me to Hay House; Patty Gift, who accepted me; and Anne Barthel, who brilliantly edited my work. In times of turbulence, I could always count on my true friends Dr. Loren Duffy and Sherry Hoskins.

About the Author

D r. **Mario Martinez** is a licensed clinical psychologist and best-selling author of two books, *The MindBody Code: How to Change the Beliefs that Limit Your Health, Longevity, and Success* and the psychological novel *The Man from Autumn*. He lectures worldwide on his pioneering work in biocognitive science, a new mind-body paradigm that investigates the inherited causes of health, how longevity is culturally learned, and how our cultural beliefs affect our immune, nervous, and endocrine systems. Based on how the immune system makes decisions under conditions of uncertainty, Dr. Martinez has also developed a unique model of organizational science he calls The Empowerment Code to teach executives of global companies how to maximize productivity while enhancing wellness. Website: www.biocognitive.com

Hay House Titles of Related Interest

YOU CAN HEAL YOUR LIFE, the movie, starring Louise Hay & Friends
(available as a 1-DVD program and an expanded 2-DVD set)
Watch the trailer at: www.LouiseHayMovie.com

THE SHIFT, the movie,
starring Dr. Wayne W. Dyer
(available as a 1-DVD program and an expanded 2-DVD set)
Watch the trailer at: www.DyerMovie.com

*THE BIOLOGY OF BELIEF 10th ANNIVERSARY EDITION: Unleashing the
Power of Consciousness, Matter, and Miracles,* by Bruce H. Lipton, Ph.D.

*GODDESSES NEVER AGE: The Secret Prescription for Radiance,
Vitality, and Well-Being,* by Christiane Northrup, M.D.

*RESILIENCE FROM THE HEART: The Power to
Thrive in Life's Extremes,* by Gregg Braden

YOU ARE THE PLACEBO: Making Your Mind Matter,
by Dr. Joe Dispenza

All of the above are available at your local bookstore,
or may be ordered by contacting Hay House (see next page).

We hope you enjoyed this Hay House book. If you'd like to receive our online catalog featuring additional information on Hay House books and products, or if you'd like to find out more about the Hay Foundation, please contact:

Hay House, Inc., P.O. Box 5100, Carlsbad, CA 92018-5100
(760) 431-7695 or (800) 654-5126
(760) 431-6948 (fax) or (800) 650-5115 (fax)
www.hayhouse.com® • www.hayfoundation.org

Published and distributed in Australia by: Hay House Australia Pty. Ltd.,
18/36 Ralph St., Alexandria NSW 2015
Phone: 612-9669-4299 • *Fax:* 612-9669-4144 • www.hayhouse.com.au

Published and distributed in the United Kingdom by: Hay House UK, Ltd.,
Astley House, 33 Notting Hill Gate, London W11 3JQ
Phone: 44-20-3675-2450 • *Fax:* 44-20-3675-2451 • www.hayhouse.co.uk

Published and distributed in the Republic of South Africa by:
Hay House SA (Pty), Ltd., P.O. Box 990, Witkoppen 2068
info@hayhouse.co.za • www.hayhouse.co.za

Published in India by: Hay House Publishers India,
Muskaan Complex, Plot No. 3, B-2, Vasant Kunj, New Delhi 110 070
Phone: 91-11-4176-1620 • *Fax:* 91-11-4176-1630 • www.hayhouse.co.in

Distributed in Canada by: Raincoast Books,
2440 Viking Way, Richmond, B.C. V6V 1N2
Phone: 1-800-663-5714 • *Fax:* 1-800-565-3770 • www.raincoast.com

Take Your Soul on a Vacation

Visit www.HealYourLife.com® to regroup,
recharge, and reconnect with your own magnificence.
Featuring blogs, mind-body-spirit news, and
life-changing wisdom from Louise Hay and friends.

Visit www.HealYourLife.com today!

Free e-newsletters from Hay House, the Ultimate Resource for Inspiration

Be the first to know about Hay House's dollar deals, free downloads, special offers, affirmation cards, giveaways, contests, and more!

 Get exclusive excerpts from our latest releases and videos from *Hay House Present Moments*.

 Enjoy uplifting personal stories, how-to articles, and healing advice, along with videos and empowering quotes, within *Heal Your Life*.

 Have an inspirational story to tell and a passion for writing? Sharpen your writing skills with insider tips from *Your Writing Life*.

Sign Up Now!

Get inspired, educate yourself, get a complimentary gift, and share the wisdom!

http://www.hayhouse.com/newsletters.php

Visit www.hayhouse.com to sign up today!

 HAYHOUSE RADIO *radio for your soul*

 HealYourLife.com

you can

HEAL YOUR LIFE

make your soul smile

Visit HealYourLife.com daily and meet the world's best-selling Hay House authors; leading intuitive, health, and success experts; inspirational writers; and like-minded friends who will share their insights, experiences, personal stories, and wisdom.

- ♥ **DAILY AFFIRMATIONS**
- ♥ **UPLIFTING ARTICLES**
- ♥ **VIDEO AND AUDIO LESSONS**
- ♥ **GUIDED MEDITATIONS**
- ♥ **FREE ORACLE CARD READINGS**

FEEL THE LOVE...

Join our community on Facebook.com/HealYourLife

www.HealYourLife.com®